Grounding Human Rights
in a Pluralist World

Advancing Human Rights

Sumner B. Twiss, John Kelsay, Terry Coonan, Series Editors

Grounding Human Rights in a Pluralist World

Grace Y. Kao

Georgetown University Press/Washington, D.C.

Library of Congress Cataloging-in-Publication Data

Kao, Grace (Grace Y.)
  Grounding human rights in a pluralist world / Grace Kao.
      p. cm.—(Advancing human rights)
  Includes bibliographical references (p.) and index.
  ISBN 978-1-58901-733-7 (pbk. : alk. paper)
1. Human rights. 2. Cultural pluralism. I. Title.
  JC571.K336 2010
  323—dc22   2010036734

♾This book is printed on acid-free paper meeting the requirements of the American National Standard for Permanence in Paper for Printed Library Materials.

15 14 13 12 11   9 8 7 6 5 4 3 2
First printing

Printed in the United States of America

Contents

Acknowledgments

Thanks are due to several persons and institutions that have been vital to bringing this project to completion. While I was an undergraduate at Stanford University, Philip J. Ivanhoe, Van Harvey, and Timothy P. Jackson first pointed me toward graduate school to pursue further work on the relationship between philosophical and religious ethics—a concern that animates this book. The central problem and basic frame of *Grounding Human Rights in a Pluralist World* was conceived when I was a doctoral student at Harvard University, where I was again challenged and nurtured by many fine teachers and advisors. I thank Francis Schussler Fiorenza, David Little, Ronald F. Thiemann, David C. Lamberth, and Hilary Putnam for their time and careful shepherding of me throughout my program of study. Of the many fine colleagues I had while working as an assistant professor of religious studies at Virginia Tech, Elizabeth Struthers Malbon especially stands out for her judicious mentorship and holistic investment in my well-being. A National Endowment for the Humanities summer institute on human rights in conflict under the direction of John R. Wallach and a University of Notre Dame Erasmus Institute summer faculty seminar on justice under the direction of Nicholas Wolterstorff also provided me with lively conversation partners with whom to test out ideas when the manuscript was still in its nascent form. And many other friends I have made throughout my formal schooling, the institutions at which I have worked, or professional organizations such as the American Academy of Religion and the Society of Christian Ethics have provided me with a constant stream of support and encouragement. I regret that I cannot name them all here.

I am especially grateful to the Georgetown University Press staff and their director, Richard Brown, and the Advancing Human Rights series editors, especially Sumner B. Twiss, for all of their assistance and patience, particularly as the book went through several periods of hibernation.

Grounding Human Rights in a Pluralist World is dedicated to six people: to my parents, Luke and Catherine Kao, for literally crossing an ocean to provide a better life for my brother and me, and for all that they continue to do to that end. To my older brother, John Kao, for sharing all of the important milestones of life together. To my husband, Nathaniel Walker, for his loving-kindness and willingness to endure the life of a faculty spouse alongside of his own professional ambitions. And to my two sons—Preston Jia-Ying and Keenan Chuan-Sheng—to whom I gave birth during this book's long gestation and whose zest for life continues to enrich my own.

Introduction

On December 10, 1948, the General Assembly of the United Nations adopted the Universal Declaration of Human Rights (UDHR) without a single dissenting vote. The document was novel in declaring that every human being, without "distinction of any kind," possesses a set of morally authoritative rights and fundamental freedoms that ought to be socially guaranteed. Along with the 1946 Nuremberg Principles and the 1948 Genocide Convention, the UDHR was radical in helping to construct a new geopolitical framework to hold states more accountable for the manner in which they treated their own citizens, foreign nationals, and members of other states.[1]

Today, human rights have arguably become the most important cross-cultural moral concept and evaluative tool to measure the performance and even legitimacy of domestic regimes. Most UN member-states have ratified the two international covenants that subsequently gave the UDHR legal form: the International Covenant on Civil and Political Rights (ICCPR) and its optional protocols and the International Covenant on Economic, Social and Cultural Rights (ICESCR). Other international human rights conventions or treaties cover topic-specific concerns about torture and punishment, racial discrimination, children, women, migrant workers, persons with disabilities, and enforced disappearances. Consequently, states that are "named and shamed" for their persistent human rights violations could suffer adverse effects either in their diplomatic ties with others or in their petitions for economic assistance from international financial institutions such as the World Bank and the International Monetary Fund. A people's prospects for statehood could even hinge upon their willingness or ability to honor human rights. Even non-state actors such as multinational corporations increasingly face pressures to comply with international human rights standards, such as when labor activists and human rights watchdog groups inspire

1

consumer boycotts of certain products because of the sweatshop conditions under which they were manufactured.

Despite the increasing rhetoric and expanding institutionalization of human rights, worries persist about their universal validity.[2] Even before the UDHR was officially promulgated, the American Anthropological Association (AAA) had already expressed wariness that the proposed document would represent nothing but a "statement of rights conceived only in terms of the values prevalent in the countries of Western Europe and in America."[3] An anti-Western backlash by formerly colonized peoples soon followed upon the heels of the UDHR and was detectable during the first international conference of Asian and African nations in 1955 in Bandung, Indonesia (Burke 2006). Samuel Huntington's thesis regarding a "clash of civilizations" between the "West and the Rest" is now well known, as is his claim that the values of "individualism, liberalism, constitutionalism, human rights, equality, liberty, the rule of law, democracy, free markets [and] the separation of church and state, often have little resonance in Islamic, Confucian, Japanese, Hindu, Buddhist or Orthodox cultures" (1993, 40–41; see also Huntington 1998).

Are human rights concepts actually Western ones masquerading under a cloak of ethical universalism or otherwise concealing a disreputable claim to power? Admittedly, the post–Cold War superpower, the United States, has historically minimized or even ignored the human rights violations of regimes believed to be friendly to its interests (e.g., Israel, Egypt, and Iran under the Shah) but has publicized the abuses of others in order to discredit them (e.g., China occasionally, Cuba, Burma, Iran under Ruhollah Khomeini or Mahmoud Ahmadinejad, and Iraq under Saddam Hussein), despite its own nonexemplary human rights record.[4] All rhetoric aside, much has also been made about the uneven enforcement of human rights. For example, critics have questioned why the United States through the North Atlantic Treaty Organization engaged in forms of "humanitarian intervention" in Bosnia in 1995 and Kosovo in 1999 but apparently looked the other way in Rwanda in 1994, when extremists in the Hutu-dominated government massacred approximately 1 million Tutsis and moderate Hutus in the span of ten to thirteen weeks. The United States has not yet (at the time of this writing) come to the rescue of the defenseless in the Darfur region of the Sudan, even though top U.S. officials have since September 9, 2004, used the word "genocide" to describe the crisis. Still others have been more chagrined that the "line of complicity" between state perpetuators of mass violence and those purportedly intervening to stop it has increasingly been effaced (Balfour and Cadava 2004, 288; Zizek 2004; and Brauman and Petit 2004).[5]

The world community continues to face a crisis of legitimacy with respect to human rights. In the mid-twentieth century, French Catholic philosopher Jacques Maritain had already observed a pervasive disbelief in the fundamental "rights of the human person," in addition to a "temptation toward skepticism" even among those amenable to rights talk (1951, 80–84). But one need not endorse moral skepticism in full to balk at either the very idea of human rights or specific human rights provisions, particularly when the latter involves matters of family law, the status of women, criminal justice, democratic institutions, certain economic or social benefits, or the extension of rights to entire peoples. Doubts about the universal validity of human rights cannot even be appeased by pointing to the worldwide consensus that the International Bill of Human Rights purportedly reflects since a genuine, universal endorsement of those standards still is arguably uncertain. Many states either have signed onto those documents without intending to fulfill their contractual obligations for merely face-saving or other self-serving reasons (e.g., to appease more powerful states), or have only ratified them after registering significant reservations on full compliance.[6]

According to Jerome J. Shestack (1998), a former ambassador to the United Nations Commission on Human Rights, the peoples of the world would be more amenable to the authority of international human rights law if its underlying reasons were better understood. Whether Shestack proves correct on this score, the moral or conceptual underpinnings of human rights do remain subject to considerable uncertainty. Why do we have human rights? What makes each individual human being entitled to certain liberties, procedures, or benefits that all others must respect? Must the very idea of human rights be premised upon a religious or metaphysical idea in order to be conceptually intelligible, sufficiently protected, or practically stable over time? Or might we ground our conception of human rights upon reasons that we could all share or at least not conscientiously reject?

Although plenty and varied, responses to this crisis of legitimization can be divided into two general types. The first type is the maximalist approach to justification. Maximalists do not intend to reduce "thick" philosophical doctrines into "thinner" ones but seek to embed human rights claims within a richer and more substantive set of religious commitments. The Organisation of the Islamic Conference's Cairo Declaration on Human Rights in Islam (1990), the papal encyclical *Pacem in terris* (1963), and the Parliament of the World's Religions' Declaration toward a Global Ethic (1993) all exemplify the maximalist approach because each contextualizes its understanding of human rights and any accompanying schedule of provisions within the comprehensive vision and values of their respective religion or religions.

Theorists who endorse maximalism do not only contend that human rights *can* be grounded religiously, but they further insist that human rights *must* be grounded accordingly if they are to retain their theoretical coherence, normative force, or practical efficacy. Michael Perry, a human rights theorist, U.S. constitutional law scholar, and Roman Catholic, characterizes the very idea of human rights as "ineliminably religious" and concomitantly brands all secular versions of the idea conceptually incoherent (2000b, 2006). Hans Küng, a leading German Catholic theologian and ecumenicist, contends that the absoluteness and universality of any global ethic can only be secured if grounded upon something that transcends the finite conditions of human existence—an Ultimate Reality (1991, 1998). Protestant theologian Max Stackhouse and Protestant Christian philosopher Nicholas Wolterstorff not only locate the deep roots of the idea of human rights within biblical texts but further hold that particular theological convictions are still now required to provide an adequate justification for them (Stackhouse 1998, 2005; Wolterstorff 2008a). These examples, of course, do not exhaust the maximalist approaches to human rights justification that are in circulation and of influence today.

The other major strategy of justifying human rights is, in contrast, overtly minimalist by design. In the wake of postcolonial resentment toward forced "Westernization," modern and postmodern attacks against appealing to human nature or essentialist metaphysics in ethics, and widespread doubt that any common philosophical presumptions—much less shared religious beliefs—can be presumed in our pluralistic world today, minimalists hope to avoid having to rely upon any contentious philosophical or religious premises in their defense of human rights. They aim to defend their universal validity without chauvinism concerning the myriad tradition-specific ways of protecting human worth and without slipping into modes of argumentation that they judge to be outmoded. Given the persistent charge that human rights are Western, many theorists who adopt minimalist strategies of justification endeavor to separate the concept of human rights analytically from the larger matrix of either Western Enlightenment liberal values or monotheistic beliefs with which human rights are so commonly—but, as they see it, unnecessarily—identified.

This book is principally concerned with the question of whether minimalism can provide a sufficient justification for human rights, or whether the maximalist assumption is correct that the project of advancing universal human rights requires a religious premise to serve as its underlying rationale. After clarifying in chapter 1 some basic challenges that any universalistic account of human rights must address and overcome, I turn in chapter 2 to a deeper discussion of the maximalist approach to human rights justification as articulated by the aforementioned documents and theorists, making sure to explain the ways in which they do and do not regard religion to be inextricable to the task. I then spend the next three chapters addressing the adequacy of three accounts of justification with significantly broad appeal that respond in their own way to the maximalist challenge.

The first of these approaches is the most minimalist among the three in its specification of the content and justification of human rights in accordance with the limited but serious role they are to play in a just international order. John Rawls, among others, adopts this enforcement-centered approach to human rights. His work is important for our purposes not only because of his continued place of prominence within political philosophy but also because of his conscientious attempts to refine his critically acclaimed theory of justice to be amenable to what he has called the "fact of reasonable pluralism" today. In chapter 3 I carefully examine John Rawls's theory of "human rights proper" as well as the larger account of international justice from which it emerges. While Rawls's concern not to exploit the concept of human rights through overextension will prove instructive for our purposes, his privileging of the interests of entire peoples over individual persons, his reduction of the various roles that human rights could play to that which merely sets the limits of acceptable behavior within societies, and his elimination of many internationally recognized human rights from his list of genuine human rights leave much to be desired. Most problematic for our purposes is his curiously incomplete account of justification. Rawls neglects to demonstrate how even his pared-down list of human rights could withstand the very charge of ethnocentrism that it was designed to overcome. He also fails to explain why "humanitarian intervention" to stop systematic and gross abuses of human rights would still be legitimate if it were advanced for reasons that the interveners would be officially precluded from having. In light of these and other difficulties, I ultimately advise that Rawls's account of human rights only be selectively retrieved for our purposes.

The next strategy under consideration, consensus-based approaches to human rights, also attempts to avoid wading into seemingly intractable debates about religion, human nature, or the ultimate ends of social and political life. By seeking intercultural agreement among diverse parties only at the level of practical human rights standards or norms, this two-tiered approach preserves conceptual freedom for each political, religious, or philosophical-moral tradition to supply its own rationale for the area of overlap. This manner of justifying human rights is often touted as being well suited for our pluralistic context and with its potential to satisfy both maximalists who would contextualize human rights within a robust account of the good and minimalists who would keep any official doctrine or public account of human rights sufficiently detached from commitments that are likely to be perceived as sectarian. I demonstrate in chapter 4 why consensus of this sort is important, practically necessary, and even sufficient for a variety of purposes, but I conclude that consensus cannot exhaust the issue of normative human rights justification on its own. I thereby close this chapter with a suggestion that we remedy this shortcoming by returning to the work of those who originally inspired the turn to consensus for human rights: Jacques Maritain and John Rawls.

The final approach under examination is the universalistic capability approach, which is increasingly being used today in the fields of development economics and political philosophy and is steadily gaining traction among proponents of human rights. We might describe the capability approach (also known as the capabilities approach) as simultaneously neo-Aristotelian and neo-Kantian, given its Aristotelian-inspired emphasis on human flourishing and Kantian-like respect for persons as choosers of their own ends. In particular, feminist philosopher Martha Nussbaum's version of the capability approach seeks to straddle the minimalist–maximalist divide by defending essentialism and an objective account of the good, on the one hand, while insisting upon the "free-standing" or nonmetaphysical character of those ideas, on the other. In chapter 5 I discuss the capability approach in general and its relationship to the more familiar human rights framework in particular, taking care to illuminate points of contact and divergence between them. I ultimately propose that what is most instructive about the capability approach is neither any enumerated list of central human capabilities, nor any particular translation of the language of capabilities into that of rights or vice versa. Rather, the capability approach helps to clarify what it actually means to secure a human right to someone, correctly acknowledges the unavoidability of presupposing a conception of the good for human beings in the process, and properly situates human rights claims alongside of the moral entitlements that nonhuman animals might be said to have. While Nussbaum is correct that persons of diverse (including no) religious affiliation could endorse the capability approach, I conclude that her version is more philosophically comprehensive and thus nonreligiously maximalist than even she is willing to admit.

The central argument of this book is inspired by, although ultimately distinguishable from, these aforementioned approaches, and I suggest most directly in chapter 6 which elements of each should be retrieved. These include, but are not limited to, the following ideas: the enforcement-model caution over inflating the concept of human rights through overextension, the consensus-based defense of both pragmatism and plural foundations for human rights, the capability approach's unabashed exploration of that which is characteristically and essentially human, and the maximalist commitment to the real worth of human beings.

The account of human rights justification that I defend accordingly negotiates between the minimalist–maximalist divide by rejecting the extremes of either pole. *Pace* minimalists, I urge resistance to the temptation to either blunt the critical edge of human rights in order to evade controversy or downplay the level of philosophical commitment that the idea of human rights requires in order to increase their reception among disparate audiences. But *pace* maximalists, I also call for an end to their exaggerated claims that noncosmologically grounded rationales for human rights invariably lack sufficient theoretical coherence or motivating force. My position is maximalist-leaning in concluding that we can make the most sense of the powerful claims that human rights make when we embed them within an ethically realist framework, but it is minimalist-leaning in insisting that value realism itself could be supported on either religious or nonreligious grounds.

What remains to be said here is how I will use the term "human rights." Unless otherwise stated, I will follow convention in using that term to mean the set of entitlements and justified claims that every human being has simply by virtue of being human, independent of anything else that might follow as a result of national citizenship, social status or differentiation, individual accomplishments or lack thereof, or specific speech acts and transactions with others. So understood, we should regard human rights as a special class of moral rights that would ideally be recognized in, and protected by, the law and other institutions. Like other kinds of rights, we should also conceive of human rights as having prima facie priority over social goals or collectivist ends. However, because rights claims can and often do conflict with one another, we should acknowledge that an individual's exercise of her rights could justifiably be overridden in some cases for carefully circumscribed reasons. For example, even if we were to count the freedoms of movement and association as fundamental human rights, a severe outbreak of an infectious disease could warrant temporary restrictions on those freedoms for reasons of public health.[7] While international human rights law has recognized that some human rights, including the right not to be tortured, are absolute in that they can neither be traded away nor overridden even in times of emergency (Art. 4, ICCPR), the absoluteness of even those rights remains controversial and will be discussed in subsequent chapters.

Now the claim that membership in the species Homo sapiens alone yields a series of individual entitlements says nothing on its own about their content—the kinds of treatment or forbearance thereof that are due each human *qua* human. Thus, without begging the question whether internationally recognized human rights really are genuine human rights, I will often allude to the provisions stated in the International Bill of Human Rights and other core treaties to provide a common framework on which to base the following discussion. My unwillingness to simply sign off on their moral validity stems from the possibility that their framers and signatories might have gotten the matter wrong—perhaps the list of genuine human rights or their manner of specification or both needs to be curtailed, expanded, or otherwise amended. Indeed, once we become clear what human rights *are* and are supposed to *do,* we will see why any official account of human rights should remain subject to ongoing revision.

One

PROLEGOMENA
TO ANY PHILOSOPHICAL
DEFENSE OF HUMAN RIGHTS

This book is concerned with the prospect of justifying human rights. As such, it defends the twin ideas that there are moral claims and demands that apply to everyone and that those involving human rights can be safely counted among them.

This first chapter is offered in the spirit of prolegomena: it will not set out to establish the universal validity of human rights but will instead lay groundwork for their eventual defense by demonstrating how two of the most common objections to such prospects ultimately fail to devastate. These are the cultural relativist arguments against the existence of any universal values or ethical norms and the ethnocentrist identification of human rights as merely and inherently Western. After interrogating the cultural relativist and ethnocentrist theses in their descriptive and prescriptive varieties, I discuss the legitimate but misplaced fears that likely account for their enduring popularity.

CULTURAL RELATIVISM

The first charge against the universal validity of human rights falls under the umbrella term "cultural relativism." As a variant of ethical relativism, cultural relativism denies the possibility of truth in ethics by relativizing all moral judgments about social behavior to each culture's prevailing beliefs about them.[1] Whether baffled by or deeply impressed with the vast differences in customs among the myriad peoples of the world, cultural relativists insist upon the impossibility of objective adjudication between and among competing norms. They accordingly reason that all assessments of the conduct of others could only be tied to idiosyncratic standards of measurement. In the words of anthropologists Clifford Geertz and Melville Herskovits, respectively, "One cannot read too long about Nayar matriliny, Aztec sacrifice, the Hopi verb, or the convolutions of the hominid transition and not begin at least to consider the possibility that, to quote Montaigne again, 'each man calls barbarism whatever is not his own practice . . . for we have no other criterion of reason than the example and idea of the opinions and customs of the country we live in'" (Geertz 1989, 14); and "Evaluations are relative to the cultural background out of which they arise" (Herskovits 1948, 63). In short, if all social practices, behavioral norms, or moral ideals could only be evaluated in culturally delimited ways, then universalism in ethics would be illusory and the post–World War II attempt to establish one "common standard of achievement for all peoples and nations" through the UDHR should be regarded as totally problematic.

Descriptive Problems with Cultural Relativism

We can begin to interrogate descriptive or empirical claims of irreducible difference across cultures by observing how such arguments generally "succeed" only through exaggeration.[2] Consider the following putative examples of radical cross-cultural difference. Purportedly, some African and Asian cultures greatly revere their elders and even practice forms of "ancestor worship," whereas other cultures, such as the Inuit, engage in senilicide by abandoning their elderly to die when they can no longer hunt or travel with the group (Steckley 2008). Some Western societies legally prosecute cases of animal cruelty and enact statutory measures to protect animal welfare, whereas other societies, such as the Hopi, apparently show no compassion for animal suffering and sometimes take pleasure in it (Brandt 1959; Moody-Adams 2002). Despite these reports of widely divergent practices and attitudes about them, moral common ground might still be found at the level of higher principles. Non-Inuits and Inuits alike might subscribe to the idea that it is wrong to prolong an inevitable death in desperate circumstances; after all, medical practices ranging from passive euthanasia to physician-assisted suicide have won a range of popular support in the West and are currently legal in the Netherlands, Belgium, Switzerland, and in several U.S. states (e.g., Oregon, Washington, and Montana). Alternatively, non-Inuits and Inuits alike might concur that every society must determine how to distribute health care when resources are scarce, just as first responders and medical triage units do in times of national disasters, war, or other public emergencies. With respect to the second example of humane treatment versus cruelty toward animals, many of us in the United States arguably show considerable concern for our "companion animals" or pets. But let us not forget our overall societal indifference to the production and slaughterhouse conditions of the estimated 9.8 billion animals we consume for food alone each year, not to mention the less than idyllic living conditions of the 17–100 million other animals we use annually for research and experimentation in science and industry.

In other cases, cultural relativist reports of radical difference across cultures overlook or deliberately exclude voices of dissent from within any given culture. An illustration of this false picture of homogeneity can be found in one of the many pro-"Asian values" assertions by the founding father and former Prime Minister of Singapore, Lee Kuan Yew:[3] "The fundamental difference between Western concepts of society and government and East Asian concepts . . . is that Eastern societies believe that the individual exists in the context of his family. He is not pristine and separate. The family is part of the extended family, and then friends and the wider society. The ruler or the government does not try to provide for a person what the family best provides" (quoted in Zakaria 1994, 113). In contrast to Lee's observations, certain strands of feminist political theory and communitarianism—the latter, a political-philosophical movement commonly associated with theorists such as Michael Sandel, Alasdair MacIntyre, Charles Taylor, and Michael Walzer—would contest this linkage of the West with liberal individualism.[4] Feminists and communitarians alike maintain that an atomistic conception of the self is not only philosophically indefensible but also an inaccurate portrayal of the range of what Western thought has to offer. Lee's characterization of East Asia as essentially family-oriented further ignores the historical record of East Asian movements that were and still are supportive of liberal values, not to mention China's now-abandoned attempt to detach itself from all vestiges of its feudal Confucian past during the Great Proletarian Cultural Revolution of the late 1960s and 1970s (Bary 1983, 1994). To be clear, the point is not to deconstruct Lee's statements as an end in itself but to show how any abstraction or idealization about a society's mores can distort just as it can illuminate.[5] This example should further reveal how philosophical disagreement about the nature of the self or society will often occur within cultures and not merely between or among them.

Prescriptive Problems with Cultural Relativism

The question remains whether cultural relativism in either of its two prescriptive versions fares any better than the descriptive varieties discussed earlier. Strictly speaking, relativism is not a normative ethical claim that entails practical consequences (i.e., it does not provide moral instructions about how to act) but a meta-ethical proposition about the nature of truth and justification in ethics. Thus, by prescriptive varieties of cultural relativism, I mean to signify the social attitudes, practices, or policies that are likely to be adopted by those who hold the cultural relativist position that moral values and judgments are relative to sociocultural context.

In the first formulation of prescriptive cultural relativism, the cultural and linguistic entanglement of all norms and values is believed to portend failure for any attempt to understand them from the "outside." But this objection can be summarily dismissed in the following manner: there may be Quinian-inspired uncertainties about the proper translation of foreign words or customs because "translations are more delicate than heart transplants," as interreligious dialogue expert Raimon Pannikar once famously quipped (1982, 77). Nevertheless, any sensible, well-traveled, or multilingual person should readily acknowledge that certainty or proof in matters of translation is not required for successful communication. As philosopher Amelie Rorty (1989) explains by way of a literary example, even if certain connotations of Shakespearean English cannot be captured perfectly in other languages, and even though there are cross-cultural variations in the criteria for and experiences of illness and pain, we outsiders can still appreciate Shylock's plaintive "If you cut me, do I not bleed?" in the *Merchant of Venice* because we can empathize with his fears and vulnerabilities.

In the second formulation of prescriptive cultural relativism, due recognition of the myriad tradition-specific norms or conventions is believed to compel equal respect for, or at least toleration of, them all. It is widely believed that anthropologists by discipline are committed to tolerating the world's great diversity of religiocultural rites and social customs—however odd, offensive, or immoral these might appear when judged from their own perspective. As missionizing imperialists attempted to Christianize and "civilize" various indigenous peoples by imposing Western forms of dress, abolishing "pagan" rituals, and prohibiting polygamous practices, anthropologists such as Franz Boas, Ruth Benedict, and Melville Herskovits interrogated the presumed superiority of modern Western civilization and combated the racist notions of human evolutionary progress implicit in such campaigns (Hatch 1983; Renteln 1988).[6] Given postcolonial loathing of these assumptions of Western civilizational superiority and widespread desires to avoid repeating the injustices that were committed in the name of Western or Christian expansionism, should toleration now be regarded as the morally appropriate posture and public policy?

While the question is timely and merits a sound response, we would be wise to remember that cultural relativists are unlikely to be able to provide one. This is because an embrace of toleration in accordance with their own logic would have to face the same restricted applicability as well. Cultural relativists could only urge each culture to tolerate the differing social practices or customs of all others by succumbing to a (universalist) form of argument to which they are supposed to be principally opposed. Now cultural relativists

could avoid self-refutation by advocating only for their society's toleration of all others on culturally specific grounds, such as when
Western cultural relativists recommend a policy of toleration for the
West because they conceive of toleration as a Western liberal virtue
or prudential "best practice." Even if revised and reformulated accordingly, however, two new problems would emerge. First, since both
the noninterfering "tolerant" attitude and the intolerant "imperial-
istic" one are found in abundance in Western culture and society, it
would remain unclear why the former position should prevail. Second, even if cultural relativists could make the case that Western
thought and society either already does or now should bend more
toward tolerance than intolerance, the reasons they could marshal
for such a position would fail to capture something important: genuine respect for the *Other*. Put in the form of a question, how could
cultural relativists demonstrate *that* if they could only support tolerating the *Other* in ways that merely referred back to their own
subjective assessments without ever transcending them, such as by
appealing to the objective worth of foreign peoples and their ways
or the real harm done to them when subjected to unwarranted forms
of intervention? Despite all appearances, then, the principle of toleration is neither a natural ally nor a logical extension of the cultural
relativist thesis. Those who would encourage greater, not lesser, toleration of cross-cultural differences would thus be wise to base their
support for toleration on other grounds.

Postscript on Cultural Relativism

Cultural relativism as a thesis might not only be descriptively problematic and prescriptively incoherent but might also be pernicious
to the extent that it could be deployed to shield certain harmful but
well-entrenched social practices from external critique: untouchabil-
ity, child marriage, patriarchy, religious intolerance, racial suprema-
cism, slavery or forced servitude, honor crimes, and human sacrifice.[7]
Fortunately, most human rights proponents have not succumbed to
the lure of cultural relativism out of any misguided respect for pluralism. Instead they have accused political or religious leaders of

"bad faith" if and when the latter have rationalized their patently oppressive practices or authoritarian regimes through appeals to deep-seated tradition (Gyatso 1998; Kelsay and Twiss 1994; Muzaffar 1999).

Although anthropologists might initially have offered cultural relativism as a counterpart to Western imperialism, today it is dated to believe that they are still committed to it by trade or discipline. The American Anthropological Association has since 1999 officially reversed its position on the existence of cross-cultural moral principles, endorsed several international treaties on human rights, and encouraged the expansion of the human rights framework to include issues that are not conventionally prioritized (Engle 2001). Thus, when some anthropologists continue to employ the term "cultural relativism," philosopher John Tilley (2000) observes that they usually do not intend any of the formulations discussed earlier. Instead, they usually mean to assert either methodological contextualism (the idea that customs, beliefs, or actions should be understood in cultural and historical context) or methodological neutralism (the idea that social scientists should try to suppress their own moral evaluations when studying other cultures, even though an eradication of all bias is hermeneutically impossible).

In demonstrating that cultural relativist claims cannot withstand critical scrutiny, we must be careful not to exaggerate what we have and have not shown. First, cultural relativism may be untenable as a philosophical thesis, but situationism, the view that an act could be right or wrong depending on the circumstances, need not be. In fact, situationism could even be compatible with universalism in ethics because the soundest course of action when determining the permissibility of any given proposal might still involve recourse to a universal principle (Tilley 2000). Second, even a successful demonstration of the improbability or undesirability of relativism could not itself imply the truth of ethical universalism, for expressivist and nihilist possibilities remain that moral claims are not the kinds of things that are true or false, whether for discrete cultures or for humanity as a whole (Ayer 1952; Blackburn 1993; Mackie 1977; Joyce 2001).

Finally, even if ethical universalism could be established against its alternatives, nothing yet would have been said about the status of human rights because it remains possible for universal moral values to exist even if human rights are not to be counted among them.

ETHNOCENTRISM

The next oft-heard objection to human rights takes its point of departure from this last possibility by identifying human rights as Western in origin or substance and then dismissing the need to apply them outside of the West.[8] Charges of ethnocentrism were most prominent during the height of the Cold War, when Western democracies accused Communist states of neglecting to honor civil and political rights while Communist states retorted that their differing ideological commitments led them to privilege economic and social rights instead. Although those disputes more or less died with the Soviet Union, equally impassioned debates have reemerged elsewhere, especially in parts of Africa and Asia. These allegations of ethnocentrism are sometimes bundled with a denunciation of the "colonial syndrome," or the continued measurement of all cultures and civilizations against the standards, achievements, and theoretical constructs of the West. In short, the fear is that the legal framework and conceptual apparatus of human rights will continue to intrude hegemonically, whether by intent or inevitable consequence, upon all the peoples of the world, including those who would rather do without them.

The charge that "human rights are Western" can itself be understood in at least two separate but related ways. The first is through narrative, or by locating the genesis and development of the idea of human rights within and among Western soil. The second is through content, or by identifying Western bias in contemporary human rights formulations or standards. In either case, critics are not so much denying that the burgeoning post–World War II movement for human rights was spearheaded by what political philosopher Johannes Morsink (1999, 2009) has described as the world's—not merely the West's—moral outrage over the atrocities committed by the Nazis and fascists. Rather, their primary complaint is that the sociophilosophical precursors of human rights are to be found in Western natural rights doctrines of the seventeenth and eighteenth centuries or even earlier, in the Christianized and classical theories of natural law that preceded them.

Natural Law to Natural Rights to Human Rights?

Doctrines of *ius naturale*, or natural law, served for centuries as the cornerstone of Western ethical thought. The idea of natural law entails belief in an objective morality that need not be formally instantiated into positive law for its legitimacy or trumping authority. Although the precise origins of natural law thinking are contested— some point to its beginnings in Sophocles (496–406 BCE) or Aristotle (384–322 BCE) whereas others refer to the writings of Cicero (106–43 BCE)[9]—many scholars credit the Stoics and Roman jurists for being the first to have elaborated upon several of its key ideas: a common humanity; nature as a source of moral knowledge; universal epistemic access to the basic truths of morality; and its eternal, immutable, and unwritten content.

When formulated in explicitly theological terms, natural law conceives of God as the highest lawgiver and requires the subordination of all human laws or other social conventions to the intrinsic moral order established by divine will. St. Augustine (354–430 CE) appealed to natural law to defend his idea of a "just war" as well as to absolve God of the blame God would have incurred had humankind been created ignorant of the basic principles of morality. St. Thomas Aquinas (1225–1274 CE) conceived of natural law as a "participation in the eternal law" and used it, among other things, to defend the naturalness of *dominium*, or private property, against the rival Franciscan ideal of apostolic poverty (*Summa theologica* II-I, 91.2, 94; II-II, 66. 2). As seen in canon law and in subsequent reflections by the likes of Duns Scotus and William of Ockham, the interrogation of the ideal of apostolic poverty eventually led to a radical theory of natural rights as the meaning of *ius* shifted from signifying that which was objectively right in the world to an interior ability, faculty, or power inherent in every individual (Tuck 1979; Tierney 1997; Witte 2007). To illustrate, Dominican priest Bartolemé de Las Casas (1474–1566) grafted a theory of natural rights onto the Thomistic conception of natural law to protest the theft, murder, and genocide of the indigenous populations of South America and thereby defend their equality and freedom.

European moralists of the seventeenth century, most famously Hugo Grotius, Samuel Pufendorf, and Thomas Hobbes, essentially laid the foundation for secularizing natural law thinking by grounding the idea into human nature and thereby reducing the need for a transcendent referent. Hugo Grotius (1583–1645), the first to reconstruct an actual legal system composed of rights rather than laws, conceived of natural law as a "dictate of right reason." What conformed to our nature as rational and social beings was believed to be right while whatever opposed it was deemed wrong. Although Grotius maintained the traditional theological belief in God as the author of nature, his position concerning the validity and immutability of natural law should God fail to intervene in government or even exist paved the way for the more secularized and rationalistic theories of both natural law and natural rights that ensued.

As in the case of their natural law predecessors, natural rights theorists claimed for them universal accessibility to their content without any need of special revelation, and their universal legitimacy without any need to be codified into positive law. John Locke (1632–1704) argued that the Law of Nature serves as the source of our inalienable rights of life, liberty, and property; his writings gave philosophical support to the overthrowing of absolute monarchy in the 1688 Glorious Revolution in England (1690). Lockean thought also heavily influenced the U.S. Declaration of Independence (1776) against England's George III and the French *Déclaration des Droits de l'Homme et du Citoyen* (1789, 1793, 1795)—the latter of which ended King Louis XVI's rein and proclaimed the "natural and imprescriptible rights of man." These political triumphs notwithstanding, the idea of natural rights was not accepted without protest within the West. To name a few famous dissenters, Karl Marx (1818–1883) denounced the bourgeois character of those French declarations, and proto-utilitarian Jeremy Bentham (1748–1832) dismissed the idea of natural, imprescriptible rights as "rhetorical nonsense, nonsense upon stilts" (Waldron 1988). More recently, moral philosopher Alasdair MacIntyre (b. 1929) has pejoratively compared belief in natural rights as "universal features of the human condition" to belief in witches or unicorns (1984, 64–68).

While the "rights talk" that emerged in the aftermath of World War II centered on human as opposed to natural rights or law, the conceptual continuity among these concepts has been observed by many with either approval or suspicion. Michael Ignatieff, the first director of the Carr Center for Human Rights Policy at Harvard University and the leader of the Liberal Party of Canada since 2008, has characterized the human rights revolution as a "return by the European tradition to its natural law heritage" and described the "global diffusion of Western human rights [as] a sign of moral progress" (2001, 4–5). Christian ethicist and human rights scholar David Little has argued that the recognition in international law of "universal peremptory principles" or *jus cogens,* norms that protect individuals everywhere against brutalities such as apartheid, slavery, torture, and genocide, is "closely reminiscent of the idea of natural rights" (2006, 296–300). To be sure, the documents of the International Bill of Human Rights refer to neither God nor nature as their foundational underpinning, and in this sense are conceptually distinguishable from those earlier traditions of ethical reflection. But the documents still resemble the natural law and natural rights talk of the Enlightenment and earlier periods in their stipulation of humanity-at-large as the relevant moral community, placement of normative constraints upon the workings of positive law, and use of analogous language. To illustrate these continuities with respect to the UDHR, the first clause of the preamble recognizes the "inherent dignity" and "equal and inalienable rights" of all members of the human family as the "foundation of freedom, justice and peace in the world," and the third clause contains a submerged right of rebellion—a right demanded and historically won by various Europeans and North Americans when attempting to overthrow their nonrepresentative forms of government. Article 1 echoes the U.S.

Declaration of Independence and the French declarations of the *Droits de l'Homme et du Citoyen* in its assertion that humans are "born free and equal in dignity and rights," and Article 16 conceives of the family as the "natural" unit in society. That the UDHR intentionally as opposed to coincidentally contains these traces of Western philosophy is supported further by the fact that many African and Asian nations did not have a voice in the drafting period of 1946–48 because they had yet to win their independence from their Western colonizers.[10]

What are we to make of this popular genealogy of the idea of human rights? Does it confirm the suspicion that human rights are either thinly disguised or newly updated ways of speaking about natural rights or natural law? If so, would such conceptual continuity be to the world's benefit, or should we instead regard the global promotion of human rights as an undesirable imposition of Western institutions and ethical traditions everywhere? To respond to these questions, we must assess the validity of the brief narrative sketched earlier as well as the merits of the ethnocentric objection itself.

Descriptive Problems with the Ethnocentrist Objection

> To please the Western governments . . . non-Western governments sign on to a list of values that their people do not know about, their preachers do not preach, and their jurists and scholars do not accept. If we add up China, North Korea, most of Southeast Asia, and the whole Muslim world from Morocco and Nigeria to Indonesia, we have a "vast majority of the international community" that does not subscribe to the liberal, democratic, Enlightenment values of the UDHR, whatever documents their governments might have endorsed.
>
> —Robin Fox, "The Ground and Nature of Human Rights"

There are three primary ways to counter the charge that human rights are provincially Western and thus neither deserves universal recognition nor protection. The first is by demonstrating how Western

perspectives were not the only ones represented during the formation of the UDHR. The second is by showing areas of conceptual
compatibility between human rights and the values that undergird
a wide diversity of religions, philosophies, and cultures. The third is
by examining how the persistent identification of human rights as
Western not only inaccurately treats various Western articulations of
human rights monolithically, but also ignores notable discontinuities between the postwar declarations of human rights and the earlier traditions of ethical reflection discussed earlier.

Let us turn, then, to the actual drafting process of the UDHR. Admittedly, some portions of the historical record work to substantiate, rather than repudiate, persistent accusations of Western privilege
and bias. A former U.S. first lady and Episcopalian (Eleanor Roosevelt) chaired the Economic and Social Council's Commission on
Human Rights from which the UDHR emerged. Many of the rights
on which the Canadian professor of law and director of the UN Division on Human Rights (John Humphrey) based the original draft
first appeared in various European and Latin-American documents
on rights.[11] And a French secular Jew and eventual Nobel Peace Prize
Laureate (René Cassin) was responsible for revising successive drafts.
These facts notwithstanding, it was actually the smaller nations
(smaller in political clout) and various religious and humanitarian
associations that first agitated for an actual list of human rights beyond the nominal references to the idea within the UN Charter.[12] The
"big three" at that time—the United States, the United Kingdom, and
the Soviet Union—did not originally intend for the fledgling United
Nations to prioritize the promotion of human rights because they
were more concerned with the prevention of war and other matters
of collective security.

A closer look at the drafting process of the UDHR would also reveal the not insignificant contributions by representatives from
non-Western and less powerful states. For instance, the Philippines's
Gen. Carlos Romulo campaigned incessantly for the rights of peoples under colonial rule as well as for a solid position against racial
discrimination—much to the discomfort of the then officially

segregated United States and other colonial powers. The results of his lobbying can be seen in the many stipulations in Article 2 that prohibit discrimination of any kind in the rights to which each individual should be recognized as being entitled. To give another example, India's Hansa Mehta lobbied effectively, even against Madam Chairperson Eleanor Roosevelt herself, for what we would now call (gender) inclusive language.[13] The results of her persistence can be seen in the first sentence of Article 1, which reads "All human beings [not "all men"] are born free and equal in dignity and rights." Finally, the Republic of China's Peng-chun Chang pushed for a social and not simply rational basis for how we come to understand the content of our moral obligations by advocating for the Confucian concept of *ren* or "two-man-mindedness."[14] Although the delegates settled for the term "conscience" in the second part of Article 1—as in "They are endowed with reason and conscience and should act towards one another in a spirit of brotherhood"—there is reason to believe that they did so in part to accommodate Chang's concerns (Twiss 1998a, 40–41; and Morsink 1999, 296–302; 2009, 55).

In addition to the ways in which non-Western perspectives were incorporated into the final text of the UDHR, human rights could also be said to be conceptually congruent with a variety of norms or values that are prized beyond the West. I will address this matter in greater detail in chapter 4, when we turn to consensus-based approaches to human rights. But to illustrate this point now with Confucianism, a tradition still popularly believed to be antithetical to rights talk, many scholars have argued the case for nonhostility or even basic compatibility between key Confucian ideas and contemporary human rights norms. Among others, political theorist Joseph Chan (1999, 2000) acknowledges the traditional Confucian emphasis on role-specific duties rather than on abstract individual rights, but he finds in the Confucian classics a privileging of the ideal of *ren* (humanity, humaneness) over an excessive preoccupation with *li* (ritual practice, propriety). Chinese philosophy expert Irene Bloom regards the Mencian concept of common humanity, which is based on the four incipient moral tendencies inherent in us all (i.e., compassion, shame, courtesy/deference, a sense of right and wrong), to be an important connecting link between classical Confucian ideals and contemporary human rights norms (Ivanhoe, *Mencius* 2A.6; and Bloom 1996, 1998). Comparative philosopher Julia Ching regards human rights as recent products of earlier developments in the West that had analogs elsewhere, such as in traditional China. She argues that both Confucian China and Christian Europe subscribed to a doctrine of "vicarious authority in kingship," wherein rulers only ruled by divine mandate and misgovernment could lead to a loss of rightful power (Ching 1998; Ivanhoe, *Mencius* IB.8, IB:12, 1A:7, 7B:14). Although the Confucian idea falls short of the Enlightenment notion of a people's right of revolution, and although related notions of popular sovereignty did not make it into the political structure of China as they did in the West, Ching's point is that the Confucian heritage of several other East Asian countries has not prevented them from endorsing representative forms of government and human rights. Thus, other nations with a Confucian legacy could just as well follow suit.

Of course, Confucianism as a longstanding tradition has texts, rites, and other resources rich enough to allow its adherents to justify a wide range of positions on many issues. It should therefore come as no surprise that other scholars of Confucianism, such as Roger T. Ames (1988) and Henry Rosemont Jr. (1988, 1998), have not only judged Confucianism to be fundamentally at odds with contemporary notions of human rights, but have also implied that rights-obsessed Westerners would do well to learn from the traditional Confucian preference for harmony over litigious conflict and social cohesion over possessive individualism (see Dallmayr 2002, 178–82). Elsewhere, pro-democracy activist Fang Lizhi (1990) regretfully reports that Chinese Communist leaders have interpreted the Mencian idea of the four moral sprouts with which all humans are natively endowed to mean that everyone can be taught to think alike—not to provide grounds for the right of freedom of thought and expression. As can be seen in these examples, one could interpret Confucianism in ways either congruent with human rights norms or as cutting against the grain of contemporary human rights standards. Still, the very fact of scholarly disagreement on whether Confucianism is ultimately more critical than supportive of human rights or vice versa should effectively demonstrate why the case for compatibility or incompatibility between any non-Western tradition and human rights must be affirmatively made and not merely presumed.

Finally, the persistent identification of human rights as Western reifies the West by unproductively treating it as static and monolithic. But it took centuries and a great deal of internal resistance for Westerners to overcome once-dominant views concerning the natural superiority of some groupings of humans over others, and the rule of the one or the few over the many. Moreover, even after many Western societies legally recognized individual rights, the class of persons entitled to make claims to them only expanded in a painstakingly slow manner: from first only white propertied men from certain Christian denominations, to eventually all male and female citizens, regardless of property-owning status, religious affiliation, or race. The pervasive characterization of rights talk as Western further glosses over real differences that remain today between and among various Western societies in the diverse ways that they interpret their citizens'—and in some cases every human being's—right to life, to bear arms, to privacy, to free speech, to express or exercise religion in the public square, to bodily integrity and reproductive freedom, and so forth.

Prescriptive Problems with the Ethnocentrist Objection

Returning now to the question of the origins of human rights, we should note here that the answer, though important for historical or sociological reasons, holds only questionable normative weight. Assuming for the sake of argument that the idea of human rights originally emerged in the West, it is not clear how or why this fact would necessarily undermine its prospects for universal validity because to think so would be to succumb to the genetic fallacy.[15] Of course, a combination of postcolonial defiance and nationalist pride for things homespun might motivate some non-Westerners to attempt to prevent Western-originated ideas from influencing the shape of their institutions, practices, or attitudes about either. Yet wherever the concept of human rights originated or whichever group articulated it first, we would be wise to think twice before dismissing an idea simply because it is not indigenous—or even endorsing it simply because it is. As philosopher Martha Nussbaum has aptly observed, people are "resourceful borrowers of ideas": Marxist thought originated in the British Library but has influenced powerful social movements in Cuba, China, and Cambodia; Christianity originated in a dissident sect of Judaism in Asia Minor but has become a world religion; and a comparable phenomenon obtains with respect to the global spread of Islam (2000b, 48–49). This is all to say that the posture that a people or society adopts toward any concept or social practice already is, and arguably should continue to be, influenced by more substantive considerations than when and where it made its debut.

Critics who object to human rights on account of their purportedly Western roots may not only be conflating the source of an idea with its validity but may also be guilty of other types of faulty reasoning. For example, in the "Asian values" debates that dominated the discourse on human rights in the early to mid-1990s, some Asian dignitaries rejected certain human rights provisions on suspicion of their Western roots but uncritically appealed to the idea of national sovereignty in the process (Langlois 2001). But in doing so, they failed to notice that the concept of national sovereignty is itself modern Western in origin; the prevalent forms of social organization in the world had been tribes, kingdoms, empires, city-states, protectorates, and colonies—but not the modern state until various Western expansionist campaigns divided up much of the world's territory accordingly. Whether owing to reconstitution or to the lasting effects of colonization, today it is an empirical fact that this Western-originated model of the sovereign state has been reproduced around the world, with its notion of centralized power, control over resources, and agenda of modernization. To avoid charges of inconsistency or selective rejection, then, those who would reproach human rights for ethnocentrism would have to either condemn all "Western" ideas not original to their respective traditions (e.g., the concept of human rights and national sovereignty) or find a separate reason to ground their objection.

Postscript on Ethnocentrism

Might charges of ethnocentrism against the universal validity of human rights ironically be trading upon a reverse form of orientalism? Recall that the "the Orient" was concocted by nineteenth-century Western academicians—with the help of writers, artists, bureaucrats, and representatives of imperial powers—to serve as a mirror image of what was considered backward, inferior, scandalous, or otherwise alien in or to the West (Said 1979). Today, however, many critics who denounce the human rights project for its purported ethnocentrism keep the misguided dualism between "East" and "West" intact but simply change the appraisal in the East's favor.[16] Some scholars have offered a sociopsychological explanation for this reversal of valorization: it helps to heal the wounded self-esteem and humiliation of formerly colonized peoples and is thereby part of a process of self-emancipation (Tatsuo 1999; Freeman 2000). Rather than reify this unproductive dichotomy between East and West, however, genuine emancipation might require the dismantling of this dualism altogether.

As with the previous case of cultural relativism, the purpose of interrogating the charge of ethnocentrism was not to establish the universal validity of human rights but only to show how such prospects remain credible. We must accordingly resist the temptation to exaggerate what we have and have not shown, particularly in light of three possible areas of overstatement. First, we must fully acknowledge that that the universal validity of any given ethical concept cannot be established by a series of successful comparisons (e.g., Confucian virtues compared to Enlightenment values), however many of these we make and however important comparative work might be for other purposes. For even if we could demonstrate a wide-ranging, cross-cultural, and interreligious convergence on basic moral standards of conduct, the sheer popularity of those results would still not count as sound evidence for their truth or justification.[17] Second, we must not forget that claims of conceptual compatibility (or incompatibility) between any particular religiocultural tradition and human rights can and often will be contested by others even within the same tradition, as we saw in the case of Confucianism. Finally, we would be wise to remember that we have largely dismantled the specter of ethnocentrism only on the most general level: we have directed nearly all of our attention to the opponent who disputes the very idea of human rights *tout court*, not to the more nuanced critic who alleges cultural bias in only particular interpretations of human rights.

The more sophisticated critic who accepts the universal validity of the idea of human rights but takes issue with certain articulations of what the idea entails must therefore have some way of distinguishing between the universal and the merely local. Relatedly, supporters of human rights themselves will need to be able to determine what constitutes a legitimate cultural implementation of a human right and what represents an unacceptable deviation from a globally valid standard. Since these issues remain hotly debated even among human rights proponents themselves, we will address them later in greater detail. In the next chapter we will see how maximalist approaches to human rights justification do not merely ground them with reference to an explicitly religious vision or account of the good but also interpret their meaning and extension in light of those deeper loyalties.

Two

THE MAXIMALIST CHALLENGE TO HUMAN RIGHTS JUSTIFICATION

Maximalist approaches to human rights make direct appeals to matters of first philosophy or religion for their ultimate justification. These premises affect their underlying rationale for human rights as well as the set of liberties or goods that will even be counted as human rights. Further distinguishing maximalist from minimalist approaches is a robust articulation of our common humanity and what it is about us as human beings that entitles us all to this special class of rights called human rights.

Recall that the maximalist approach's primary claim is not simply that human rights *can* be conceptualized within a larger vision of the good than what is explicitly stated in international human rights conventions or treaties but that they *must* be so embedded. Those who argue accordingly insist that minimalist strategies of justification are inevitably bound to fail because they fall short of their own desiderata in not being able to provide either a true theoretically "freestanding" account or one that adequately safeguards the rights of all human beings at all times. I examine in this chapter the maximalist challenge to human rights justification, and I discuss, to that end, three maximalist declarations and four theoretical defenses of the central maximalist contention that the human rights project requires a religiously grounded or metaphysical rationale of some kind or other: the Organisation of the Islamic Conference's Cairo Declaration on Human Rights in Islam (CDHRI); the papal encyclical *Pacem in terris*; the Parliament of World Religion's Declaration on Towards a Global Ethic; and the work of Michael Perry, Hans Küng, Max

Stackhouse, and Nicholas Wolterstorff. While leaving in reserve here whether human rights must be justified maximally, I discuss at the close of this chapter why proponents of human rights should at least attempt to defend their universal validity in ways that bypass any necessary recourse to religion.

MAXIMALIST APPROACHES IN HUMAN RIGHTS DECLARATIONS AND DOCUMENTS

Maximalist approaches to human rights do not simply exist in the minds of those who are committed to them but have functioned practically and historically in important ways on the world stage. Consider the Cairo Declaration on Human Rights in Islam (CDHRI), which was endorsed by the Organisation of the Islamic Conference (OIC) in 1990 to serve as a guide for member states and was then presented by the Saudi Arabian foreign minister for adoption at the 1993 World Conference on Human Rights in Vienna, Austria.[1] Against the conventional narrative discussed in chapter 1 of the Western origins of human rights, the CDHRI attributes their source to divine revelation in seventh-century Arabia instead, when the "last of His Prophets" (i.e., the Prophet Muhammad) received the "Revealed Books of God," thereby completing previous "divine messages." The Cairo Declaration names the Islamic Shariah as the ultimate foundation of and reference for all the human rights and freedoms declared therein. This is why "Shariah-prescribed reasons" explicitly constrain the scope of many of its enumerated provisions, including the human rights to life, to safety from bodily harm, to freedom of movement, to the fruit of one's labor, to various criminal proceedings, to freedom of expression, and to assume public office (preamble, Art. 2, 12, 16, 19, 22–25).[2] Other maximalist elements of the CDHRI include an Islamic description of our moral worth and common humanity, that we are all "united by submission to God and descent from Adam," and an embedding of both the concept and implementation of human rights within a comprehensive way of life (i.e., Islam) such that their observance becomes an "act of worship and their neglect or violation an abominable sin" (preamble, Art. 1a, 1b).

One of the most famous papal encyclicals of the twentieth century, *Pacem in terris,* could also be regarded as a maximalist document. As issued by Pope John XXIII on April 11, 1963, and addressed to the Catholic faithful as well as to "all men of good will," the encyclical interprets human rights to be wholly compatible with both natural and special revelation. Our conscience reveals that our universal rights and duties flow from our nature as human beings, and the Bible confirms that it was indeed the "Father of the universe" who originally inscribed these "laws which govern men" upon us (par. 5–7, par. 9, par. 28, par. 30, par. 85). The encyclical accordingly explicates all human rights provisions, including those pertaining to the worship of God and religion, work and welfare, property, the formation of groups, and civil and political participation, with reference to the requirements of reason via the natural law, on the one hand, and scripture and the social teachings of the Catholic Church, on the other (par. 14, 20–21, 24, 26–27, 46–52, 56). When compared to the CDHRI, the encyclical provides an even more theologically robust description of who we as bearers of these universal rights and duties essentially are: we human beings are comprised of "body and immortal soul," we have each been created in the image of God and endowed with intelligence and freedom, we are "by nature social" and "equal in natural dignity," and we stand united in our "redemption by Christ" and "supernatural destiny" (par. 3, 10, 23, 31, 44, 48, 59, 121). Indeed, the encyclical expresses its grand teleological hope that a society properly "formed on a basis of rights and duties" and characterized by truth, justice, freedom, and love will be conducive to everyone's ability to attain a "better knowledge of the true God— a personal God transcending human nature" (par. 35–37, 45).

Although not emerging out of only one religious tradition but purportedly from the "ancient wisdom" of all major world religions, the Declaration Towards a Global Ethic issued by the 1993 Parliament of the World's Religions could also be described as a maximalist document.[3] Without intending to replace each religion's "supreme ethical demands" or deny the irreducible differences that remain among them, the declaration's diverse signatories turn to their respective traditions to come to a consensus on human rights. They justify their endorsement of the UDHR among other universal values, standards, and attitudes by demonstrating how transreligious teachings or principles such as the Golden Rule give way to a range of universal human rights and responsibilities. For instance, the ancient directive "You shall not kill!" and its positive formulation "Have respect for life!" ground the signatories' commitment to the human rights to life, safety, development of personality, and freedom from arbitrary injury, torture, and genocide. Likewise, the ancient directive "You shall not steal!" and its positive formulation "Deal honestly and fairly!" ground the signatories' commitment to the right of private property and to the duty to serve the common good with it and so forth.

Now the Declaration Towards a Global Ethic differs from both the CDHRI and *Pacem in terris* in providing neither an account of who we human beings essentially are, nor a telos toward which all life is directed. Nevertheless, the declaration promotes an "authentically human" ideal in light of our demonstrable weaknesses by calling for mutual respect and compassionate consideration for others, moderation and modesty and not "greed for power, prestige, money, and consumption," and an active pursuit of truth as opposed to indifference toward it. As in the case of the other maximalist documents, the Declaration Towards a Global Ethics calls for much more than fidelity to human rights norms. It expressly hopes that a "spiritual renewal" will take place in the "inner orientation, the whole mentality, the 'hearts' of people" to promote peace among all persons, religions, and states, to improve the welfare of the entire "community of living beings" (not just humans), and to care for the entire earth.

As we have seen in this brief sampling, maximalist declarations of human rights collectively issue mutually incompatible claims about the theoretical foundations of human rights. But this lack of conceptual agreement should come as no surprise because the maximalist declarations themselves envision radically different higher ends: The Cairo Declaration would have the Islamic *Ummah* "guide a humanity confused by competing trends and ideologies" to live in harmony, knowledge, and faith. The papal encyclical expressly hopes for humankind to "form one Christian family." And the Parliament of World Religions encourages transcendent spiritual renewal while remaining noncommittal on the question whether God or gods even exist. In light of these internally divergent commitments, any maximalist advantage of connecting the abstraction of human rights to the deeply held convictions of many of the world's religious traditions must be held against the reality of significant disagreement about which rights we all have, how are they to be interpreted or applied, and what is their underlying conceptual basis.

WHY HUMAN RIGHTS NEED RELIGION: A SAMPLING OF FOUR THEORETICAL ACCOUNTS

Despite the reality of deep and protracted disagreement about religion, a number of theorists have defended the maximalist claim that human rights must still be grounded religiously. Some understand this unavoidable dependence on religion in practical or existential terms, their argument being that only religion can sufficiently respond to the limit question of morality—why be moral?—when expedience tempts us instead toward indifference or the immoral course of action. Others provide a conceptual analysis of what the very idea of human rights entails and then argue that its presuppositions remain inescapably religious. Variations of these two arguments appear in the work of Michael Perry, Hans Küng, Max Stackhouse, and Nicholas Wolterstorff, among others, with the latter two theorists arguing further for the necessity of particular theological convictions to the possible exclusion of all others.

Michael Perry and the "Ineliminably Religious" Character of Human Rights

Michael Perry is a prominent Catholic legal scholar whose major contribution to human rights theory lies in his insistence that prima facie secular international human rights documents are actually premised upon an "ineliminably religious" idea. Perry reads what he calls the "morality of human rights" in the International Bill of Human Rights as making a twofold claim: (1) each and every (born) human being has inherent dignity, and (2) certain things ought not to be done to any human being, and certain other things ought to be done for every human being because the claim of inherent human dignity has normative implications for social conduct (2000b, 5; see also 2006, 5). While Perry acknowledges that these documents do not specify *why* human beings have dignity (i.e., they say nothing about in *what* our dignity inheres), he nonetheless interprets talk of inherent human dignity to be tantamount to the claim that all human beings are sacred, inviolable, and ends-in-themselves (2000b, 5, 13). That the idea of human rights not only can but, more importantly, must be grounded religiously thus follows from what Perry interprets to be the unintelligibility or otherwise inadequacy of all secular justifications for these two component ideas.

What exactly does Perry mean by a religious vision or worldview? In the existential search for the meaning of life—a struggle that often begins when one has a profoundly personal (even if vicarious) experience with sickness, old age, evil, suffering, or death—Perry defines a religious response as one that finally trusts that the world is ultimately purposeful and meaningful "in a way hospitable to our deepest yearnings" (2000b, 16). A religious cosmology offers a "vision of final and radical reconciliation" through a set of beliefs about "how one is or can be bound or connected to the world—to the 'other' and to 'nature'—and above all, to Ultimate Reality in a profoundly intimate way" (2000b, 15-16). In contrast, a nonreligious or secular worldview regards value as something that human beings must instead make, construct, and impose upon the world, either because the world is ultimately bereft of meaning or because one is cosmologically agnostic about whether the world is in the final analysis absurd or purposeful (2000b, 24-25).

To be sure, Perry is neither assuming the plausibility of every religious account of humanity's place in the cosmos, nor the compatibility of the teachings and "professsed ideals" of all the world's religious traditions with contemporary human rights standards (2000b, 22). While he also provides for explanatory purposes a Christian account of human dignity that is centrally premised upon God's love for humanity,[4] his mention of the Buddhist tenet that the Other should always be regarded as the subject of infinite compassion is expressly designed to disclaim any need for theism when grounding human rights (2000b, 20–21, 116n48, 117n49).[5] All that is required is belief that one's conviction about universal human worth discloses a fact about the way the cosmos really is, not simply as we have merely imagined or socially constructed it to serve our own ends (2000b, 29). Thus, the problem with secular persons is not that they would be fundamentally incapable of honoring human rights but that any support on their behalf would require them to live out existentially what they could not in principle affirm and thus trade upon unacknowledged religious ideas.

What remains to be seen is why this is so—why Perry believes that secular analogs to religious cosmologies could not be equal to the task. Although Perry concedes the difficulty of proving a negative, he concludes that it is "far from clear" that there could be a sufficient secular justification for human rights after canvassing and quickly dismissing several nonreligious attempts: Ronald Dworkin's secular notion of human sacrality, Martha Nussbaum's understanding of compassion as a basic social emotion, John Finnis's natural law approach, the definitional turn to the impartial "moral point of view," the self-regarding strategy of justifying human rights according to a desirable end state of affairs, and even Richard Rorty's attempt to dispense entirely with "human rights foundationalism" or theory (2000b, 25–41; and 2006, 16–29). Whether Perry is correct about these matters ultimately depends upon several factors: The merits of his interrogation of the aforementioned secular accounts of justification, the feasibility of other secular possibilities left unexamined, and the adequacy of his understanding that talk of the inherent human dignity upon which the "morality of human rights" rests are truly equivalent to talk of human sacredness.

Hans Küng and the Declaration Towards a Global Ethic, Revisited

The aforementioned Declaration Towards a Global Ethic invites the religious and nonreligious alike to work for a new global order and repeatedly insists that its norms can be affirmed by anyone with ethical convictions, whether religiously grounded or not. Despite this apparently equal embrace of the religious and the secular, even the declaration gestures toward maximalism. That is, when certain of its passages are read alongside of the writings of its chief architect, the reform-oriented German Catholic theologian and priest Hans Küng, the declaration seems to be implying that something crucial to the human rights project would be lost if pursued in religion's absence.[6]

Admittedly, neither the declaration nor Hans Küng in his single-authored work holds that religion alone can solve the world's complex social, political, and environmental problems. Both also acknowledge the many ways in which the world's religious traditions have been petty, inhumane, and violent as opposed to champions of inclusion, solidarity, and peace. Still, while the declaration repeatedly affirms the need for "unconditional" and "irrevocable" ethical imperatives that apply to everyone, Küng in his own work provides two reasons why religion must be invoked to support them, given the limitations of philosophy alone to accomplish the same.

In the first case, Küng argues that philosophy continues to encounter difficulty with providing the "foundation for an ethic which is practicable for a larger strata of the population" (1991, 42; and 1998, 96).[7] The modern liberal social order has historically relied upon a "thick 'cushion' of pre-modern systems of meaning and obligation" to cultivate basic civic virtues among the populace, such as respect for the authority of the state, obedience toward its laws, and a strong work ethic (1998, 132). But now that the "common convictions, attitudes, and traditions" that traditionally formed the basis of public spiritedness have largely been lost and citizens cannot reasonably be expected to "invent everything all over again today," Küng rhetorically asks where the "moral resources" and "pre-legal conditions" for social cohesion and a consensus on ethical standards are to be found (ibid.). Without rejecting other possibilities for "strengthening the awareness of values" or suggesting a reversion to Christendom, Küng recommends a (re)turn to religion, since religious traditions have historically played a major role and "integrating function" in providing guidance about human well-being, moral motivation in pursuing the good, criteria for evaluating various ideals or states of affairs, and an "all-embracing horizon of meaning" that trusts that there is an "ultimate ground, ultimate content, and ultimate meaning of the world and human life" (Küng 1998, 133, 142, 275; 1991, 54–64; 1987, 231; Parliament of the World's Religions 1993, 5–7). In short, only religion gives shape to the entirety of human existence by disclosing a "certain 'more' in human life" and by responding to the perennial questions "where have we come from and where are we going?" in the midst of life's joys, sorrows, triumphs, trials, and other significant experiences (Küng 1991, 54; 1998, 140–43).

Beyond the practical difficulties that philosophy continues to encounter in mobilizing people toward the good, Küng raises deeper conceptual concerns about the limits of secular theorizing to ground any universally and unconditionally binding ethic. While secular moralists such as humanists or Marxists could still respect and defend human rights and accordingly lead lives that are "authentically human and in this sense moral," they would still purportedly be unable to justify the "absoluteness and universality of ethical obligation" even if they were to accept unconditional norms for themselves (Küng 1991, 51).[8] In his own words:

> Philosophical models easily fail precisely at the point where
> an action is required of human beings in a specific instance—
> and this happens quite often—which is in no way to their
> advantage . . . but rather can require of them an action against
> their interests, a "sacrifice" which in an extreme case can even call
> for the sacrifice of their life. Philosophy quickly ends with the

"appeal to reason" where ethical obligation "hurts" existentially. So can one face any danger of spiritual homelessness and moral arbitrariness with pure reason? (1991, 43)

No ethic in itself, but only religion, can guarantee unconditionally values, norms, motivations and ideals and at the same time make them concrete. Ethical directives are unconditional only on the presupposition of an unconditional. A "pure" human reason can also provide a basis for values, norms, motivations and ideals. But, like everything human, they remain conditional. They become unconditional only by being tied to an unconditional, the first and last reality. In other words, religion gives an answer to the ultimate question of why we are responsible and what for. (1998, 142–43)

Küng simply has no confidence that an ethic grounded within the "finite conditions of human existence" could create authoritative and universal obligations that applied "without any ifs and buts, unconditionally; not 'hypothetically' but 'categorically'" (1991, 51). When rejecting the adequacy of secular accounts of justification, Küng concludes that an "independent abstract 'human nature' or 'idea of humanity' (as a legitimating authority)" could not itself create unconditional obligations for any particular individual, that a "duty for humankind to survive" could neither be rationally proven, nor answered without appealing to humanity's real metaphysical worth, and that other philosophical attempts to justify a universal and binding ethic have failed to proceed beyond "problematical generalizations and transcendental-pragmatic or utilitarian pragmatic models" (1991, 43, 52–53, 151–52n78).[9] Even the accounts of postmetaphysical philosophers, such as Karl Otto-Apel and Jürgen Habermas, who dispense with a "transcendent principle" would not suffice. They are purportedly too abstract to be practical and overconfident that they have uncovered universally valid principles in their turn to discourse ethics, consensus, and an "ideal community of communication," even though their "long path of horizontal communication" might just as well be leading them "in a circle" (Küng 1991, 42–43).

While Perry had reached a similar conclusion about the conceptual indispensability of religion for human rights but did not attempt to prove the validity of any religious vision in particular, Küng explicitly disavows that such a task could ever be accomplished. Although only the Ultimate Reality provides an "over-arching meaning and . . . embraces and permeates individual, human nature and indeed the whole of human society," Küng concedes that this "mysterious absolute" or "revealer figure" that different religions interpret to be their Ultimate Reality cannot be rationally demonstrated, only "accepted in a rational trust" (1991, 53).[10] As with Perry, whether Küng is ultimately correct about these matters depends upon several factors: the propriety of his dismissal of the aforementioned secular justifications, the feasibility of other secular accounts left unexamined by his analysis, and even the desirability of conceptualizing all global ethics as absolute.

Max Stackhouse and the Indispensability of Theology for Human Rights

Max Stackhouse, a leading Christian ethicist and ordained minister in the United Church of Christ, offers a maximalist account of human rights that echoes some of the previous arguments and makes some comparatively bolder claims. Like Perry, Stackhouse regards the idea of human rights as representing a "belief about what is sacred in human relations and the pattern of civilization," which is why he also opposes the "standard secularist account" that denies religion's indispensability to matters of justification (Stackhouse 1984, 2; 2005, 26–31).[11] Like Küng, Stackhouse argues historically that religious traditions have traditionally presented "metaphysical-moral vision[s] of what is 'really real'" upon which the idea of human rights rests, and practically that proponents of human rights today will still need the "concrete institutional footing" that religions provide in order to "actualize these normative visions" in society (Stackhouse 1984, 6; Stackhouse and Healey 1996, 505).[12] These similarities notwithstanding, Stackhouse argues for a necessary link between human rights and the Christian theological tradition in ways that the other two theorists, although fellow Christians, do not. Only Stackhouse interprets the idea of human rights as having "developed nowhere else than out of key strands of the biblically-rooted religions," as still essentially theological, and as only sufficiently recognized and implemented within those cultures, philosophies, and religions that have been shaped by that original biblical and social legacy (2004, 25; 2005, 26–40).[13]

According to Max Stackhouse's genealogy, the Christian tradition with its Hebraic roots is the first to have formulated and then institutionalized key ideas about God, humanity, and morality in ways that proved crucial to the worldwide promotion of human rights. He reads the biblical proclamation of God's existence as tantamount to an acknowledgment that all human beings live under an ultimate spiritual power and moral reality that we neither created nor could ignore.[14] Because everyone has been created in the image of God, the God of the biblical traditions enjoins moral conduct from us, from minimally abstaining from patently harmful activities such as theft and murder to prodigiously loving our neighbor and even enemy. Stackhouse interprets the *imago Dei* as ontologically distinguishing human beings from all other creatures, somehow reflected in our capacities to reason, to will, and to love, and ultimately conferring upon us a dignity that we would otherwise not have, as seen in the following passage:

> The *imago Dei*, the image of God . . . means that there is something holy, that is sacred that is not an inherent dignity, but a bestowed dignity. If it were an inherent dignity you could look around and find examples of people in infancy or people in the aged who hardly seem to manifest any of these characteristics of inherent dignity as an empirical mater, still, there is a real sensibility we ought not wantonly destroy them and the way of speaking symbolically about *imago Dei* points to that sacred respect that we should offer them. Why do we do that? We think that in principle each person has some residual capacity to use reason, with flaws, with difficulty, obscured by interest. If one has

a chance to exercise will, freedom is somehow there, so there is
some possibility of choices there. Furthermore, people have a
capacity to love, to bond with others, so the capacity to think,
to will and to love are seen to be very distinctive capacities so far
as we know, of the human species. (2003, 8; cf. 2004, 27–28;
2005, 38)

Although the institutionalized church has not always exemplified the
prophetic message it professes, Stackhouse contends that this biblically rooted vision of human dignity led the Christian tradition to
pursue both "personal regard for each person" and particular sociopolitical arrangements that protected each individual's endowments in ways that ultimately proved hospitable to the worldwide
promotion of human rights (2004, 27).[15]

Beyond insisting upon the Christian origins of human rights in
ways that Perry and Küng do not, Stackhouse's other comparatively
bolder claim involves his understanding of their essentially theological character. He often explains theology's indispensability to human
rights in terms of content, as when he characterizes them as based
on "nothing less than decisive theological convictions" or describes
them as a modern way of speaking about "cross-cultural ethical concepts that actualize certain valid theological presuppositions . . .
where theology is understood to be the critically examined and systematically stated interpretation of what humanity is—sinful creatures . . . [who] know we live under a God who establishes moral
laws and ends and contexts of life we cannot attain alone" (Stackhouse and Healey 1996, 490–94). Stackhouse elsewhere explains
theology's indispensability less in terms of propositional content
than upon its mission and method, which is to "judge bad faith from
within and provide the moral architecture of civilization without"
by using the discipline that the early church created through the fu-
sion of rational (Greek) thought with the biblical tradition to offer
a rational set of tools to guide the selection, ordering, and application of insights from the past (1984, 34–38; 2005, 28). So understood, it is theology's task to evaluate competing religious and ethical

claims to determine which ones are false or trivial and which ones have "greater validity or importance" (2005, 28). Indeed, Stackhouse's book-length study on human rights is expressly devoted to determining "which fundamental vision is most true and most fully meets the widest range of basic human needs and thus *ought* to be adopted universally as creed and institutionalized in every society" (1984, 20–21).

Given longstanding disputes about religion or matters of ultimate concern, this line of inquiry remains fraught with controversy. But Stackhouse persists in charging those who would methodologically refuse to "raise critical questions about the most decisive levels of human existence" with a lamentable "failure of intellectual nerve" (Stackhouse and Healey 1996, 512). He concludes that several religions in their present forms, including Islam, Hinduism, and certain branches of Judaism and Christianity, are unlikely to sustain a commitment to human rights in the long run, although there is potential for them all to reform (Stackhouse and Healey 1996, 490–95; see also Stackhouse 2005, 26–33). Stackhouse optimistically believes that the "theological motifs" upon which the idea of human rights rests have been "scripted into the deepest levels of the human soul, even if they are overlaid by obscuring other doctrines, dogmas, practices and habitual ways of thinking in many of the traditions of the world's religions." Thus, the task for theologians and human rights proponents alike is to identify "where, in the depths of all these traditions, that residual capacity to recognize and further refine the truth and justice of human rights insights lies" (2004, 28; see also 2005, 40).

Nicholas Wolterstorff and the Pearl of Great Price

One of the most distinguished Christian philosophers of our time, Nicholas Wolterstorff, provides his own version of maximalism that shares notable similarities with the others. Like Stackhouse, Wolterstorff not only traces the conceptual origins of human rights to key biblical claims about God and justice but he also doubts that society will be able to protect them sufficiently if severed from their theological roots. Like Perry, Wolterstorff contends that the most plausible justification for human rights is one that successfully defends the notion of inherent human worth, presents a theological articulation of that idea that turns centrally on God's love for everyone, and somberly concludes that no adequate secular grounding has yet to emerge. Like Küng, Wolterstorff refrains from attempting to prove the existence of the God upon whom his understanding of human rights rests, defending theism instead from the charge of irrationality without providing foundationalist evidence or argument. Despite these notable areas of overlap, Wolterstorff's account cannot be assimilated to these other approaches without remainder.

While details of their genealogy differ, Wolterstorff parallels Stackhouse in tracing the deep origins of human rights not to seventeenth century discussions of political individualism in the modernizing West, nor to the nominalism of the fourteenth century following debates about apostolic poverty and private property, but to ancient themes in the Hebrew and Christian scriptures (Wolterstorff 2008a, 62–64, 393). Although the biblical writers did not explicitly conceptualize the idea of natural human rights, or entitlements to certain goods that all humans have by virtue of being human and thus independently of any social conferral by legislation or specific speech-acts, Wolterstorff insists that they nonetheless embraced what we would today call natural human rights (2008a, 33, 313, 388–89).[16] His test of whether any given individual has an inherent right to a certain good is whether deprivation of that good would constitute a moral wrong, would treat that individual with "under respect" or less than her worth, and thereby would alter her "moral condition" (2008a, 25, 374–75). Wolterstorff accordingly interprets the Bible in support of the concept of inherent human rights because it regards every human being as "irreducibly precious" and as accountable to God for meeting the basic demands of justice; everyone must treat all others in ways that properly reflect their worth (2008a, 86–89, 361, 386; 2008b, 673–74). For biblical evidence for this first claim

The Maximalist Challenge to Human Rights Justification

about universal worth, Wolterstorff points to the placement of human beings as only "a bit lower in the cosmic scale of worth than divine beings (or angels)" by the writer of Psalms 8; the grounding of the proscription against murder in Genesis 9:6 not in God's law but in the divine image in which everyone has been created; and Jesus's appeals to our inherent worth to explain why he heals on the Sabbath and why God cares for us (2008a, 95, 130–31; see Lk. 12:24, Mt. 6:26, 10:31, 12:11–12). For biblical support for this second claim about universal accountability, Wolterstorff points to its predating the giving of the Torah and thus its conceptual nonreliance upon formal membership into the "covenant people" (2008a, 82–88).[17] Although Wolterstorff does not follow Stackhouse's methodology in examining whether ancient non-Western cultures or religions also had a comparable "framework of conviction" upon which to justify the idea of human rights, he nevertheless echoes Stackhouse's suspicion that rights cannot, "over the long haul, float free of its theistic origins" if they are to be properly recognized and protected today (Wolterstorff 2008a, 65, 393; 2008b, 675).[18]

These similarities notwithstanding, Wolterstorff offers a markedly different account of the *imago Dei* and the role it should play in any attempt to justify human rights. Although the biblical profession that we have been created in the divine image is of great theological and moral significance, even a correct understanding of what constitutes the *imago Dei* would purportedly be insufficient to ground the idea of natural human rights (2008a, 352). Popular attempts to articulate the nature of our imaging in terms of particular capacities, such as in those required to exercise the blessing or mandate of dominion over the animals, may have the virtue of ontologically distinguishing human beings from non-human animals (see Gen. 1: 26–27; Stackhouse 2003, 8; 2004, 27). But such attempts could only come at the expense of excluding certain human beings from properly resembling God as well, including those who were severely mentally impaired from birth, who never properly developed those capacities, or Alzheimer's patients and those in a deep coma and so forth, who no longer possessed them (Wolterstorff 2008a,

348–49). Even the "nature-resemblance" as opposed to "capacities-resemblance" interpretation of the *imago Dei* that Wolterstorff himself favors would still be unable to ground the idea of natural human rights. For it would be difficult to see why a malfunctioning or malformed human being who still possessed a human nature, albeit one where "the mature and properly formed possessors of that nature resemble God with respect to their capacities for exercising dominion," would still be of inestimable worth simply because of shared species membership (Wolterstorff 2008a, 350). In light of these difficulties, Wolterstorff turns to the biblical idea of God's redemptive love of every creature that bears the *imago Dei* as that which correctly bestows each human being with great and equal worth—and directly references Michael Perry's work when doing so (2008a, 352–53, 393).

Unlike Stackhouse and Küng, then, Wolterstorff's position is neither that human beings have rights because of "some socially transcendent norm extrinsic to themselves," nor because God has conferred various rights upon all of humanity by an act of divine legislation (Wolterstorff 2005, 10, 23–37). Rather, his view is that all human beings have rights because of their inherent worth, and the property or relation common to all in which this worth inheres or supervenes is precisely that each is beloved by God (2008a, 10–11, 319–20, 352–53).

Finally, although Wolterstorff's account of human rights resembles Michael Perry's in notable ways, Wolterstorff's primary critique of secular approaches does not concern their ultimate coherence or intelligibility. Instead, his concern is whether even their most philosophically promising candidates would be able to explain why all members of the species *Homo sapiens* have human rights—and have them equally.[19] To demonstrate why secular rationales for human rights would remain vulnerable in ways that his theistic grounding purportedly would not, Wolterstorff draws our attention to the following observation: the most common way to ground human rights is to appeal to an idea of human dignity, and the most common way to ground *that* is to specify some uniquely human property or capacity in which our dignity inheres.

The Maximalist Challenge to Human Rights Justification

According to the well-known Kantian framework of human worth, for example, our dignity as human beings arises from our capacity for rational action—our ability to act autonomously in accordance with various moral imperatives that we give to ourselves and to others. But Wolterstorff charges Kant's capacities approach, like all other capacities approaches, with two fatal problems. First, because the capacity for rational agency comes in degrees (i.e., some exercise it better than others, others lack it entirely), those who would ground human dignity upon it would be hard-pressed to explain why an individual's worth or dignity—and thus, her schedule of rights—should not similarly reflect her comparatively better or worse use of those faculties (Wolterstorff 2008a, 327–28, 390–91). Second, without explicitly using the term, Wolterstorff faults all capacities approaches with a fundamental inability to withstand what has been called the "argument from marginal cases," or the observation that there is no morally relevant property or capacity that could successfully distinguish *all* human beings from *all* other animals because there are "marginal" human beings who are cognitively and socially underdeveloped, profoundly mentally retarded, irreversibly comatose, or otherwise severely brain-damaged, just as there are highly intelligent and sociable animals such as dolphins, whales, and the great apes (2008a, 331–33). Thus, it is not simply that capacities approaches cannot adequately protect the equal moral worth of all human beings due to the undeniable variation among our possession and use of the relevant capacities. But it is also that such approaches would unwittingly elevate certain nonhuman animals above the threshold of moral dignity and standing while it would simultaneously demote other human beings below it, namely those who either lack the capacities entirely or only possess them in severely diminished and thus nonimpressive ways. Still worse is the fact that Wolterstorff charges other prominent secular justifications for human rights that are either dignity-but-not-capacities-based, or capacities-but-not-dignity-based, with succumbing to similar problems of unintentionally protecting the inherent worth, and thus the inherent rights, of only some (not all) human beings.[20]

What remains to be said is how Wolterstorff's account compares with Hans Küng's. Although not an area of emphasis, Wolterstorff follows Küng (and the others) in doubting that secular accounts of justification could ever have the practical "power over imagination and action" that the religious vision of God's love for everyone historically has had (Wolterstorff 2008a, 393). Wolterstorff also similarly stresses the importance of not subsuming the concept of rights into that of duties because they symmetrically evoke two different dimensions of the moral order: the patient dimension in the case of duties, when others come into our presence bearing morally legitimate claims upon us about how we are to treat them; and the agent dimension in the case of rights, as we bear morally legitimate claims upon others when we come into their presence (2008b, 671; 2005). His rejection of the "evidentialist challenge" to theism and concomitant Reformed epistemological defense of both the rationality and justifiability of belief in God despite lack of foundationalist argument can also be compared to Küng's position that the Ultimate Reality can never be rationally demonstrated but only accepted in rational trust.[21]

These similarities notwithstanding, Wolterstorff's version of maximalism is arguably the boldest among those that we have canvassed thus far. He does not stop at identifying deficiencies in secular accounts of human rights but uses what he concludes to be the comparative superiority of these religious justifications to advance the religious claims in question. In his own words: "if one believes that there are natural inherent human rights, then the fact that the secularist cannot account for those rights, whereas the theist who holds the convictions about God's love that I have delineated can do so, is an argument for theism (of that sort)" (2008a, 361).

A PRELIMINARY ASSESSMENT
OF THE MAXIMALIST CHALLENGE

These four maximalists have issued formidable challenges. If human rights can only be justified religiously or even theologically, then attempts to promote or secure them everywhere must be described as religious or theological activities. While I will leave in reserve in this chapter whether the maximalist challenge to human rights justification is truly insurmountable, we should identify here certain areas of vulnerability or overstatement so we can put aside those arguments that critics of maximalism need not overcome.

Let us begin by reconsidering Michael Perry's assumption that a religious vision of one kind or another is required to sustain the idea of human rights. Perry reached that conclusion because he could find no adequate secular justification for belief in the "inherent dignity of the human person" of which the International Bill of Human Rights speaks. But he also reached that conclusion because he assumed talk of inherent dignity to be equivalent to talk of sacrality, and he thereafter judged the very idea of secular sacredness to rest upon a conceptual confusion.[22] But it is neither analytic nor beyond contestation why the concepts of "inherent dignity" and "sacrality" must be treated synonymously. While the idea of the sacred has conventionally been linked to that of the holy, of things "set apart" by or for God or the gods, it remains an open question whether the concept of "inherent dignity" should be as well (see, e.g., Kohen 2007, 77–81; Jackson 2003, 2005). Thus, unless we were first to establish conceptual equivalence between the concepts of inherent dignity and sacrality, those who would oppose Perry's maximalism need not also articulate a nonreligious conception of the sacredness of all human beings. They need only supply an adequate secular defense of the idea of inherent human dignity from which international human rights law proclaims itself to have been derived.[23]

Let us now recall one of Hans Küng's arguments for religion's indispensability: only an appeal to the Ultimate Reality can ground the unconditional and absolute character of any universally binding ethic. While Küng rhetorically dismissed the value of any global ethic that "does not apply without any ifs and buts, unconditionally; not 'hypothetically' but 'categorically,'" it is worth noting that the International Bill of Human Rights does not (Küng 1991, 52). Article 29 of the UDHR states that the exercise of one's rights and freedoms may be legally subject to certain limitations or conditions: the purposes and principles of the United Nations, respect for the rights and freedoms of others, and fulfillment of what is necessary to meet the "just requirements of morality, public order and the general welfare in a democratic society." The ICCPR contains similar language about restricting the exercise of some human rights when necessary to preserve national security, public order, public health or morals, or the rights and freedoms of others.[24] The ICESCR even explicitly aims for "progressive [not absolute] realization," given empirical limitations in the available resources of developing countries (Art. 2). Thus, in contrast to the conditionality that international law affords in the implementation of the vast majority of human rights for carefully circumscribed reasons, any suggestion that all global ethical standards must be met under every imaginable scenario would seem dogmatic and severe by comparison.

Beyond acknowledging the ways in which the call for absoluteness far exceeds what is required by international human rights law, it is worth noting the intuitive plausibility of, and wide-ranging public support for, conditionality in the realization of many human rights. The exercise of an individual's rights should minimally be subject to the ability of others to enjoy theirs, and this may require society to set limits or priorities when rights and other potentially countervailing considerations (including other rights) come into conflict. We might imagine a case where we affirm the universal human right to movement, assembly, and association but still permit local law enforcement authorities to diffuse a dangerous situation of overcrowding in a public space by peaceably ordering the masses to disperse. We might also imagine affirming the universal right to freedom of religion, together with the right and obligation of public authorities to regulate the killing and disposal of animals for reasons of public health, even if such legislation directly affects the religious rites of animal sacrifice or slaughter.

Admittedly, international human rights law requires the unqualified and categorical protection of some human rights, such as the rights to life and to be free from enslavement and torture, even in the most challenging of times—including "public emergenc[ies] which threaten the life of the nation" (Art. 4, ICCPR).[25] It remains hotly contested today whether there truly are no possible circumstances under which it would be morally permissible to transgress what the ICCPR has classified as nonderogable rights. Consider the (nonderogable) human right to life (Art. 6, ICCPR). Several liberal political philosophers, most prominently Michael Walzer and John Rawls, have courted both widespread support and controversy for their defense of a "supreme emergency exemption" from the traditional just war principle of discrimination. Their argument is that a political community truly threatened with annihilation should be able to directly target noncombatants for harm in order to save itself (Walzer 1977, ch.16; Rawls 1999b, 98–99; Toner 2005). Consider contemporary unresolved debates about the use of torture to obtain intelligence. While organizations such as Amnesty International and Human Rights Watch strenuously insist upon maintaining an absolute ban on torture, endless philosophical speculation and social commentary about the "ticking time bomb scenario" reveal that a sizable portion of the public would support a temporary lifting of the prohibition under such truly rare and extreme circumstances.[26] In light of these unsettled debates and to return to Küng's original concern with absoluteness in global ethics, we might revise his maximalist charge, so now it is only that secular reasoning would be unable to sustain the unconditionality of those nonderogable provisions in question. If they were reformulated accordingly, those who would hope to justify human rights on minimalist grounds would no longer have to defend the exceptionless quality of all international human standards, only a special class of them (i.e., the nonderogables).[27]

Three other claims in these maximalist accounts, particularly Wolterstorff's, merit some attention here. First, because the question of grounding human rights in a pluralist world does not depend upon the adequacy of either Wolterstorff's or Stackhouse's historical reading of the emergence of the very idea or concept, it is not necessary for our purposes to verify (or interrogate) either genealogy. To reiterate a point made previously, we can separate historical inquiry into the origins and development of the idea of human rights from conceptual or theoretical questions about what might be required today for their truth or justification. Second, to return to the question of the adequacy of capacities approaches in light of the argument from marginal cases, we should note that Wolterstorff overstates his case with respect to the property or relation for which we must to look to ground the idea of natural human rights.[28] He is correct that the property or relation should be one that all (not merely some) human beings possess, but he is wrong to stipulate further that it should also be one that "no non-human animal has," such that everyone's "non-instrumental worth" would be greater than that of any human animal (2008a, 321). The idea of human rights does not require a concomitant belief in either the superiority or uniqueness of *Homo sapiens sapiens* in comparison to all other species. The idea entails universal recognition of a set of rights for every human being without distinction of any kind but it need not say anything else about whether other species possess moral worth or even rights of their own. I return to a discussion of the ways in which claims of animal rights do and do not affect those of human rights in chapters 5 and 6.

Third and finally, we would be wise to remember that much of Wolterstorff's maximalism is devoted to defending the idea of natural human rights, not human rights *simpliciter,* even though he fully concedes that the latter need not be based on a conception of the former. That is, rather than ground the idea of human rights on the worth that inheres in every human being (i.e., on a conception of natural human rights), even Wolterstorff acknowledges that an international treaty could simply confer upon all human beings a set of rights that they might or might not (already) possess by nature, and then could justify doing so by consequentialist considerations (2008a, 317–18, 340–41). Although Wolterstorff implies that declarations on human rights that proclaim more than natural rights are not proclaiming "truly human rights," he elsewhere concedes that the extensions of natural rights and human rights "do not necessarily coincide" (2008a, 314–17).[29] Thus, whether the idea of human rights should track so closely with that of natural rights remains an open question, and defenders of human rights—whether maximalist or minimalist—need not follow Wolterstorff's lead in this regard without argument.

RISING TO THE MAXIMALIST CHALLENGE

As we have seen, claims about equivalence between the concepts of sacredness and inherent dignity, the absoluteness of all universal ethical standards, the historical development of the idea of human rights, humanity's exalted status over all other animals, or even the close linkage of human rights with natural rights transcend the basic maximalist challenge under consideration in this book and thus are not critical to its success or failure. We are left, then, with the primary maximalist conviction that will command the remainder of our attention—that the human rights project requires either some underlying religious vision or even a specific theological vision to the potential exclusion of others for its long-term success. Whether the maximalist challenge is understood in a religiously ecumenical or more exlusivistic fashion, human rights proponents would be wise to marshal their energies into overcoming it.

In insisting that human rights are necessarily premised upon religious assumptions, maximalists have essentially implied that the legitimacy of the human rights project itself turns on the truth or at least the feasibility of those religious convictions themselves (see Perry 2006, 161n3). If such a (maximalist) conclusion were correct and widely known, however, the project of globalizing human rights would surely encounter more resistance than it already does in some quarters, particularly among those who profess different views about religion than those purportedly undergirding the entire project. In addition, states that are officially secular, have no established religion, or have an established religion that differs from the religious tenets upon which any given maximalist justification for human rights would be based would also experience great difficulty in accepting the moral legitimacy and legal authority of human rights. To be sure, the truth-value of the maximalist contention that the idea of human rights requires some religious cosmology or other for its very intelligibility does not turn on whether large scores of people acknowledge or repudiate that claim. Nevertheless, strong practical incentives would remain for proponents of human rights to avoid appealing to controversial and seemingly indeterminate religious premises when attempting to justify their implementation everywhere, especially if some satisfactory nonreligious basis could be offered instead in their defense.

Beyond the practical problems of acceptability that the global human rights project would encounter if maximalism were both true and widely known, there would still be the deeper issue with which all human rights proponents, including maximalists themselves, would have to contend. Because one of the most widely cherished human rights today is freedom of religion and conscience, the maximalist proclamation that the idea of human rights inescapably rests upon one or other religious premise would appear to exist in some tension with that putative genuine provision. While it is, of course, logically possible that the right to religious freedom itself requires or presupposes a particular religious vision (e.g., belief in a tolerant and inclusivist God), the insistence upon the "ineliminably religious" character of human rights would still seem to work at cross-purposes with the putative right, especially since religious freedom is normally understood to encompass freedom *from* religion as well. What is more, given various maximalists' warnings that human rights are likely to be insufficiently recognized and protected wherever their religious roots are obscured, it is not unreasonable to suppose that those persuaded by maximalist arguments would subsequently seek a privileged place for the religious commitments that are purportedly sustaining the very idea, thereby raising concerns of bias and privilege.[30] Thus, in light of the seemingly intractable debates on religious matters as well as the cherished human right to religious freedom, advocates of human rights would be wise to search for a workable, nonreligious justification.

The remaining chapters of this book attempt to do just that, and in ways that are not adequately addressed by the aforementioned maximalists. Michael Perry briefly discusses and then dismisses Martha Nussbaum's understanding of the basic social emotion of compassion as a possible secular ground for human rights, but he does not consider her extensive work since the 1990s on the capability approach as a way to guarantee many of the same individual entitlements that are already protected by various international human rights treaties and conventions. This I seek to do in chapter 5. All of these maximalists argue for the conceptual and practical dependency of human rights upon some religious claim or other, but they do not (with the exception of Hans Küng) seriously consider whether universal human rights standards might be justified by an ecumenical "overlapping consensus" instead. I turn to consensus-based approaches to human rights in chapter 4. Finally, Wolterstorff very briefly describes Rawls's well-known theory of justice as an "inherent natural rights theory" (2008a, 15–17) but does not consider his more recent writings on human rights in the *Law of Peoples*, wherein he aims to defend their universal validity without having to weigh in on contested religious or philosophical claims about inherent human worth or dignity. I turn to Rawls's analysis and attempted evasion of maximalism in the next chapter.

Three

AN ENFORCEMENT-CENTERED APPROACH TO HUMAN RIGHTS, WITH SPECIAL REFERENCE TO JOHN RAWLS

What if we were to justify a doctrine of universal human rights according to the political role they were to play in the international arena and not on any account of inherent human dignity or worth? We would presumably evade the need to identify the dignity- or worth-making feature common to all human beings, bypass seemingly intractable philosophical or religious debates about why each human being merits our respect, and thereby provide a minimalist response to the maximalist challenge to human rights justification. And what if the primary function of human rights were to govern relations between political communities by setting the limits of tolerable pluralism so that a state's systematic failure to secure them would be sufficient to warrant diplomatic censure, economic sanctions, or even military intervention in extreme cases by others? Those who were intent on preserving a strong sense of state sovereignty would have strong incentives to avoid proliferating the range of goods or liberties that would be counted as genuine human rights. They would most likely even seek to curtail the existing catalog of internationally recognized human rights so that a state's refusal or inability to provide certain benefits, such as "periodic holidays with pay" or free and compulsory primary education, would not automatically give license to outsiders to intervene in their internal affairs (Art. 24, 26, UDHR).

John Rawls, who is widely regarded as the most important political philosopher of the latter half of the twentieth century, offers an account of human rights that essentially adopts this scenario. Although he is best known for developing principles of justice for a (single) liberal democratic society, his account of justice between and among peoples is more relevant for our purposes. Rawls's toleration of a type of nonliberal society that he calls "decent" leads him to reject an articulation of human rights that would be "peculiarly liberal or special to the Western tradition" (1999b, 65). As a result, only a subset of the various liberties and entitlements that are recognized today in core international human rights instruments meet his criteria for "human rights proper." An encounter with Rawls's work compels us to ask whether human rights must not only be justified on minimalist grounds to secure their universal validity but also have its list of provisions abridged for the same. While selective retrieval of Rawls's work is possible and will be pursued in subsequent chapters, I suggest here that his positive answers to those questions, together with his systematic privileging of the interests of "peoples" over "persons," betray the central insights of the human rights revolution of the twentieth century and beyond in ways that impair the overall attractiveness of his account.

A PRIMER ON RAWLS'S CONCEPTION
OF GLOBAL JUSTICE

The central problematic of Rawls's *Law of Peoples* is how to extend his social-contract inspired idea of "justice as fairness" for one constitutional democracy to cover international principles of justice for the world of nations. In comparative fashion to the difficulty discussed in his earlier *Political Liberalism*, the sheer diversity of cultures and traditions of thought complicates the search for and public justification of such principles. Rawls's ideal of "public reason" and its concomitant "criterion of reciprocity" require that we reason collectively "from premises we accept and think others could reasonably accept to conclusions we think they could also reasonably accept" (1999d, 155; see also 1999b, 14, 121–22; and 2001, 27).

Following Immanuel Kant's lead in "Perpetual Peace" (1795), Rawls does not aim to construct a world-state to satisfy the demands of global justice but rather a more modest federation of peaceful nations that is governed by its own "Law of Peoples," or political principles of international law and practice that are to regulate relations among societies (1999b, 3n1,10, 36; 2001, 13). Although he employs his familiar devices of the "original position" and the "veil of ignorance" to determine their content, it is surprisingly entire peoples and not individual persons who become his basic units of legal and moral concern.[1] This is why it is peoples and not persons who are modeled as free and equal parties behind the veil.[2] Rawls further presumes that liberal peoples would not push to globalize their liberal egalitarian commitments when granted the opportunity to do so. Instead, they concur with nonliberal but "decent" peoples upon the following eight intersocietal norms:[3]

1. Peoples are free and independent, and their freedom and independence are to be respected by other peoples.
2. Peoples are to observe treaties and undertakings.
3. Peoples are equal and are parties to the agreements that bind them.
4. Peoples are to observe a duty of non-intervention.
5. Peoples have the right of self-defense but no right to instigate war for reasons other than self-defense.
6. Peoples are to honor human rights.
7. Peoples are to observe certain specified restrictions in the conduct of war.
8. Peoples have a duty to assist other peoples living under unfavorable conditions that prevent their having a just or decent political and social regime. (1999b, 37)[4]

A central novelty of Rawls's *Law of Peoples* is his construction of an idealized Muslim republic called "Kazanistan" to illustrate what a hierarchically ordered "decent society" might resemble if a nonliberal comprehensive doctrine were widely endorsed by its citizens as well as built into its "basic structure."[5] Kazanistan officially gives pride of place to Islam in such a way as to underwrite its common good conception of justice, to view its citizens as responsible and cooperative members of groups instead of as "separate individuals" in possession of "equal basic rights as equal citizens," and to exclude non-Muslims from occupying upper positions of governmental authority and influence (1999b, 66, 71–78). While Kazanistan is not "as reasonable and just" as well-ordered liberal societies for these reasons, it is "not fully unreasonable" and decent nonetheless because it enjoys peaceful relations with its neighbors, honors all human rights that are recognized in the Law of Peoples, and allows for a form of civic participation through its consultative hierarchy (1999b, 74, 78, 83).[6]

Under Rawls's conception of international justice, then, a society's meeting the requirements of decency wins it the right to be left alone by others in addition to official recognition in the Society of Peoples as a "bona fide member" in "good standing" (1999b, 61, 79). Because decent societies are not inferior to liberal ones when evaluated from the perspective of compliance to international law (i.e., the Law of Peoples, including its particular schedule of human rights), Rawls instructs liberal peoples to refrain from exerting any kind of official sanction or incentive—whether diplomatic, economic, or military—for decent societies to reform along more liberal democratic lines (1999b, 59, 84–85; see also principles #3 and #4 of the Law of Peoples in 1999b, 37). This call of toleration is premised upon moral considerations and not simply a realist concession to a world already divided into sovereign states, as evidenced by Rawls's refusal to extend similar respect for the three other societies in his typology: outlaw states that wage wars of aggression and violate the basic human rights of their own subjects; societies burdened by unfavorable conditions that are neither expansive nor aggressive but cannot become well-ordered by their own efforts; and benevolent absolutisms that observe basic human rights but do not permit their citizens any meaningful role in politics.

What remains to be said in this primer is what Rawls means by the term "peoples." In ordinary usage, a people refers to an ethnic or national group with its own history and customs but generally without a clearly demarcated or internationally undisputed territory of their own, for example, the Palestinians, the Roma, the Kurds, the Dalit, the Chechens, and so forth. In contrast, a people in the Rawlsian sense is a corporate entity with an established system of governance, whose jurisdictional territory coincides with present-day boundaries, however "historically arbitrary" they might be (1999b, 8). While Rawlsian peoples are thus essentially coterminus with states, Rawls deliberately uses the former term instead of the latter to emphasize each people's cultural unity, willingness to refrain from wars of aggression or expansion, and recognition of others as equals (1999b, 27–30, 35).

HUMAN RIGHTS IN THE *LAW OF PEOPLES* COMPARED TO INTERNATIONAL HUMAN RIGHTS LAW

Rawls premises his account of human rights upon many of the same guiding convictions of the post–World War II international community that led to the founding of the United Nations and the UDHR: the scope of legitimate war must be severely curtailed, religiously incited violence must end, and otherwise sovereign states must be subject to some measure of scrutiny in their internal affairs. His refusal to ground human rights on any particular religious, philosophical, or metaphysical tenet also parallels the decision of the framers of the UDHR to avoid resolving debates about religion, human nature, or the ultimate ends of social and political life. Consider the following ways in which Rawls takes pains to distinguish his approach from various maximalist alternatives:

> These rights do not depend on any particular comprehensive religious doctrine or philosophical doctrine of human nature. The Law of Peoples does not say, for example, that human beings are moral persons and have equal worth in the eyes of God; or that they have certain moral and intellectual powers that entitle them to these rights. . . . Still, the Law of Peoples does not deny these doctrines. (1999b, 68)

Comprehensive doctrines, religious or non-religious, might base
the idea of human rights on theological, philosophical, or moral
conception of the nature of the human person. That path the Law
of Peoples does not follow. (1999b, 81)

Though the Law of Peoples could be supported by the Christian
doctrine of natural law, its principles are expressed solely in terms
of a political conception and its political values. (1999b, 104)

These similarities notwithstanding, although the International
Bill of Human Rights repeatedly invokes the "inherent dignity of . . .
all members of the human family" to ground the provisions stated
therein, such a refrain would prove too philosophically robust and
maximalist of a commitment for the Society of Peoples. Rawls's
minimalist strategy of justification is thus to keep the official defense
of human rights "political" by remaining conceptually nonreliant
upon "comprehensive doctrines" of any kind, while permitting each
member of the Society of Peoples to appeal to their deeper philosophical or religious commitments when justifying human rights for
themselves.[7] To illustrate, liberal peoples might accept and regard
human rights as a "proper subset" of the more extensive rights and
liberties that their constitutional regimes honor in the domestic
case because they already view their citizens as free and equal persons in possession of "'two moral powers'—a capacity for a sense of
justice and a capacity for a conception of the good" (1999b, 82; see
also 2001, 18–19; and 1996, §5). Although decent peoples do not
subscribe to the (liberal) ideas of individual freedom and equality
but view persons instead more as "members of groups" than as
"atomistic units," they would still presumably endorse human
rights, thereby enabling their citizens to "meet their duties and obligations" and to participate in a "decent system of social cooperation" (1999b, 66, 68, 71–73).[8]

Perhaps the most striking contrast between Rawlsian human rights
and the body of internationally recognized human rights is that
Rawls regards only a "special class of urgent rights" to be human
rights proper (1999b, 79). His list of real as opposed to counterfeit

claims includes the group rights to be free from mass murder or genocide as well as the individual rights to life, liberty (i.e., freedom from slavery, serfdom, and forced occupation), a "sufficient" but "not equal" liberty of conscience, personal property, and formal equality before the law wherein similar cases are to be treated similarly (1999b, 65, 78–79). Although Rawls repeatedly enjoins all peoples to respect the human rights of women, his plea is weakened by the Society of People's refusal to count as genuine human rights the freedoms of opinion, expression, association, and political participation and even the principle of nondiscrimination on the basis of sex or gender (1999b, 75, 111).[9] To be clear, Rawls considers as genuine only Articles 3–18 of the UDHR and their "obvious implications" (viz., the conventions on genocide and apartheid) while dismissing the universal validity of the remainder because they either "presuppose specific kinds of institutions" such as social security or describe mere "liberal aspirations" (1999b, 80n23).[10] In sum, Rawls's account not only omits key civil and political rights that are already recognized in many international human rights conventions and treaties, but it further excludes economic and social rights of any kind beyond what the "means of subsistence and security" might imply in the right to life.[11]

What can account for Rawls's austere list when compared with the more extensive protections afforded by the International Bill of Human Rights and other international treaties or conventions? While there are many possible answers, three in particular stand out for their explanatory value: a primary concern to manage relations among political communities instead of among individual human beings, a desire to avoid ethnocentrism, and an offering of a highly enforcement-centered interpretation of human rights.

First, recall Rawls's decision to prioritize the rights and interests of entire peoples over individual persons when determining principles of global justice, most notably by methodologically situating the representatives of only the former but not the latter in the international original positions. Such a construction would work to legitimate the discriminatory but lawful treatment that minorities and nonconformists would encounter under each decent society's established religion or philosophy. It would also render noncitizen inhabitants of liberal societies more vulnerable given their lack of a more robust conception of human rights to which they could appeal should all the rights and liberties guaranteed in their liberal democratic constitutional regimes fail to apply to them (as is generally the case). Surprisingly, Rawls nearly concedes as much when he acknowledges that his theoretical framework is "fair to peoples and not to individual persons"—a surprising remark from someone who once famously argued against utilitarianism that "each person possesses an inviolability founded on justice that even the welfare of society as a whole cannot override" (1999b, 17n9; 1999c, §1 at 3). Despite the strong liberal egalitarianism of his earlier writings, Rawls explicitly rejects the ideal of liberal cosmopolitan justice for the world, and thus the prospect of either symmetrically situating all persons in a global original position or otherwise internationalizing "justice as fairness" so that everyone would be regarded as free and equal, granted equal basic liberties, and ensured a principle of distributive justice across societies (1999b, 82–83, 118–20).[12]

Second, Rawls's decision to guide the selection and justification of the international principles of justice by the "criterion of reciprocity" leads him to strike from the catalog of genuine human rights all those he surmises would be reasonably rejected as politically parochial or biased toward liberalism or the West. That decent hierarchical peoples do not subscribe to a liberal view of justice wherein individuals possess "equal basic rights as citizens" thus explains the many differences between Rawlsian human rights and his standard of decency, on the one hand, and international human rights law, on the other. Case in point: neither the *Law of Peoples* nor Rawls's paradigmatic decent society (Kazanistan) protect universal and equal suffrage in genuine and periodic elections, the right of equal access to public service in his country, or the equal freedom of thought, conscience, and religion (see Art. 2, 18, 21, UDHR). Although liberals might bemoan the exclusion of these civil and political rights from the purview of the *Law of Peoples*, Rawls insists that omissions of this kind would bring rewards of its own: namely, the maintenance of "mutual respect between peoples and of each people maintaining its self-respect, not lapsing into contempt for the other, on one side, and bitterness and resentment, on the other" (1999b, 122, 61).[13]

Third, recall that for Rawls to call a liberty, benefit, opportunity, or process a genuine human right is to identify what the Society of Peoples has a legitimate interest to protect—by diplomatic or economic sanctions or even by military force, if necessary, in cases of grave and systematic violations (1999b, 36, 80–81). Because chronic and egregious abuses of human rights provide in-principle justifications for outsiders to intervene, those wishing to minimize legitimate causes for interference would obviously refrain from couching all real or worthwhile public policy goals in the language of rights (see Tasioulas 2002, 384–85). Philosopher Joseph Raz understands parsimony of this kind to be a virtue. He reasons that the strategy of identifying something as a human right only if it would functionally disable an argument against third-party interference in the (otherwise) sovereign affairs of a state would render the idea of human rights more determinate. More specifically, if we were to follow Rawls's lead in conceptualizing human rights more narrowly through their interference-justifying role, we would have a method for determining which claims were genuine human rights and which were not, we would forstall what some have judged to be an excessive proliferation of human rights that has given the whole enterprise a "bad name," and we would put an end to the increasingly common tendency today of articulating everything of importance in morality or justice in terms of rights (Raz 2007).

Whatever the real reason for Rawls's highly constrained account of what human rights are essentially supposed to *be* and to *do*, the consequences of his rereading are considerable. As alluded to earlier, his comparatively anemic account of the rights we all possess as human beings would serve to support rather than challenge each well-ordered society's existing schedule of liberties or other entitlements. Imagine, for example, a liberal society that failed to recognize any economic and social rights beyond the aforementioned "means of subsistence and security"—it neither recognized the right to work and to receive equal pay for equal work, nor the right of children to enjoy the "same social protection" whether born "in or out of wedlock" (see Art. 23, 25, UDHR). Such a society might be judged deficient from the perspective of what particular conceptions of liberalism or social justice would require but would be fully compliant with all universally valid principles of justice in the Society of Peoples. Consider also the legal requirement in decent hierarchical societies that dissenters "stay within the basic framework of the common good idea of justice" when expressing political protest—a stipulation tantamount to obliging dissenters to voice their criticisms from within the confines of the state-established comprehensive doctrine (e.g., Islam or a certain interpretation of it in Kazanistan) to which they most likely already conscientiously object (1999b, 72). Civil rights advocates would undoubtedly object to those constraints on free speech, but they would be without the backing of international law in their critique because the *Law of Peoples* does not recognize any such human right to the freedom of opinion and expression (see Art. 19, UDHR).

A separate but closely related consequence of Rawls's comparatively downsized account of human rights is that it would obstruct certain types of criticism that would otherwise be warranted. To illustrate this concern, consider the Republic of Zimbabwe—a state widely considered at the time of this writing to be one of the poorest and most repressive regimes in the world. Zimbabwe would most likely be classified as either a "society burdened by unfavorable conditions" or an "outlaw state" or both under Rawls's fivefold schema. It would be a society burdened by unfavorable conditions because of its hyperinflation, high unemployment rate (estimated in 2005 at 80 percent), HIV/AIDs and cholera pandemic, low life expectancy (thirty-four years for women and thirty-seven years for men, according to the World Health Organization's 2008 statistics), ongoing food shortage crisis, and other severe problems. It would be an outlaw state because of the widespread international consensus that

Zimbabwe for many years has been systematically violating even what Rawls would regard as urgent human rights.

While Zimbabwe would neither be eligible for membership in Rawls's Society of Peoples nor immune from reform-oriented intervention by others, we should be clear about what the Society of Peoples could and could not legitimately criticize per its principles of international justice (i.e., the *Law of Peoples*) if the following widely reported allegations of systematic human rights abuses have any basis in truth. The Society of Peoples could justifiably object to President Robert Mugabe and the ruling party's (the Zimbabwe African National Union–Pacific Front) use of security forces and war veterans to arbitrarily arrest, detain, torture, and even kill known political dissidents or those believed to be sympathetic to the opposition party, the Movement for Democratic Change, since those atrocities violate the "urgent rights" that the *Law of Peoples* recognizes (see Articles 3, 5, and 9, UDHR). They could also legitimately intervene on behalf of the government's manipulation of the Grain Marketing Board to routinely and publicly deny maize meal to suspected opposition supporters on the grounds that withholding the nation's food staple in times of low production and drought-induced food shortages violates the right to "subsistence and security" implied by the universal right to life. Nevertheless, from the same standpoint of what respect for Rawlsian human rights requires, they would ironically be precluded from criticizing what is most likely driving these systematic human rights abuses in the first place—the ruling party's attempts to stifle political opposition in order to preserve its own hegemony—since the right to freedom of expression or to "hold opinions without interference" is not recognized as universally valid in the *Law of Peoples* (see Art. 19, UDHR). Indeed, the Society of Peoples would have to truncate its critique of Zimbabwe in still other ways. They could not justifiably object to the ruling party's attempts to crack down on independent reporting by journalists per se because the *Law of Peoples* does not recognize the human right to "seek, receive, and impart information and ideas through any media" (Art. 19, UDHR). Nor could they denounce widespread reports of voter intimidation and electoral fraud in recent parliamentary, general, and presidential run-off elections (in 2005 and 2008) because the *Law of Peoples* does not recognize any universal right to "take part in the government of [one's] country" or to have "periodic and genuine elections" that are determined by secret and free suffrage (Art. 21, UDHR).[14] In Zimbabwe or elsewhere in the "realistic utopia" that Rawls envisions, it would be supererogatory at best—required by neither any universal principles of justice nor any standards of "decency"—for any society to guarantee a genuinely free press, allow for more than a single-party system, or arrange its domestic political institutions in such a way where "the will of the people shall be the basis of the authority of government" (ibid.).

RAWLSIAN HUMAN RIGHTS: AN ASSESSMENT

As we have seen, Rawls's account of human rights fares poorly when judged from the perspective of both international human rights law and conventional wisdom in many quarters about the broader range of rights that we all have as human beings. However, since it remains to be seen whether international law and our intuitions about such matters are correct to begin with, we cannot dismiss the viability of Rawls's account for failing to live up to those standards without begging the crucial question.

How might we then evaluate Rawls's approach to human rights in ways that would not presuppose the legitimacy of extant international human rights law? One way to do so would be to consider the adequacy of Rawls's overall approach to global justice, with the aim of assessing the impact of his theoretical framework upon his resultant conception of human rights. Another way to do so would be to identify certain vulnerabilities in the inner logic of Rawls's account of human rights, to determine whether Rawls ultimately provides a satisfactory answer to the very problems he was intent on solving. On my reading on either front, Rawls leaves much to be desired.

Let us begin, then, with the overall conception of international justice within which Rawls's account of human rights is framed.

Beyond the criticisms already noted of his consideration of peoples and not individual persons as the basic units of moral and legal concern, Rawls's failure to adjust the abstraction of a people as a culturally, morally, and politically unified entity suggests a return to the Westphalian system of national sovereignty that the founding of the United Nations and the human rights revolution of the mid-twentieth century and beyond have generally sought to transcend.[15] Rawls's theoretical framework thereby obscures the fact that many of our world's most intense and violent conflicts occur within legally recognized though hotly disputed borders and not so much between them—for example, the post–civil war genocidal conflict in the Darfur region of Sudan; the land and sovereignty disputes between Israelis and Palestinians, especially in the occupied territories; Hindu–Muslim outbreaks of violence in Kashmir; the Sinhalese-Tamil ethnoreligious conflict in Sri Lanka; the "ethnic cleansing" and various sites of balkanization in the former Yugoslavia; the Basque separatist movement in Spain; the Corsican independence movement against France; the centuries-old conflict between Catholics and Protestants in Northern Ireland; and the relatively bloodless struggles between Francophones and Anglophones in Montreal, Canada, to name a few well-known cases. Whatever the value Rawls's concept of a people might have had then—and philosopher Stephen Macedo has eloquently suggested the "moral significance of collective self-governance (2004)[16]—has been compromised by the empirical falsehood that the identities and boundaries of peoples coincide with that of states in any one-to-one relationship (see Benhabib 2004).

While some critics have faulted Rawls's conception of peoples for these reasons alone, our primary concern is that these limitations cannot but adversely affect his account of human rights because the concepts are intertwined in such a way that observance of the latter (human rights) is largely what justifies toleration among the former (peoples). Rather than connect human rights primarily to a people's foreign policy in governing relations with others, however, why not tie them directly to meeting what justice to individuals requires

(1999b, 10, 82–83)? As Allen Buchanan (2000) has forcefully argued, we must maintain the conceptual and moral prioritization of individuals over states, especially since individuals in our contemporary world do not always live their whole lives in their country of origin due to the effects of globalization, migration, and mass exodus as a result of natural disasters, war, or civil strife.[17]

Turning now to a direct assessment of Rawls's account of human rights and not just the larger global justice framework on which it depends, let us consider anew his conflation of the concept and extension of human rights with the morality of humanitarian intervention. Because those two concepts have historically been distinct, it remains to be seen why the answer we give to the former should determine the response we give to the latter. Of course, Rawls could be correct that a society that honors a "special class of urgent rights" but precludes women or members of minority groups from holding certain offices, bans trade unions, disallows a free press, does not provide universal education, or fails to guarantee a range of democratic freedoms should not automatically be subject to economic sanctions or military interference by others. After all, a variant of this scenario is certainly how Catholic social ethicist David Hollenbach reads Rawls when he likens present-day Thailand to a Rawlsian-type decent society, and then encourages Westerners to object to Thailand's legal prohibitions against criticizing the Thai king without resorting to force when doing so (Hollenbach 2003, 250–54).[18] But Rawls overlooks the fact that third parties could still refrain from intervening in the internal affairs of others without having to deny that there were any genuine human rights at stake that were being systematically violated or left unfulfilled. Indeed, Sally King has argued that socially and politically "engaged Buddhists" in Tibet, Burma, and elsewhere might find much to commend in Rawls's duty of nonintervention (i.e., principle #4 of the *Law of Peoples*) because of the suffering that such intervention would likely inflict, although they would still find "sobering" Rawls's paltry schedule of human rights, given their likely support of all (not merely some) of the provisions of the UDHR (King 2006, 654–55).[19]

To underscore this point about the difference between making a normative judgment and enforcing it, Martha Nussbaum (2002) has constructed a different decent society from Rawls's paradigmatic Kazanistan—a counterfactual "Kerala" that became an independent Roman Catholic nation instead of part of India at the time of India's independence in 1947. While she believes that a counterfactual Kerala's institutionalized forms of sex-based discrimination would be problematic but still insufficient to justify forceful interference by outsiders, her point is that Rawls need neither to have curtailed his list of human rights so severely nor to have regarded decent peoples as coequal members in good standing in the Society of Peoples in order to display such cautiousness. Instead, nonintervention could be justified by a host of other legitimate considerations: limited resources, other important priorities, countervailing desires for postcolonial self-determination, or a diagnosis that coercive intervention would most likely cause more damage than good and even set a deleterious precedential effect (1999b, 59; Nussbaum 2006b, 255–56.)[20]

In turning to the second major difficulty with the inner logic of Rawls's account of human rights we now face its most serious problem from the perspective of the central question animating this book. The principal fault with Rawls's account of human rights is neither its meager offerings when compared to the standards of international law and other instruments, nor its nonconformity with existing practices of providing a more extensive list of protections than what might be appropriate to intervene coercively in their defense, nor even that it is housed under a problematic conception of internally homogenous peoples who purportedly exist in the world under a collection of nation-states. Rather, the fundamental flaw is Rawls's failure to deliver what he set out to do: provide an adequate account of justification. Rawls's approach ultimately remains vulnerable to the charge of ethnocentrism, even though his reduced schedule of human rights provisions and narrow circumscription of their role were expressly designed to overcome it. His account also cannot avoid implicitly committing itself to the real moral worth of all individual persons, even though the public justification for human rights that he champions repudiates the need to do precisely that.

To see why Rawls's account ultimately remains susceptible to suspicions of ethnocentrism, recall first his understanding that the Law of Peoples would be "universal in its reach" if its principles could be endorsed by liberal and decent peoples alike, without requiring the latter to "abandon or modify their religious institutions and adopt liberal ones" (1999b, 121). As we have seen, Rawls does not hold decent societies to the same standard of reasonableness that is operative in liberal societies. Kazanistan can legally establish Islam even though it would be "oppressive" for a liberal society to use the state's coercive power to do the same, and it can legally prohibit non-Muslims from occupying certain positions of governmental power even though "justice of fairness" would require parallel offices and positions in liberal societies to be formally open to all (1996, 37, 60–61; 1999c, §11–§12; and 2001, §11.3, §13). Now one of the many problems with this less demanding standard of decency is that Rawls has not adequately explained why "decency" should pass the test of universally validity when "reasonableness" could not. If Kazanistanis could rightly object to the parochial nature of liberal principles of justice, what would prevent nonliberal but nondecent peoples from analogously objecting to the ethnocentric bias of decent standards (Hayfa 2004)? Rawls has not even attempted to justify global principles of justice to this latter group: he has situated only the representatives of liberal and decent peoples, but not all possible types, in the international original positions.

This concern about ethnocentrism reveals what is woefully missing in Rawls's account: a principled explanation for why certain goods or rights should be counted as universally valid requirements of justice and why others should not. Put simply, any response to the first question of the form "because liberal and decent societies would agree to them" would only answer it by definitional fiat. Rawls sometimes writes to substantiate rather than undermine this concern that his standard of decency stems from a parochial (i.e., nonobjective) source, such as when he repeatedly emphasizes that the *Law of Peoples* is developed within political liberalism as an extension of a liberal idea of justice but is less stringent than what globalized principles of liberalism would require (1999b, 3, 55). Rawls also persists in his criticism of "benevolent absolutisms" in contradistinction to "decent societies" because the former fails to offer their citizens any meaningful role in politics (1999b, 4, 63). And yet, because nothing in the eight principles of intersocietal justice (i.e., the *Law of Peoples*) or in Rawls's list of "human rights proper" requires societies to grant their citizens the right to participate in the political decision-making process, both the judgment that benevolent absolutisms are not "well ordered" for this reason and their exclusion from membership in the Society of Peoples remain unjustified in his own account.

Sympathetic readers of Rawls are likely to retort that the international principles of law and justice that are to regulate the Society of Peoples are not in fact ethnocentric. They might counter that Rawls rejects the universal validity of some provisions of the UDHR for principled, not merely parochial, reasons: the excluded provisions either state mere "liberal aspirations" or else "presuppose specific kinds of institutions" (1999b, 80n23). I would argue that if the aforementioned criteria of exclusion redeem Rawls from the charge of ethnocentrism, they do so at the price of exposing him to new charges of either argumentative incompleteness or arbitrariness or both. For if it is truly the presupposition of "specific kinds of institutions" that precludes certain provisions such as the "right to social security" or the "right to equal pay for equal work" from counting as human rights proper (Art. 22–23, UDHR), other human rights that presuppose other specific institutions should be invalidated as well, though they are not. Instead, Rawls implicitly acknowledges the universal validity of particular institutions: those associated with criminal justice (e.g., public trials, national tribunals, penal codes), those associated with a world divided into sovereign states (e.g., the right to seek asylum, the right to a nationality), and others mentioned within the Article 3–18 range of the UDHR that he endorses as universally valid.

Most importantly, concerns about argumentative incompleteness and arbitrariness are not limited to Rawls's isolation of "human rights proper" but adversely affect the public political justification of human rights that stands at the heart of his minimalist approach to the topic. Recall Rawls's fundamental conviction that the Society of Peoples could defend the universal validity of human rights without having to either rely upon "comprehensive doctrines of truth or of right," or specify why each human being qua human being is entitled to this special set of protections. At the public, official level, international society could promote and defend human rights simply for contributing to a "decent scheme of political and social cooperation" and thus to international peace and security (1999b, 55, 65, 68).

This concern about international peace and security is why outlaw states, or states that refuse to comply with the *Law of Peoples* and thus "deeply affect the international climate of power and violence," are not to be tolerated by others (1999b, 5, 81). Surprisingly then, when considering a hypothetical scenario of an outlaw state that systematically violates the human rights of its members but poses no external aggression or danger to others because it is "indeed quite weak," Rawls concludes that "a prima facie case for intervention of some kind" still exists (1999b, 81n26; 93–94n6).[21] Now the problem with Rawls's interventionist inclination is that it would remain without proper justification because the actions of the weak outlaw state would neither be compromising the scheme of "political and social cooperation" among the world's peoples nor be negatively affecting the international climate of power and violence. Still worse is the fact that the best or strongest reason for third-party intervention in that or any other case—a desire to protect the lives and well-being of human rights victims because of their moral worth—is one that the Society of Peoples would be officially prohibited from having, much less acting upon.

In sum, Rawls's account contains two fundamental convictions that appear to be working at cross-purposes with each other. He wants the "political (moral) force" of human rights to be valid everywhere, which is to say human rights would apply to all persons in the world, even if all peoples do not support them locally (1999b, 80). But he also wants to offer a public justification of human rights that is based only upon the mutually desirable outcomes that it holds for all peoples while evading all questions of why all persons would be entitled to such protections in the first place (1999b, 80–81). As discussed previously, what further complicates these difficulties is Rawls's prima facie commitment to defend the human rights of individuals in the case of externally weak outlaw states. This commitment reveals that Rawls has either reached a conclusion that his theory cannot support, or that he has been invested in the real worth of individual human beings all along but could not "own" that conclusion in light of his constitutive understanding of a publicly defensible reason. We must conclude, then, that Rawls has not provided us with a satisfactory response to the maximalist challenge of human rights justification and thus we should be prepared to look elsewhere for a more suitable alternative.

CONCLUSION

There is much to admire about John Rawls's serious engagement with diversity and difference, whether in the context of modern liberal democracies or between and among myriad peoples of the world. There is also much to appreciate in Rawls's attempt to defend human rights against persistent charges of Western bias. However, Rawls's reinterpretation of human rights as a special class of urgent rights that the international community has sufficient reason to enforce has led, unfortunately, to a dismissal of all that transcends that bare minimum. Human rights would accordingly serve as a corrective and aspirational goal to the positive law and institutional structures of only two ideal types of societies in the world (i.e., burdened societies and outlaw states) but not all of them. If only Rawls had followed Kant's lead in "Perpetual Peace" even more closely than he claimed to have done, given Kant's stipulation that perpetual peace would require each member state to have a republican form of government that would respect, among other principles, the "legal equality for everyone (as citizens)."

I have argued that Rawls's principal fault was to make peoples and not individual persons his basic units of moral-political analysis and concern, and then to defend international principles of justice in accordance with a predetermined standard of "decency" that was not fully just on his own reading, and was either arbitrary or potentially ethnocentric according to mine. Other peculiarities of Rawls's approach include a refusal to specify what it is about us as human beings that would morally require others to come to our aid in cases of systematic and egregious violations of our rights and a refusal to provide explicit protections against legal discrimination based on categories such as religion, race, or sex.

Thus, it remains an open question whether we could preserve a more extensive catalog of human rights and a broader understanding of their purposes (beyond their interference-justifying role) while still being able to justify them in ways that entailed minimum philosophical commitments. Our next two approaches, the first of which we now turn, attempt to do precisely that.

Four

CONSENSUS-BASED APPROACHES TO HUMAN RIGHTS

I am quite certain that my way of justifying belief in the rights of man and the ideal of liberty, equality, fraternity is the only way with a firm foundation in truth. This does not prevent me from being in agreement on these practical convictions with people who are certain that their way of justifying them, entirely different from mine or opposed to mine . . . is equally the only way founded upon truth.

—Jacques Maritain (1949)

Consensus-based approaches to human rights retain an insight discussed in the previous chapter that different peoples can endorse the same list of provisions for markedly dissimilar final reasons. Such ecumenicism requires the official account of human rights to be theory-thin at the level of practical standards, thus allowing different parties to draw from their deeper philosophical or religiocultural beliefs in their support of those shared norms. By permitting each community to ground human rights in their own terms and perspectives, the Western philosophical or theological commitments from which the idea of individual rights is popularly believed to have originally sprung would represent only one out of many possible ways of justifying human rights today.

Ideas of consensus and attempts at consensus-building have largely been embraced for their pragmatism and respect for religious and cultural diversity. Many, but not all, who seek to justify human rights in this fashion draw inspiration from John Rawls's conception of

obtaining an "overlapping consensus" on political principles of justice, though not particularly from his own application of the concept
in the *Law of Peoples* and thus not necessarily in ways that he would
avow. While the search for and successful demonstration of a cross-
cultural consensus on human rights will remain important for many
reasons, this approach cannot settle the issue of human rights justification if it fails to provide a common rationale that transcends
the myriad local varieties and if it neglects to explain why its results
should have justificatory force. Still, whether the consensus on human rights is to affect the actual list of practical standards or only
their manner of justification or both, we will have much to learn
from the important disparities between both Rawls's and Maritain's
understanding of the role of consensus for human rights and contemporary appropriations of their ideas for the same.

OBTAINING A CROSS-CULTURAL CONSENSUS ON HUMAN RIGHTS

As this chapter's epigraph suggests, French Catholic natural law theorist Jacques Maritain originated the idea that "men mutually opposed in their theoretical conceptions can come to a merely practical
agreement regarding a list of human rights" (1951, 76). As a key
player in discussions leading up to the formation of the UDHR, Maritain once keenly observed that delegates with "violently opposed
ideologies" could surprisingly agree upon rights, but "on condition
that no one asks [them] why" (1949, 9).

While consensus-based approaches to human rights today have
largely retained many of Maritain's insights, they instead more commonly refer to Rawls's idea of obtaining an "overlapping consensus"
on political principles of justice. Confucian scholar Joseph Chan, for
one, encourages all cultures to "justify human rights in their own
terms and perspectives, in the hope that an 'overlapping consensus'"
on their norms could emerge from "self-searching exercises as well
as common dialogue" (1999, 212). Sudanese Muslim legal scholar
and former executive director of Human Rights Watch in Africa Ab-

dullahi A. An-Na'im seeks to build a Rawlsian-inspired consensus with plural foundations "around the normative content and implementation mechanisms of human rights" (2002, 16). Catholic Canadian philosopher Charles Taylor also ponders what a "genuine, unforced international consensus on human rights" would look like; he reasons that it would resemble "what Rawls describes . . . as an 'overlapping consensus'":

> Different groups, countries, religious communities, and civilizations, although holding incompatible fundamental views on theology, metaphysics, human nature, and so on, would come to an agreement on certain norms that ought to govern human behavior. Each would have its own way of justifying this from out of its profound background conception. We would agree on the norms while disagreeing on why they were the right norms, and we would be content to live in this consensus, undisturbed by the differences of profound underlying belief. (Taylor 1999, 124)

Others who refer in some fashion to the Rawlsian idea of obtaining an "overlapping consensus" on human rights include Tore Lindholm (1992), Sumner Twiss (1998b), Amy Gutmann (2001), Jack Donnelly (2003), David Hollenbach (2003), Joshua Cohen (2004), Farid Abdel-Nour (2004), Martha Nussbaum (1999, 2006b), Rory O'Connell (2005), and Ari Kohen (2007).

Before evaluating the adequacy of these appropriated Rawlsian ideas for human rights, it is worth pausing to consider why Rawls's work in political theory might have attracted such a large and diverse following. Recall from the previous chapter that Rawlsian political liberalism requires the political conception of justice regulating the basic structure of society to be presented in a "freestanding" manner. It must be accessible to and compatible with the reasonable "comprehensive doctrines" that are held among its citizenry but conceptually independent of any of them as well as silent on the question of their underlying truth or falsity. A Rawlsian modern liberal democracy that, for instance, legally banned the institution of slavery would provide conceptual space for its citizens to affirm the legitimacy of that prohibition out of their dissimilar—even if mutually incompatible—theoretical commitments. Its Christians might support the ban out of an interpretation of what social justice or love of neighbor requires, its Buddhists out of an ideal of compassion to all sentient beings, its Kantians out of an imperative to treat all persons as ends in themselves, its utilitarians out of a calculation that slavery would decrease rather than augment the total welfare, and so forth. Now the consensus against slavery (or concerning any other matter affecting society's basic structure) need neither be universal nor complete, which is why Rawls speaks of an overlapping, not total, consensus to be formed by society's "reasonable" citizens, in addition to the need to contain all "unreasonable" views as they would "war and disease" (1996, 59–61, 64n19; 2001, §57.4).[1] Rawls's point is that a politically liberal society could justifiably prohibit slavery and even promote the legal equality of all citizens so long as it refrained from taking an official stand on the metaphysical question of the real or equal moral worth of all would-be slaves in relation to their would-be masters.

Thus, when proponents of consensus-based approaches to human rights appropriate these concepts of Rawlsian political liberalism, they loosely map Rawls's "political conception of justice" with international human rights standards and then "comprehensive doctrines" with the myriad cultural, philosophical, or religious traditions of the world. Just as Rawls argued for the legitimacy of liberal democratic values in a modern constitutional democracy in spite of the diverse and even mutually incompatible beliefs about them among its citizenry, so consensus-seekers defend the universal validity of human rights even in the absence of global agreement on their theoretical foundations by those who would nonetheless be bound by them.

To repeat, whether Rawls would actually endorse the aforementioned manner of appropriating his work for human rights remains a separate matter.[2] That question aside, we should acknowledge at the outset that there are at least two ways to conceptualize what this two-tiered approach to human rights would entail procedurally. In the first, the world community would attempt to generate anew a list of universally valid human rights standards while allowing each party to justify the results of the consensus idiosyncratically. In the second, the world community would presume that current international human rights law (viz., the International Bill of Human Rights and the nine core international human rights instruments[3]) already represents a suitable consensus on universally enforceable standards of conduct and thus would use this approach as a way to legitimate plural foundations for human rights.

OPTION 1: CONSENSUS-PRODUCING NEW UNIVERSAL HUMAN RIGHTS STANDARDS

Any search for a cross-cultural consensus on universally valid human rights provisions could itself be conducted in either a narrow or broad manner. The former alternative would involve attempts to isolate a common core while the latter would use a more relaxed standard of consistency.

Consensus Construed Narrowly; Consensus Construed Broadly

If pursued narrowly, the task of achieving cross-cultural consensus would involve identifying a set of core moral principles to which all the cultural and religious traditions of the world already subscribe to serve as the basis for an official and public catalog of human rights. Charles Taylor appears to have something like this procedure in mind when he surmises that we can "find in all cultures condemnations of genocide, murder, torture, and slavery, as well as of, say 'disappearances' and the shooting of innocent demonstrators" (1999, 125). Taylor believes the insight that "humans are especially important, and demand special treatment" to be present in some form everywhere because he regards it to be a "basic human reaction" that is developed further in various ways: a conception of the worth of each human being, an injunction to treat humans always as ends only and never as merely means, or a doctrine of universal rights

(1993, 227). Michael Walzer has similarly suggested that a comparison of the world's "thick" moral codes might yield a "thin" set of "standards to which all societies can be held . . . [such as] rules against murder, deceit, torture, oppression, and tyranny" (1994, 10). While Walzer does not directly connect his comments to human rights, he supposes that contemporary North Americans and Europeans would express these standards in that language, believes that the moral vocabulary of rights is translatable, and concludes that rights-talk is not a "bad way of talking about injuries and wrongs that no one should have to endure" (ibid.). According to Michael Ignatieff, we can retain the universality of human rights if we restrict ourselves to a "decidedly 'thin' theory of what is right, a definition of the minimal conditions for any life at all" (2001, 56). His own drastically pruned list includes putting an end to "torture, beatings, killings, rape and assault" and improving "as best as we can, the security of ordinary people" (ibid., 173).

As these musings by Taylor, Walzer, and Ignatieff suggest, the restriction of genuine human rights to the area of preexisting agreement among the myriad traditions, cultures, or political moralities of the world would yield a very short list of provisions—one markedly smaller than what the International Bill of Human Rights, other core human rights treaties, and even Rawls's aforementioned *Law of Peoples* aim to protect. This search for the "lowest common denominator" would undoubtedly exclude many rights that are widely regarded today to be of paramount importance, including the right not to be discriminated against on the basis of race, religion, or sex, because there are extant cultural, religious, and political traditions that discriminate accordingly.

If we were to conduct the search for consensus more broadly, however, a norm or standard would not need to be explicitly present in every culture to count as a genuine human right, provided it was minimally consistent with each culture's preexisting values or commitments. Ethicists, philosophers, theologians, jurists, sociologists, and other scholar-activists would then seek to locate affinities, analogues, or theoretical precedents between the values of the religious or cultural traditions under examination and contemporary human rights standards. Such a search might involve attempts to assimilate Christian teachings on agape and human dignity, the Jewish prophetic tradition, the Islamic Shari'ah, the Buddhist ideal of compassion, the Hindu *dharma*, the spirit of the African *ujamaa* or traditional extended family, and so forth into the language of human rights (Alves 2002; see also Falk 1992).

While this broad construal of consensus would most likely yield a more extensive list of human rights protections than would the previous version, it is worth recalling that convergence on human rights norms *within* any given tradition would most likely remain imperfect or incomplete. Just as we saw in chapter 1 how conceptual resources within Confucianism could be marshaled either in favor of or against contemporary human rights standards, so a mixed reception would presumably be obtained in other traditions as well. Within the Christian tradition, for example, opinions on the issue of conceptual compatibility with contemporary human rights norms range from outright rejection to support conditional upon embedding human rights within a larger framework of biblical or theological principles, to wholesale endorsement without further qualification (see, e.g., Little 1990; Johnson 1996; Villa-Vicencio 1999–2000). Still, even if one's particular cultural, philosophical, or religious tradition has not (yet) affirmed any consensus-driven statement on human rights, history has shown that even the staunchest critics can be turned. To cite a well-known example, certain modernist freedoms that were vigorously opposed by the Catholic Church for centuries, most famously by Pope Pius IX's *Syllabus of Errors* (1864), have since been embraced as wholly consistent with Catholic social thought, as the Second Vatican Council's *Dignitatis humanae* (1965) and *Gaudium et spes* (1965) amply demonstrate. The possibility of ongoing change and adaptation in religion also leads Abdullahi An-Na'im to hope for continual transformation in his own tradition of Islam because, on his view, "every form of Sunni, Sufi (mythic), or Shi'a belief held by its adherents today as 'orthodox' was, at some point in history, a dissident view which survived against the opposition of the 'orthodoxy' at that time"

(1996, 339). In any event, while scholar-practitioners internal to the traditions themselves are probably in the best position to encourage reform for reasons of competence and credibility, nothing should preclude culturally sensitive and informed outsiders from engaging in what John Rawls has called "arguing from conjecture." He writes: "We argue from what we believe, or conjecture, are other people's basic doctrines, religious or secular, and try to show them that, despite what they might think, they can still endorse a reasonable political conception that can provide a basis for public reasons" (1999d, 155–56).

Evaluating Consensus-Restricted Lists of Human Rights

Why might some proponents of human rights seek to restrict their content to the area of overlap among the world's extant moralities under the narrow "core" or broad "consistency" models discussed earlier? Perhaps it is because the scaled-back list would allow human rights claims to appear more urgent and serious. It might also prevent any people, culture, or tradition from rejecting the results of consensus on complaint of ethnocentric partiality or prejudice. In addition, given an increased willingness among UN member-states to regard gross abuses of human rights as a sufficient rationale for "humanitarian intervention," a restriction of this sort could also help to justify reform-oriented interference into the internal affairs of a sovereign state.[4] Admittedly, "humanitarian intervention" in both concept and practice remains controversial to many for its overriding of state sovereignty, often-unclear juridical status, the interveners' not uncommon mixture of other-regarding and self-interested motives, and the loss of life and other forms of destruction that the resort to force normally brings. But however the moral propriety and legal status of any "humanitarian intervention" is to be resolved, third-party intervention would likely be even more controversial if it were pursued in defense of values that the invaded people did not share or that were not minimally consistent with their other commitments.[5] Indeed, leading just war theorist Michael Walzer would not support armed intervention into the affairs of a sovereign state in pursuit of loftier goals (viz., democracy, economic justice, the right of voluntary association) although he would endorse such intervention to aid the defenseless against extreme suffering or cruelty when local forces appear incapable of, or unwilling to, handle the crisis (2004, 67–81).

While both morality and prudence demand no call to arms to ever be entertained lightly, the international community need not have a restricted catalog of human rights in order to display such cautiousness. To reiterate a point made in the previous chapter, there is no reason why the international community could not retain a sufficiently robust account of human rights and exercise restraint when contemplating the use of coercive measures to defend them. Rather than have the official list of human rights conform to the area of current agreement among the world's traditions and cultures, then, it is arguable that the direction of influence should go the other way. Such a reversal in procedure and priority would certainly cohere more with Rawls's original understanding of what the search for an "overlapping consensus" should involve because, for Rawls, the political conception of justice was always to be worked out and justified *"pro tanto* without looking to, or trying to fit, or even knowing what are, the existing comprehensive doctrines" (1996, 389).[6] Although political liberalism does look for a "political conception of justice that . . . can gain the support of an overlapping consensus of reasonable religious, philosophical and moral doctrines," Rawls explicitly warned that the political conception of justice would be "political in the wrong way" if it were to first examine "particular comprehensive doctrines presently existing in society and then tailor itself to win their allegiance" (1996, xlvii, 10; see also 2001, 188–89). Rawls's preprocedural distinction between "reasonable" and "unreasonable" comprehensive doctrines should further confirm that the maintenance of neutrality between and among all philosophical and religious beliefs was never his primary objective.

Fortunately, important human rights documents such as the UDHR were neither pieced together nor justified thereafter by appealing only to what was reportedly present in or compatible with the moral philosophies or sociopolitical structures in the world at that time. Admittedly, several delegates had leveled their own "arguments from culture" during the drafting process of the UDHR. The South African representative contested the proposed right of full equality and nondiscrimination (Art. 1 and 2), given South Africa's then-impending codification of its system of apartheid law (Glendon 2001, 141–49). The Saudi Arabian delegate objected to the proposed rights to free and full consent in marriage and to change one's religion freely (Art. 16, 18) on the grounds that the former was "at variance with patterns of culture of Eastern States" and that the latter violated Islamic Shari'ah (Glendon 2001, 153–55; Mayer 1999; Artz 1996). And the American delegate took issue with the proposed right of the worker to receive "just and favorable remuneration for himself and his family" (Art. 23), given the provision's incompatibility with regnant business practices (Glendon 2001, 141–49). Despite these and other complaints, the drafters did not ultimately limit which goods or liberties would be counted as genuine human rights to the area of overlap already present or latent among themselves as evidenced by the UDHR's official adoption of these and other contested clauses.[7]

Still, we should reject neither the "minimal core" nor the "broad consistency" notions of consensus for their inability to account for the drafting process of the UDHR or other important human rights instruments, for it remains to be seen whether any of those documents are universally valid. The more important point to make, then, is the following: any required methodological restriction of the content of human rights to what can be the current object of agreement among the world's diverse traditions carries the risk of compromising the normative force of what human rights are supposed to mean and do. To better understand this danger, recall that many of our most cherished rights today, such as freedom of religion and nondiscrimination based on sex or race, only developed after a great struggle in opposition to prevailing social views and were promulgated in advance of universal consent to their norms.[8] Thus, if we were to strike from our official catalog of human rights any currently contestable claims (viz., the presence or extent of certain economic and social human rights, women's rights, participatory rights in democratic institutions, and rights pertaining to criminal law and punishment), we would be stripping the international human rights community of its ability to stand in judgment of positive law, the world's extant moralities, and even any populist conception of human rights. Political philosopher Charles Beitz might have put it best when he observed the following: "Human rights are supposed to be universal in the sense that they apply to or may be claimed by everyone. To hold, also, that a substantive doctrine of human rights should be *consistent* with the moral beliefs and values found among the world's conventional moralities is to say something both more and different, and potentially subversive, of the doctrine's critical aims" (emphasis added; 2001, 274).[9] Thus, the dismissal or invalidation of any human rights claim simply because there is demonstrable opposition to it in some quarters is to concede the point prematurely without deliberating on their merits—or their lack thereof.

OPTION 2: CONSENSUS-ENCOURAGING PLURAL FOUNDATIONS FOR HUMAN RIGHTS

We have rejected the search for consensus on human rights as a way to circumscribe and restrict their content. Let us now consider the desirability of this two-step procedure for the purposes of justification only.

How and Why

Recall that the framers of the UDHR did not provide any official theory of human rights but instead made room for a plurality of views by their silence on the question of their theoretical foundations. Their commitment to universal standards of conduct but ultimate evasion of matters of first philosophy is illustrated well by the debates during the drafting process over Article 1, which in the final version reads as follows: "All human beings are born free and equal in dignity and rights. They are endowed with reason and conscience and should act towards one another in a spirit of brotherhood."

Although some delegates had initially pushed to insert a theological referent, as in "they are endowed by their Creator with reason and conscience," others wanted to refer to nature as the source of reason and conscience instead (see, e.g., Morsink 1999, 284–90; 2009, 30–31). After successive deliberations upon the matter, the delegates concluded that they could refer to neither God nor nature if they were to proceed. Given the Soviet delegation's position that the content of the UDHR should be accessible to theists and nontheists alike, the Chinese representative's insistence that the document should be conceived in categories other than Western philosophical concepts alone, and the French delegate's continued hope for the Human Rights Commission to avoid "taking sides" on the nature of "man and society" or on other metaphysical controversies, historians generally report that the drafters were satisfied with the compromise solution they had reached (Glendon 2001, 68–69).

Others beyond the framers of the UDHR have been drawn to the idea that the concept and legal apparatus of human rights could be supported by a multiplicity of worldviews, whether secular or religious. The UNESCO Committee on the Theoretical Bases of Human Rights that was formed during the time of the drafting of the UDHR received more than seventy responses to their questionnaire on the topic. These responses covered Hindu, Islamic, and Chinese legal perspectives; socialist, American, and European points of view; and reflections by prominent thinkers such as Mohandas Gandhi, Pierre Teilhard de Chardin, and Aldous Huxley. They concluded that the draft declaration was compatible with the values of many cultural and religious traditions, even though it was "stated in terms of different philosophic principles and on the background of divergent political and economic systems" (UNESCO 1949, 258–59). Several declarations on global ethics have also explicitly supported human rights. In addition to the aforementioned endorsement of the UDHR by Hans Küng and the Parliament of the World's Religions in 1993, the Universal Declaration of a Global Ethic authored by ecumenicist Leonard Swidler also contains principles underlying the UDHR that are recast in the language of universal rights and universal responsibilities (Swidler 1999; Küng 1998, ch. 4; see also King 2001).

An official account of human rights that could successfully distinguish their practical standards at the international level from the vast complex of principles or values that could be said to undergird them might yield several advantages. First, the often-heard charge that human rights are inextricably tied to Western liberal norms or perspectives would suffer an empirical defeat. For example, when the right to freedom of thought, conscience, and religion that is recognized in both the UDHR and the ICCPR can be shown to have non-Western conceptual and historical precedents—the Bhagavad Gita's teaching that the worship of God can take many forms, the third century BCE Indian emperor Ashoka's edicts of toleration, the Qur'anic text that there should be no compulsion in religion (Sura 2:256), the millet system of legally protected religious minorities during the Ottoman Empire, Mohandas Gandhi's understanding that Hindu philosophy "enjoins an attitude of respect and reverence" for all religions, and so forth[10]—the accusation that the provision is ethnocentrically Western becomes difficult if not impossible to sustain. Similarly, when movements for women's education, the end of *purdah,* and greater political participation can be shown to have indigenous roots in non-Western contexts such as in India, those who accuse feminists from the Two-Thirds World of sycophantically emulating Eurocentric or Anglo–North American ideals betray their own West-centrism and ignorance of local histories (Nussbaum and Sen 1989). Something comparable, of course, could said with respect to Islam. When progressive Muslim intellectuals such as Fatima Mernissi (1987, 1992) and Farid Esack (2001) endorse notions of equal treatment before the law in ways that do not privilege either men over women or Muslims over non-Muslims, they undercut the popular but inaccurate view that Islam is inherently inimical to a robust account of human rights (see also Hassan 1996). They also undermine the force of Rawls's working assumption in the *Law of Peoples* that "something like Kazanistan is the best we [in the West] can realistically—and coherently—hope for" (1999b, 78).

A second and related advantage to providing an officially "freestanding" account of human rights is that the strategy could increase their reception among audiences who might otherwise shun them. Joseph Chan, among others, has articulated a specifically Confucian justification for human rights out of a conviction that the Chinese will prefer and be more apt to comply with international standards if they can be grounded in less alien sources (Chan 1999, 2000). Analogously, Abdullahi An-Na'im has consistently urged human rights advocates to work within the framework of Islam if they wish to be credible among Muslims (1990a, 1990b; see also Othman 1999). While the assumption here is that worldwide respect for human rights would increase if their "cultural legitimacy" were enhanced through indigenization, we must concede that this presumption could turn out to be wrong, especially if these or other groups might actually be attracted to the idea or legal apparatus of human rights precisely because of their real or perceived foreign character. It also remains possible that what ultimately grounds or rationally justifies human rights to particular audiences will nevertheless fail to spur them to act in their protection or defense, which is to say that questions of theoretical justification and those of moral motivation may not always converge upon the same answer.[11]

The third possible advantage of distinguishing the public and official account of human rights from its varied conceptual bases of support is that it might make more transparent the unique contributions that each cultural or religious tradition could offer to others. For instance, Charles Taylor is intrigued by "engaged Buddhists" in Thailand—the Nobel Peace Prize–nominated Sulak Sivaraksa and Prof. Saneh Chamarik chief among them—who support human rights in ways specific to their contexts. They ground their advocacy for minimal coercion and various democratic reforms not upon modern Western liberal notions of autonomy, freedom, or conscience but out of a specifically Buddhist commitment to *ahimsa,* an understanding of the need and freedom to contribute (not simply to obtain), and a conviction that each individual must take personal responsibility for his or her own enlightenment. Because Taylor finds that Western rights talk has often been accompanied by "anger, indignation, [and] the imperative to punish historical wrongdoing" in ways that have not always proved productive, this Thai Buddhist perspective might offer Westerners a "caution against the politics of anger, itself the potential source of new forms of violence" (1999, 135). In a similar vein but with respect to a different context, Joseph Chan has suggested that the traditional Confucian preference for nonlitigious means to resolve social disputes might inspire Westerners to claim their rights only as a "fall-back mechanism" if and when their relationships deteriorate, rather than as the primary way of relating interpersonally with others (1999, 220–22).[12] Finally, in terms of enhancing and advancing international discourse on human rights, Sumner Twiss has suggested that the emphasis of many indigenous religions on the interdependence of humanity and nature or on religious views such as Buddhist "dependent co-origination" (*pratityasamutpada*) might eventually guide the international community to conceptualize human rights within a larger ecological framework than the manner in which such discussions are typically framed now (1996; 1998b, 278). In sum, an account of human rights that could successfully distinguish legally enforceable standards from myriad possible ways to ground them theoretically would allow each culture or religion to retain their diverse perspectives and might also increase possibilities for cross-cultural learning and influence.

But Would a Series of Local Justifications for Human Rights Be Sufficient?

We might regard consensus-based approaches to human rights as a compromise between maximalists and minimalists—between those who wish to embed human rights within a comprehensive conception of the good and those who hope to avoid justifying them in any official sense in terms that are likely to be regarded by others as sectarian. While settling for a shared catalog of human rights but leaving everything else undetermined, the question remains whether a series of local justifications for human rights in the absence of a common rationale would in all cases prove sufficient.

One unresolved but significant issue for consensus-based approaches is why its results, however ecumenical or interreligious, should be endowed with normative force. In times past, there was arguably a cross-cultural consensus on a number of social practices that are widely seen today as inhumane and antithetical to the ethos of human rights: slavery and serfdom, the conduct of war in violation of the Geneva Conventions, the denial of equal rights and moral standing to women, severe restrictions on religious belief and exercise, widespread use of extreme forms of corporal punishment, and so forth. What assurance, then, might those invested in consensus-based approaches to human rights be able to provide that the decisions reached today would not suffer a similar fate? Confidence in the appropriateness of the results of the consensus would seem to depend, at least in part, on the fairness of the procedure itself. What proponents of consensus-based approaches to human rights must additionally do, then, is demonstrate how the consensus would be formed under conditions that would give its findings sufficient justificatory force.

While we previously rejected the proposal of methodologically vetoing from the list of genuine human rights any item that was not already endorsed in some fashion by every culture in the world, good protocol might still require all affected parties to be given the option to present their perspectives to others and accordingly receive a fair hearing. Other baseline conditions might include impartiality, the inclusion and equal representation of all parties and not only of the currently dominant voices within them, procedural rules forbidding coercion beyond the power of rhetorical persuasion, and an acknowledgment of the goods sought or purposes behind the search for cross-cultural consensus itself. I will return to these points in the next chapter.

Let us now turn to an entirely separate concern about the adequacy of this two-tiered approach to human rights as thus far described. The approach might not only achieve its desired end in granting each group conceptual space to justify human rights in their own terms but might also unintentionally substantiate their idiosyncratic implementations of human rights in ways that could compromise the universality of the standards themselves. To be clear, there is nothing in principle wrong about "different music" being played on the "same keyboard," to use Jacques Maritain's analogy, because that outcome would be practically inevitable if different members of the world community were to ground the same list of human rights on different underlying values (Maritain 1951, 106). Nevertheless, any approach to human rights that left the matter of justification to the sole discretion of each party would increase the likelihood that each group would subsequently interpret how best to actualize those standards according to their mutually incompatible conceptions of the good, and would thereafter privilege their own commitments over those purportedly universal standards in cases where the two might conflict. Indeed, in the absence of any shared official or public justification for human rights, such an approach would work to legitimize, as to undermine, the current regrettable situation where signatories to international human rights treaties register reservations on full compliance, citing greater fidelity to their preexisting political traditions or religiocultural beliefs.[13]

For a real-world example of this concern, consider ongoing debates about the prohibition against torture and other cruel, inhuman, or degrading treatment and punishment (Art. 5, UDHR; Art. 7, ICCPR; Third and Fourth Geneva Conventions; and UN Convention against Torture and Other Cruel, Inhuman, or Degrading Treatment or Punishment). In this case as well as in others, some parties have formally assented to the same ostensible standards of behavior through their signatures and ratifications but have interpreted and applied them in accordance with their mutually incompatible underlying values and beliefs in such a way as to stand accused of compromising, if not outright violating, the standards themselves. For example, much has been made of the facts that the Shari'ah serves as the proper source of and ultimate guide for all human rights for several Muslim countries, and that various Shari'ah courts have sentenced persons convicted of *zina* (unlawful sexual intercourse) with a prescribed number of lashings, imprisonment, or even death by stoning, in the case of married persons.[14] While these punishments have been widely interpreted by the world community to violate Articles 6 and 7 of the ICCPR, the human rights of women under CEDAW, and the Convention against Torture, the common retort by defenders of these punishments has been that any international standards that failed to recognize the legitimacy of *zina* ordinances are already biased against the Shariah and thus are invalid (see An-Na'im 1992). My point here is not to criticize *zina* ordinances as an end in itself but to underscore the following point: If the international community could only insist upon the universal validity of prohibition against torture without being able to provide a shared or public justification for it, they could not successfully counter the charge of either arbitrariness or religiocultural insensitivity or both in their assessment that corporal and even capital punishment for what those societies have defined as illicit sexual activity are too severe from the standpoint of what respect for human rights requires.

Something comparable could be said about the authorized use of harsh interrogation techniques on detainees suspected of terrorism against the United States in the aftermath of the September 11, 2001, attacks—tactics that have included beatings and slaps to the head, forced nudity, prolonged exposure to cold temperatures without clothing, confinement in stress positions (sometimes with insects), sleep deprivation while being subjected to loud music, and simulated drowning (i.e., "waterboarding"). While third parties such as the International Committee of the Red Cross (ICRC) have concluded that the United States has engaged in illicit acts upon prisoners held in detention sites operated by or in conjunction with the CIA, the official U.S. stance, particularly during the Bush administration, has been to deny that the United States has punished or extracted intelligence from those captured in the war on terror in ways that have run afoul of their obligations under either domestic or international law.[15] Of course, crucial to this line of defense has been their extremely narrow definition of what torture is. While Article 1 of the UN Convention against Torture defines torture as "any act by which severe pain or suffering, whether physical or mental, is intentionally inflicted on a person" for the purposes of intimidation, punishment, or obtaining a confession or information from either the person or a third party, internal legal memos from the U.S. Department of Justice have specified that the pain inflicted must be "equivalent in intensity to the pain accompanying serious physical injury, such as organ failure, impairment of bodily function, or even death," and that the interrogator must have had a "specific intent" to inflict that severe pain to amount to a violation of the Convention.[16] Under that definition, waterboarding, however excruciating and terrifying, has not been interpreted as a prohibited act.

As these two admittedly "worst-case" examples should reveal, an overlapping consensus on legally enforceable human rights standards plus a series of local justifications for them from the world's diverse communities will prove insufficient if or when questions arise about the meaning or extent of the standards themselves. In addition, because different local justifications for human rights inevitably give rise to different local applications of the provisions themselves, the official silence about deep theory that drew so many proponents of human rights to Rawlsian political liberalism will be in the end more partial than complete. Recall Rawls's concession that a politically liberal society that is officially noncommittal about the veracity of its citizens' comprehensive doctrines will not be able to avoid implying a religious tenet's "lack of truth" if it refused to organize its institutions accordingly, such as when a liberal democracy refrains from using its power to enforce the medieval Church's doctrine *extra ecclesiam nulla sallus* (there is no salvation outside the church) (1999d, 178; 1996, 138; 2001, 183–84). Despite this "method of avoidance" at the level of theory, then, the international community would analogously be compelled to imply either the falsity or inappropriateness of a tenet of a particular comprehensive doctrine if they were to conclude that an interpretation of human rights that emerged from it, such as some Muslim countries' punishment of death by stoning for adulterers or the United States' interpretation of waterboarding as consistent with the ban on torture, went beyond the pale of acceptability.

BEYOND SHARED NORMS: RETURNING TO THE ORIGINAL SOURCES OF INSPIRATION

In the consensus-based approaches to human rights that we have been considering, members of the world community would honor the same list of legally enforceable human rights standards but would retain conceptual freedom to justify the enumerated protections in their own way. In light of the aforementioned problems with relying upon a series of local justifications alone, the question remains whether diverse parties could come to a consensus on shared human rights standards as well as on genuinely shared reasons for them—even if they ultimately embedded the significance of those reasons in accordance with their own lights. An officially shared and public rationale for human rights that transcended the myriad local varieties would certainly help to address worries about ethnocentrism, arbitrariness, and special pleading by providing a principled way to distinguish acceptable from unacceptable local interpretations of human rights. It would also prove helpful in answering the question of why groups who were not yet party to the consensus on human rights should reconsider and join. If the matter of human rights justification were solely left to the discretion of each culture, tradition, or community, any contextualist reasons the current participants could offer to nonsubscribers would prove unpersuasive to those who did not already share those ecumenical values or commitments. Fortunately, the two theorists who originally inspired various consensus-based approaches to human rights—John Rawls and Jacques Maritain—foresaw why an area of deeper cross-cultural agreement beyond universal standards of conduct was desirable, possible, and even necessary. They disagreed, however, on how and when to conduct such a search.

According to Rawlsian political liberalism, the identification of an area of deeper agreement among persons of diverse but reasonable comprehensive doctrines should have preceded the very search for an overlapping consensus on the political principles of justice. That is, the political conception regulating the basic structure of society was supposed to have been premised upon a shared set of "fundamental ideas" that had been worked out in "reflective equilibrium" in congruence with, and in light of, our (ever-revisable) considered judgments or convictions (1999c, §9 at 42–44; 2001, §10).[17] These fundamental ideas would not have been drawn from the "background culture" of different philosophies, religions, or other comprehensive views but from the "public culture" of what citizens of a modern liberal democracy already hold in common: the "political institutions of a constitutional regime and the public traditions of their interpretation (including those of the judiciary) as well as historic texts and documents that are common knowledge" (1996, 13–14).[18] That Rawls always intended the overlapping consensus to encompass both the political principles of justice and the shared fundamental ideas underlying them is further confirmed by his insistence that any agreement on the former without the latter would represent neither a moral achievement nor even a genuine "overlapping consensus" but a mere modus vivendi—an inherently unstable situation should the balance of power among the different parties ever change (1996, 147–48; 2001, 192–95).

Thus, if proponents of consensus-based approaches to human rights were to apply the concepts of Rawlsian political liberalism more faithfully, they would first have to determine what the "fundamental ideas" would be for the international community to serve as a common basis for an official account of human rights. Such a task would not prove difficult according to the aforementioned UNESCO Committee on the Theoretical Bases of Human Rights because the committee interprets those who endorsed the draft UDHR as already sharing "common convictions on which human rights depend":

> They believe that men and women, all over the world, have the
> right to live a life that is free from the haunting fear of poverty
> and insecurity. They believe that they should have a more

complete access to the heritage, in all its aspects and dimensions,
of the civilization so painfully built by human effort. They believe
that science and the arts should combine to serve alike peace and
the well-being, spiritual as well as material, of all men and
women without discrimination of any kind. They believe that
given that, given goodwill between nations, the power is in their
hands to advance the achievement of this well-being more swiftly
than in any previous age. (1949, 258–59)

Political theorist Ari Kohen has similarly interpreted the UDHR as
having already achieved an overlapping consensus not only on universal human rights standards or norms but also on the "dignity of
the human person" as a "common foundation" for them, even if the
parties could not further agree upon "the reason behind the reason"
(2007, 144–45, 151). David Hollenbach likewise finds in the UDHR
a list of what claims merit universal recognition as human rights as
well as why that is so. He reads in the second clause of the preamble a shared, experienced-based rationale for the universal standards
themselves: the atrocities and "barbarous acts" committed during
World War II so "outraged the conscience of mankind," that the international community pressed for the need for human rights to be
recognized and protected everywhere (2003, 234; see also Morsink
1999, ch. 2; 2009, ch. 2; Little 2006, 296–98). Other candidates for
genuinely shared reasons include what Hans Küng has identified as
the fundamental ethical criterion of the *humanum* or the "fundamental norm of authentic humanness," common interests for peace
and security, similar views of universal human capacities and vulnerabilities, analogous moral principles, virtues, and the like (Küng
1987, 239–44; 1998, 98–99; Twiss 1998b; 2004, 63–64).

While the identification of shared fundamental ideas for Rawls was
to have preceded the formulation of enforceable human rights standards or norms, Jacques Maritain surmised that a deeper agreement
on shared values among the world's diverse groups might be possible after the consensus on practical standards had been obtained. He
had hoped that in the course of that consensus "taking root in the

Beyond Shared Norms: Returning to the Original Sources of Inspiration

conscience of the nations," one day "agreement may be reached throughout the world, not only on the enumeration of human rights, but also on the key values governing their exercise and on the practical criteria to be used to secure respect for them" (1949, 17). Maritain understood that a suitably public justification for human rights could itself emerge from cross-cultural dialogue and mutual learning (see also Taylor 1999, 136; Sen 2004b, 320).

The capability approach to human rights can be understood as an exploration of both of these Rawls- and Maritain-inspired possibilities. One prominent version articulates some "fundamental ideas" or substantive reasons for securing basic social entitlements for all human beings before turning to a political or procedural justification. The other invites the world community to shape the formation of "key values" that are to be jointly affirmed as a result of public deliberations by members of the world community. It is to that approach to human rights that we now turn.

Five

THE CAPABILITY APPROACH TO HUMAN RIGHTS

The capability approach, also known as the "capabilities approach," is a broad conceptual framework increasingly used today to compare the quality of life across nations, evaluate the design of public policies, and assess the justice of social institutions. Simply put, this framework seeks to advance the positive freedoms of all individuals to be or to do certain things that each of us may have reason to value. The approach is most commonly associated with its leading proponents, Amartya Sen in development economics and Martha Nussbaum in political philosophy, but its influence can be seen in the work of other members of the Human Development and Capability Association and in the United Nations Development Program, whose human development reports have been heavily influenced by the capabilities framework since 1990.[1]

When applied to our central question of human rights justification, the capability approach (CA) can be understood as straddling the minimalist–maximalist divide: it deliberately avoids relying upon religion, metaphysics, or externalist accounts of human nature, although it offers more than a purely procedural defense. Martha Nussbaum's specific articulation of CA, arguably the "thickest" response to the maximalist challenge under consideration in this book, advocates for the development of a set of human capabilities for everyone to be able to function in ways essential to our good as human beings.[2] Although a defense of human rights through the conceptual lens of human capabilities is not a straightforward affair, the approach's concern for human flourishing and freedom, respect for individual and communal forms of decision making, and endorsement of universal values without uniform treatment are highly germane to the task of grounding human rights in a pluralist world.

As I will demonstrate in this chapter, the capabilities framework provides constructive ways to interpret and even expand upon the discourse on human rights. Martha Nussbaum's version of CA can especialy be lauded for clarifying what it actually means to secure a human right to an individual, providing a method for determining which capabilities will be deemed worthy of protection everywhere, and contextualizing human rights claims alongside their impact upon nonhuman animals who may have moral entitlements of their own. Legitimate questions remain, however, about the approach's conceptual dependence upon unacknowledged or otherwise submerged premises that are maximalist in tone, though not conventionally religious in form. After providing an overview of CA and comparing it to the more familiar human rights paradigm in terms of the norms they both prescribe, their flexible manner of implementation, and their common philosophical justifications, I conclude this chapter with the following question. If the traditional human rights framework could be greatly enhanced by supplementing it with insights drawn from CA, but its best version ultimately trades on nonreligiously maximalist assumptions, what implications would this dependence have on our search for a satisfactory response to the maximalist challenge to human rights justification?

WHAT IS THE CAPABILITY APPROACH? A PRIMER

A useful way to describe the basic contours of CA is to contrast it with its major alternatives. While all egalitarians operate under the conviction that the political distribution of basic rights and goods should not be arbitrary from a moral point of view, proponents of CA maintain that capabilities, not other "informational bases" such as bundles of resources or assessments of subjective welfare, should be the "what" to secure and thus compare across persons and nations (Sen 1981b).[3]

Capability theorists fault resource-distribution models, such as John Rawls's much-discussed conception of "primary goods," for focusing on distribution alone and not its disparate effects. They observe that a physically disabled person could have an equal amount of resources as others but have less ability to move around if she lacked a wheelchair and an accessible environment, just as an individual could have more wealth and food at her disposal than others but still have less of an ability to be well nourished because of "higher basal metabolic rate, greater vulnerability to parasitic diseases, larger body size, or simply because of pregnancy" (Sen 1992, 81–82; and Nussbaum 2000b, 68–69).[4] Amartya Sen has observed that a person's ability to pursue her own ends will depend not only on what ends she has but also how well she is able to convert her resources into valuable functionings in light of the following five variables:

- Personal heterogeneities, such as disabilities or proneness to illness
- Environmental diversities, including climate conditions or varying threats from epidemic disease or local crime
- Variations in nonpersonal resources and social climate, such as the nature of public health care or social cohesion
- Different relative positions vis-à-vis others (e.g., being relatively poor in a rich country may prevent persons from achieving elementary functionings even though their income, in absolute terms, may be higher than the level of income of members in poorer communities)
- Distribution within the family, because the income earned and opportunities afforded may not be equally distributed (1990; 1997b, 385–86; 2004b, 332–33n29).

Capability theorists accordingly urge us to take these personal and environmental heterogeneities into account when weighing matters of distributive justice.[5]

Proponents of CA also inveigh against utilitarian models that focus instead on subjective welfare. These models fail to address the question of distribution among individuals when attempting to maximize happiness and also reduce the vast plurality of goods into one single metric of analysis.[6] Still worse from the perspective of capability theorists is the reality that an individual's desires or stated preferences neither always accurately reflect her real needs nor reliably indicate her actual well-being. Many among the wealthy would be demonstrably unhappy unless they satiated the "expensive tastes" to which they have become accustomed but do not need, just as many among the poor and underprivileged adjust their expectations to the level they can realistically achieve and thereafter report satisfaction even in the midst of various deprivations under the phenomenon known as "adaptive preferences" (e.g., women living under patriarchy who have internalized norms of misogyny).[7] Thus, if subjective assessments of welfare were to serve as the informational bases of public policy, society would be held hostage to the spoiled and self-indulgent, on the one hand, but excused from having to redress the social ills that the underserved suffer, on the other.

Of course, any theoretical model that is focused on what individuals are actually able to be or to do cannot safeguard every human capability as a matter of justice if it is to be normative or practically efficacious. Advocates of CA must accordingly determine which capabilities will be worthy of inclusion in any scheme of social protection and which will not, the latter because they are of lesser import or are even pernicious. In response to this question, Martha Nussbaum has drawn inspiration from the work of Marx and Aristotle to generate a list of ten central human capabilities, each of which is presented as irreducibly essential to living a decent and dignified human life and thus worthy of a minimal threshold of protection by the governments of all nations. Although modified and reconfigured on several occasions, a recent formulation of this list is reproduced below in its entirety:

Central Human Functional Capabilities

1. *Life.* Being able to live to the end of a human life of normal length; not dying prematurely, or before one's life is so reduced as to be not worth living.

2. *Bodily Health.* Being able to have good health, including reproductive health; to be adequately nourished; to have adequate shelter.

3. *Bodily Integrity.* Being able to move freely from place to place; to be secure against violent assault, including sexual assault and domestic violence; having opportunities for sexual satisfaction and for choice in matters of reproduction.

4. *Senses, Imagination, and Thought.* Being able to use the senses, to imagine, think, and reason—and to do these things in a "truly human" way, a way informed and cultivated by an adequate education, including, but by no means limited to, literacy and basic mathematical and scientific training. Being able to use imagination and thought in connection with experiencing and producing works and events of one's own choice, religious, literary, musical, and so forth. Being able to use one's mind in ways protected by guarantees of freedom of expression with respect to both political and artistic speech, and freedom of religious exercise. Being able to have pleasurable experiences and to avoid nonbeneficial pain.

5. *Emotions.* Being able to have attachments to things and people outside ourselves; to love those who love and care for us, to grieve at their absence; in general, to love, to grieve, to experience longing, gratitude, and justified anger. Not having one's emotional development blighted by overwhelming fear and anxiety. (Supporting this capability means supporting forms of human association that can be shown to be crucial in their development.)

6. *Practical Reason.* Being able to form a conception of the good and to engage in critical reflection about the planning of one's

life. (This entails protection for the liberty of conscience and religious observance.)

7. *Affiliation.* A. Being able to live with and toward others, to recognize and show concern for other human beings, to engage in various forms of social interaction; to be able to imagine the situation of another. (Protecting this capability means protecting institutions that constitute and nourish such forms of affiliation, and also protecting the freedom of assembly and political speech.) B. Having the social bases of self-respect and non-humiliation; being able to be treated as a dignified being whose worth is equal to that of others. This entails provisions of nondiscrimination on the basis of race, sex, sexual orientation, ethnicity, caste, religion, national origin.

8. *Other Species.* Being able to live with concern for and in relation to animals, plants, and the world of nature.

9. *Play.* Being able to laugh, to play, to enjoy recreational activities.

10. *Control over One's Environment.* A. *Political.* Being able to participate effectively in political choices that govern one's life; having the right of political participation, protections of free speech and association. B. *Material.* Being able to hold property (both land and movable goods), and having property rights on an equal basis with others; having the right to seek employment on an equal basis with others; having the freedom from unwarranted search and seizure. In work, being able to work as a human being, exercising practical reason and entering into meaningful relationships of mutual recognition with other workers. (2006b, 76–77; see also 2000b, 79–80; 1992, 222; 1990a, 225 for earlier articulations)

Alternative lists of human capabilities can be found in Elizabeth Anderson's conception of "democratic equality," Ingrid Robeyns's gender inequality assessment, and Brooke Ackerley's rights and capabilities-inspired criteria for what every human being should be able to choose to do "in order to life a life worthy of being described as human and which the liver would describe as fulfilling" (Anderson 1999, 316–32; Robeyns 2003, 71–72; Ackerley 2000, 114–16).

Rather than sign onto any of those lists, Amartya Sen has emphasized the need for any schedule of capabilities to remain relative to the context or evaluation that is to be made (2005, 158–60). According to Sen, the basic capabilities that would demand attention in any social assessment or theory of justice include "the freedom to be well nourished, to live disease-free lives, to be able to move around, to be educated, to participate in public life, and so on" (2005, 158). The pursuit of gender justice would require the development of women's capabilities to be free from the imposition of fixed, traditional family roles and to be consulted in serious family decisions (2004a; 2004b, 345). The "relevant functionings" for still other purposes might include more complex achievements such as "being happy" and "having self-respect" (1992, 39). Sen's wariness is not about the use of lists of capabilities per se but about any "proposal of grand mausoleum to one fixed and final list" or insistence that they find generic application because doing either on his reading would impede public reasoning, fail to respond to the outcome of democratic deliberation, and thereby overstate what pure theory could achieve (2005, 157–60; see also 2004b, 333n31).[8]

Despite variability among these lists and internal dispute about how they are to be used, all proponents of CA are keen to distinguish between the possession of important human capabilities and their exercise, which is why they generally push for an equal or minimal threshold of capability development, not actual functioning.[9] Individuals would accordingly be responsible for their choices in developing certain bundles of functioning over others, or in pursuing different strategies and tactics (Sen 1990, 116; 1992, 82). All societies, in turn, would work to guarantee a certain level of capability development while preserving each individual's freedom to sacrifice her well-being if desired, as when some persons were to fast for a period of time but retain the option of being well-nourished (Nussbaum 2000a, 123–24).

Martha Nussbaum offers two qualifications to this general policy of not mandating the exercise of one's capabilities. First, she insists upon certain forms of functioning in children, particularly in the areas of education, health, emotional well-being, and bodily integrity, because meaningful choice in adulthood would be virtually impossible without them (2000b, 90; see also 2006b, 172). Second, she restricts the choices of adults if they attempt to sign away one of their ten central capabilities entirely (e.g., commit suicide, bond themselves into slavery), but she adopts a more permissive line if they seek to engage in activities that could merely threaten them (e.g., smoke or use dangerous drugs, play extremely violent sports such as boxing or American football) (2000a, 130–32; 2000b, 93–96; 2006b, 171–73). Her overall point, with which I am largely sympathetic, is that a certain degree of state paternalism is both defensible and even necessary, given the value we place on our abilities to function in important ways, our recognition that it is not always wise to leave such matters to personal discretion, and (as I would add) the state's justifiable interest in our becoming and remaining contributing members of society.

COMPARING THE CAPABILITY APPROACH TO THE HUMAN RIGHTS FRAMEWORK

The international community has primarily deployed the language of human rights, not human capabilities, to address how we all ought minimally to be treated by others as well as by our own governments. Given the greater popularity, usage, and acceptance of the moral vocabulary of rights, it stands to reason that the desirability of CA will depend, at least in part, on its relationship to that more familiar language. Capability theorists are themselves keen to note the many parallels between CA and the more familiar human rights paradigm, particularly in light of the social entitlements they seek to protect, their flexible manner of realization, and their common philosophical justifications. However, even proponents of CA acknowledge that these conceptual frameworks are ultimately not reducible to one another, which is why they urge us to retain the use of both.

Overlapping Content

Human rights and human capabilities share some obvious areas of convergence in the norms they seek to protect. Nussbaum frequently describes CA as a "species" of the more familiar human rights framework and observes that her list of ten central capabilities covers the familiar terrain of the full range of civil, political, economic, cultural, and social human rights (2000b, 2006b; see also Anderson 1999, 317–18). Just as some human rights are to be secured equally (e.g., religious liberty, voting rights), whereas others do not require sameness in treatment for their satisfaction (e.g., education, housing, health care), so Nussbaum would have the governments of the world ensure an equal level of certain capabilities but only a minimum or adequate level for others (2006b, 292–95). Without weighing in on the use of equal or minimum thresholds, Sen has likewise commented upon various areas of convergence between human rights and human capabilities, in addition to the feasibility of conceptualizing human rights as rights to certain freedoms, with capabilities representing freedoms of various kinds (2005, 152, 158).

These areas of overlap notwithstanding, talk of capabilities and of rights diverge in at least two significant ways. First, because human rights protect both fair processes (e.g., the right not to be sentenced without a fair trial) and fair opportunities (e.g., the right to have access to medical treatment) but CA is focused almost exclusively upon the latter, the capabilities framework cannot exhaust all that is entailed by what international law recognizes today as our human rights (Sen 2005, 152–56). Second, not all capabilities that are valued by leading proponents of CA are protected in core human rights conventions and treaties. Consider the following capabilities that Nussbaum would have all governments of the world secure as a matter of basic justice: to "have pleasurable experiences and . . . avoid

nonbeneficial pain" (rubric #4), to form various emotional attachments with others (rubric #5), and to "live with concern for and in
relation to animals, plants, and the world of nature" (rubric #8).[10]
Sen has likewise emphasized the importance of certain capabilities
that are not explicitly protected in international human rights law:
the capabilities for women to be consulted in serious family decisions and—with reference to Adam Smith—for everyone to be able
to "appear in public without shame" (see also Anderson 1999, 318).
Whether or not an argument can be made that there are rough
analogs to these capabilities in international human rights law, those
hoping to expand the range of protected human rights might find
much to commend in CA while those opposed to rights proliferation would likely balk at the greater scope and comprehensiveness
of those demands (see, e.g., Glendon 1993; Art. 27, UDHR; and
Art. 15, ICESCR).

Flexibility in Implementation

Despite these and other discontinuities in content, both the human
rights framework and CA urge multiple realization and flexible implementation of their provisions for three primary reasons: respect
for local context and needs, an acknowledgment of suboptimal empirical realities, and the need to prioritize some claims over others in
cases of tragic conflict or emergency. To clarify, the project of globalizing either human capabilities or human rights is universal in both
form and scope—the former because it holds for all and not only
some cases of a specific domain, and the latter because it is encompasses all and not merely some human beings. But these types of universality can be satisfied without compromise in the absence of
uniform behavior or prescription. As philosopher Onora O'Neill explains, the principle that "each should be taxed in proportion to [his
or her] ability to pay" is universal in scope but would result in nonuniform payments in a world of differing cases, just as the policy
"everyone should be punctual" prescribes a degree of uniformity with
respect to timekeeping but leaves everything else undetermined, including the means one should employ to avoid being late (1996, 75).

By extension, just as states could legitimately fulfill their obligations to universal human rights standards in nonuniform ways, the governments of the world could secure one universal set of basic capabilities for their constituents but retain the right to set their threshold levels in accordance with internal processes or needs. To use Nussbaum's examples for the purposes of illustration, although every state would be required to protect the freedom of expression, it might be appropriate for Germany to ban anti-Semitic literature (given its history with Nazism) and for others to permit "hate speech" of all kinds. Likewise, although all states would be obligated to protect religious free-exercise, it might be wise for the United States to uphold its nonestablishment principle due to its founding ideals, but it might be disastrous for India to move toward disestablishment, given fears that the interests of its minority Muslim population would suffer as a result (2000b, 210–12; 2004b, 200–201).[11]

The need for flexible implementation in other cases might result more from a concession to less than optimal empirical realities than from any sensitivity to pluralism or local histories as such. For instance, we might urge states that are in a position to provide public access to the Internet and other communication technologies to do so but encourage those less-developed countries in the grip of poverty to secure elementary education and basic health first (Sen 2005, 159–60; see also Nussbaum 1997b, 19, 48). This is not, however, to recommend that we restrict the list of universal social entitlements to what could realistically be fulfilled anywhere at any given time, for as Sen is fond of observing, the very articulation of a claim as a human right could help to change the social order in question.

The third and final reason why capability theorists prescribe flexible implementation is tied to the need for adjudication when the exercise of some social entitlements conflicts with others. Neither Nussbaum nor Sen tout the standard libertarian line concerning any absolute right to private property, for they insist that individuals could not justifiably keep their surplus in situations of famine when others are starving and dying (Nussbaum 1997a, 297–300; 2006a; see also Nozick 1974). Priorities or "trade-offs" would have to be set in times of crisis: the "ability to be well-nourished" when "people are dying of hunger in their homes," but the "freedom to be sheltered" when "people are in general well-fed, but lack shelter and protection from the elements" (Sen 2005, 159).[12] As discussed in chapter 2, international human rights law already acknowledges a need for flexibility of this kind: the ICESCR (Art. 4) permits nations to take the "general welfare" of society into consideration when fulfilling the terms of the treaty, and the ICCPR (Art. 4) specifies emergency conditions wherein signatories can legitimately derogate from some of their obligations. It is, of course, uncontroversial for capability theorists and human rights proponents to call for adjudication when claims conflict. Dissension and controversy generally ensue, however, when specific judgments are rendered about how to resolve them.

JUSTIFYING HUMAN CAPABILITIES AND HUMAN RIGHTS

The strongest and most relevant area of resemblance between human capabilities and rights for our purposes lies in the same or similar philosophical grounding that leading proponents of CA offer for both conceptual frameworks. While Martha Nussbaum and Amartya Sen propose different accounts of justification, each is careful to address both substantive and procedural matters in their remarks.

Amartya Sen's Defense of Universal Norms

Although he has strongly endorsed the "perspective of freedom" in many of his writings, Sen has not so much provided a fully fledged account of justification for either human rights or human capabilities as he has a transcendental argument stating the conditions for their possibility. What Sen regards as ultimately justifying a doctrine of universal social entitlements is whatever "would survive in public discussion, given a reasonably free flow of information and uncurbed opportunity to discuss differing points of view" (2004b, 320; see also Nussbaum 2006a). He envisions a highly interactive and deliberative process of justification that would not be constrained by the boundaries of each nation or people, thus avoiding "parochial prejudices," examining a wider range of counterarguments by including perspectives "from a distance," and maintaining the universalistic character of those basic freedoms. He would also not limit the results to merely a "conjunction" or "intersection" of the world's prevailing views (perhaps as in some of the appropriated "core" or "consistency" consensus-based methods discussed in the previous chapter) because he rightly insists that no candidate for a universal norm should be disqualified simply because someone somewhere objects to it (2004b, 320, 349–50; 1999a, 12). Instead, Sen understands that the claim for any universal norm should involve a counterfactual analysis, "that people anywhere may have reason to see it as valuable" even if they have not yet encountered the specific proposal in question (1999a, 12). Finally, in ways reminiscent of Maritain's understanding of what might follow the emergence of a cross-cultural consensus on universally valid norms, Sen has also stressed how the power of public reasoning and the outcome of democratic deliberation could themselves shape the formation of social values (Sen 2005, 157–58).

Beyond these largely procedural remarks on justification, Sen has also acknowledged the substantive commitments that would be required to sustain them. Aside from the value of freedom, which he understands to be of both intrinsic and instrumental worth, he has correctly observed that any methodological insistence on an "open public discussion from which no one is excluded" would entail a prior "acceptance of equality," and that this logically prior commitment would have "substantive implications" for the content of the deliberations to follow (1999a; 1999c; 2004b, 349n57).

Martha Nussbaum's Substantive Account of Justification

Martha Nussbaum has variously characterized her version of CA as "Aristotelian in spirit," a "close relative and ally" of modern contractarian approaches, a "member of the family" of liberal conceptions of justice with Rawlsian political liberalism, a "species of the human rights approach," and a revival of the "Grotian natural law tradition"

(2006b, 6, 21, 71, 93, 285–86). She does not, however, ground each individual's entitlement to be treated in certain ways upon any natural teleology (*pace* Aristotle), hypothetical or real consent of rational contractors based upon mutual advantage (*pace* social contract theorists),[13] original position that models political ideas already implicit only in Western liberal democracies (*pace* Rawls), or the existence of God (*pace* theological articulations of natural law). Instead, Nussbaum premises these minimal, prepolitical social entitlements upon an essentialist though nonmetaphysically realist "intuitive idea of human dignity" that is principally inspired by her Marxian-Aristotelian understanding of the type of beings we are. All ten central capabilities are accordingly presented as giving shape and content to that conception of human flourishing such that no one could live a "life worthy of human dignity" if any one of those capabilities in question were lacking (Nussbaum 2006b, 74–75).

Martha Nussbaum's conceptual debt to Aristotle is substantial: she retrieves his universalist defense of nonrelative virtues, his way of combining theory with "sensitivity to the actual circumstances of human life and choice in all their multiplicity," and his understanding that some capabilities and functionings are "more central, more at the core of human life, than others" (1990b, 25–26; 1993, 242–43; 1995b, 63; 2006b, 85, 132).[14] What she draws from Marx—or more specifically, in Marx's reading of Aristotle—is not only that we are social creatures in need of a "plurality of life-activities" but also that there is something morally relevant about doing things in a human as opposed to in a mere "herd" or "flock" animal way.[15] We eat to survive but also in ways infused by "practical reasoning and sociability," just as we use our senses in ways that have been cultivated "by appropriate education, by leisure for play and self-expression, by valuable associations with others," and as she (but not Marx) would add, by the freedom of religion (Nussbaum 2000b, 72; 2006b, 74). Despite undeniable variation and difference among human beings, Nussbaum remains committed to the idea of a common humanity—to the idea that there is a "structure" to "the human personality . . . that is at least to some extent independ-

ent of culture, powerfully though cultures shapes it at every stage"
(2000b, 155).

Two additional features of Nussbaum's account deserve mention
here. First, given her commitment to the political liberalism of John
Rawls and Charles Larmore, she offers her account of the good and
conception of the human being for political purposes only and in a
purportedly "freestanding" manner; they are purportedly conceptually nonreliant upon any metaphysical or epistemological doctrines,
religious beliefs, or their rejection (2001a, 886–87; 2006b, 36, 86,
163). Although Nussbaum is clearly working out of an essentialist
framework, her conception of the human being is not based on
sources completely external to self-interpretation or evaluation, such
as appeals to nonmoral scientific facts, a purely biological account
of our species membership, or a value-free theory of human nature.
Rather, Nussbaum grounds her understanding of who we essentially
are and what is required for our flourishing on a number of intuitive
ideas that emerge from what she has variously called the "Aristotelian
procedure in ethics" or "internalist essentialism" (1992; 2004b,
197).[16] The method is basically Socratic in requiring us to examine
questions of personal continuity or identity (i.e., what changes could
I endure and still be me?), inclusion (i.e., what features must any
creature have in order to be "truly human"?), and worth in order to
determine what is indispensable to the human form of life—and to
a minimally good and dignified one at that. Beyond relying upon
thought experiments and common sense, Nussbaum finds the
world's heritage of myths and stories to be particularly instructive for
informing our public policy debates about what we might need to
live minimally good lives. This is because some of those stories commonly "situate the human being in some way in the universe, between the beasts on the one hand and the gods on the other," to
describe what it means to live as "beings like us with certain abilities . . . [and] certain limits" (1992, 215; see also 2000b, 74).

The second notable feature about Nussbaum's substantive account is her grounding of these basic social entitlements on an even
deeper level than on the intuitive idea of human dignity to which

she frequently appeals. That is, Nussbaum also repeatedly refers to the ideas of a "species norm," an Aristotelian-inspired desire to "see each thing flourish as the sort of thing that it is," and the dignity of forms of life that possess "both abilities and deep needs" (2004a, 306; 2006b, 346). So understood, the deeper moral intuition behind the capabilities framework seems to be the following: because there is "something wonderful and worthy of awe in any complex natural organism," and because it is a "waste and tragedy" when living beings are prevented from functioning in ways important to their own good, creatures who have capabilities and needs essential to their own flourishing have entitlements to them as a matter of basic justice (2006b, 93–94, 346–52).

A full exploration of this deeper justification cannot be provided here, but it is worth mentioning two major implications that follow. First, it would be incumbent upon those committed to the use of a species norm to address what obligations humans would incur with respect to the development and exercise of both human and non-human animal capabilities (see, e.g., Sen 2003a, 330). Second, when attempting to provide a philosophical justification for human rights, we could no longer simply explore why human beings have a set of fundamental rights and freedoms by virtue of their humanity alone, or what it is about us as human beings that endow us with moral worth. Instead, we would be compelled to ask how we might justify, let alone implement, the worldwide promotion and protection of human rights and capabilities given that their cultivation and exercise would in many cases adversely impede the ability of other creatures to flourish. In short, Nussbaum's view that nonhuman animals have both capabilities and a form of dignity of their own renders the question of animal entitlements relevant to the question of human ones and vice versa.

Martha Nussbaum's Procedural Account of Justification

Before turning to Nussbaum's procedural defense of these basic social entitlements, it is worth pausing to consider why this second step would even need to be taken. That is, since the ten central capabilities are supposed to be of intrinsic worth, it remains to be seen why Nussbaum insists that justification include a notion of "acceptability to all" (2006b, 163–64). Her answer is that the very search for a transnational "overlapping consensus" on these universal standards would not only show respect to persons for their stated beliefs and preferences but would also give them some assurance of their potential stability (2006b, 163–64). A two-part justification would thus avoid the pitfalls of subjective welfarism, in which the good and the right would be determined simply by canvassing opinions on the matter— perhaps democratically but without any way of accounting for the problem of "adaptive preferences." It would simultaneously avoid Platonism, in which the good would be defined in total independence from any of our informed desires or preferences (2000b, 116–17).

So understood, Nussbaum's procedural approach to justification is largely inspired by John Rawls's idea of an argument proceeding toward "reflective equilibrium": we lay out arguments for a given position, hold them up against the "provisionally fixed points" in our moral intuitions, see how those intuitions both test and are tested by the conception under examination, and then modify either accordingly. For example, if we were to discover that our "intuitive idea that human beings are stunted and 'mutilated' . . . by not having the chance to develop their faculties through education" was also reflected in our "best informed-desired approaches" about the importance of quality primary and secondary education, we would count such convergence as a good sign that we have identified worthwhile political goals (Nussbaum 2006b, 279). This search for a "reflective equilibrium" would require us to consider the viewpoints of fellow deliberators as well as alternative conceptions of the good and the right (Nussbaum 2000b, 101–5). We might even understand Nussbaum's many revisions to her list of ten central human capabilities after further reflection upon feedback from others and insistence that the list remain "open-ended and humble" as modeling the very process of what the search for a reflective equilibrium should resemble (cf. Wasserman 2006, 228–29).

To reiterate, Nussbaum's confidence that widespread agreement on these universal standards could be possible among people who otherwise diverge in their deepest loyalties and commitments rests on her presentation of them in the spirit of Rawlsian political liberalism—as "freestanding ethical ideas only" that require no contentious metaphysical or epistemological doctrines for support. I will return at the close of this chapter to the question of whether Nussbaum's account of justification is really only "political," not "metaphysical." For now, however, it is worth observing that Nussbaum tempers the importance of obtaining an actual consensus on these standards in ways that echo Sen's use of counterfactuals when she states that we do not even need to show that such a cross-cultural consensus "exists at present" but only that "there is sufficient basis for it in the existing views of liberal constitutional democracies that it is reasonable to think that over time such a consensus may emerge" (2006b, 388). As should be clear, then, the weight is placed more on the substantive defense of these universal norms than on this political and procedural one.[17]

ENHANCING HUMAN RIGHTS THROUGH THE FRAMEWORK OF CAPABILITIES

Having compared CA with the more familiar human rights framework in terms of their content, implementation, and theoretical grounding, we finally consider the important question of relevance for our purposes: why consider the capability approach at all? For in light of the areas of overlap already noted, one might surmise either that nothing of real value would be gained or that the two conceptual frameworks should be regarded instead as rivals. Against those concerns I would submit that defenders of human rights would stand to benefit from a selective appropriation of CA without first having to settle internal disputes about which list of capabilities to use, where to set the threshold for public policy, and whether talk of capabilities (rather than resources, welfare, or actual functioning) would in all cases be the best way to conceptualize egalitarian justice or to make quality-of-life comparisons across persons and societies.[18] Indeed, a selective retrieval of CA could enhance the project of advancing human rights in a pluralist world in the following three ways:

- A public policy focus on what individuals are actually able to *be* and to *do* would help to clarify what it actually means—and thus practically entails—to secure a human right to an individual.

- A focus on human capabilities would direct our attention to the conception of the human being that must undergird any theoretical justification for human rights, and its connotations of finitude and transcendence could also help to distinguish genuine claims from counterfeits.

- Martha Nussbaum's use of a species-norm and extension of CA to nonhuman animals could prove instructive in contextualizing human rights alongside of the entitlements that other beings might have as well as in providing an adequate response to the argument from marginal cases.

Clarifying What It Means to Secure a Human Right

One real contribution that a focus on individual capabilities could make to the more familiar human rights framework is by fleshing out what it would actually mean to secure human rights to individuals. As Nussbaum has aptly noted, if we were to think about a range of rights in terms of capabilities to function in various ways, we could make more intelligible the distinction between de jure and de facto protections. We might observe that individuals in some contexts legally possess the right of religious freedom but do not have it any meaningful way when they are consistently deprived of information about religion and thus cannot exercise real choice (Nussbaum 1997a, 292–94). We might also note that women in some contexts have the legal right of political participation but lack real abilities for civic engagement because they are secluded, threatened with violence if they leave the home, or prevented from pursuing educational opportunities due to the power of extant familial and cultural expectations about gender roles. Thus, if we were to regard these and other human rights (e.g., freedom of speech, freedom to seek employment outside the home) as honored only when the relevant capabilities to function were present, societies would have to engage in more extensive social and institutional reforms to propel all above the appropriate threshold.[19] To illustrate, genuine fulfillment of the rights of free speech and political participation in a previously authoritarian regime might require unobstructed access to the press and an end to the state-endorsed one-party system, whereas guarantees of the same in a wealthy and well-established democracy might necessitate certain limits on campaign contributions instead.[20] Whatever the specification, an interpretation of human rights through the conceptual lens of capabilities would obligate UN member-states to adopt measures beyond formally signing and ratifying the relevant human rights conventions and treaties or enacting their provisions into domestic law. They would also have to prevent what human rights expert Jack Donnelly (1989) has called the "possession paradox of rights," wherein individuals only recognize and claim their rights when they are absent, consistently violated, or otherwise not actionable.

Essentialism about the Good and the Language of Finitude and Transcendence

A second contribution that CA could make to our project of grounding human rights in a pluralist world lies in its recognition that any defense of universal social entitlements would have to be implicitly or explicitly guided by some notion of the good. Without a normative conception of our common humanity and commitment to an ethical ideal (e.g., a particular conception of human dignity, freedom, equality, harmony), we could neither determine which goods, processes, freedoms, or capabilities should be protected out of myriad possibilities nor could we judge certain modes of treatment to be unacceptable or even inhumane, nor justifiably apply the concept of "adaptive preferences" to those living under abysmal conditions who nevertheless overreport their contentment. Thus, in contrast to the previously discussed enforcement-centered approach to the justification, a capabilities-inspired defense of human rights could provide principled reasons for their global promotion and defense that were directly connected to the value of human beings as such. In contrast to the appropriated consensus-based approaches to human rights, these normative commitments would be understood as driving the search for an "overlapping consensus" itself, as opposed to emerging only as a result of public deliberations.

Admittedly, we need not reflect on our capabilities to function in various ways to come clean on the conception of the human being underwriting any justification for human rights. Nevertheless, the language of human capabilities points toward two helpful but seemingly different directions that the language of rights alone does not: a certain permanence about us as human beings, limited as we are by our biological needs and psychosocial vulnerabilities on the one hand, and our possibilities for invention and change on the other. As I shall argue, these opposing connotations of finitude and transcendence could help the international community expand or otherwise revise its specification of what rights we all have as human beings where appropriate.

Taking these two connotations in turn, the finitude pole of capabilities talk would recommend that we ground our common humanity and any resultant claims of rights upon our species-specific physical limitations, vulnerabilities, and psychosocial needs. Even as descriptions of these features of ourselves vary across persons and cultures, and even as our grasp of certain "facts" about us as humans beings are subject to change (e.g., the medical definition of death), there is a sense in which our capabilities—and thus any normative claim that they be cultivated—will be circumscribed by those "hard" constraints. For instance, all human beings have mobility needs, but it would be unreasonable to demand that our social institutions help us develop an ability to fly because flying unassisted is a physical impossibility for the types of creatures we are (i.e., featherless bipeds).[21] However, because we could not even live if deprived in certain ways, it would not be unreasonable for us to design a social order that provided social guarantees to meet our basic needs (e.g., to clean air, adequate shelter, potable water, a minimum caloric intake, sleep, and care by others when very young, old, infirmed, or impaired). More controversially, we might also require as a matter of justice that our social institutions enact measures to protect our bodily integrity and security, permit outlets for self-improvement or expression, and allow social interaction with others because we as creatures would suffer significant psychosocial harm if we were denied such possibilities. In these and other ways, a capabilities-influenced account of our basic human needs and aversions could serve as a springboard for subsequent claims of basic rights (see Shue 1996).[22]

The other pole of capabilities talk connotes openness, creativity, and transcendence and could prove helpful when assessing new candidates for human rights. Because what we as human beings are collectively capable of being or doing is relative to historical context and advances in technology, talk of capabilities would remind us that a good, a freedom, or a process need not be timeless to be considered universally valid today. Consider, for example, the inclusion of literacy as a basic social entitlement under Nussbaum's capability rubric #4. Centuries ago, before the rise of the middle class, invention of the movable type, and other forms of mass-produced printing, there could have been no real prospects for general literacy among the populace and, thus, no legitimate demand that literacy be promoted as a basic requirement of justice. Following the advent of new technologies and the widespread offering of compulsory and universal education, universal literacy has since become genuinely possible, although not yet universally achieved. Given literacy's direct connection today to other vitally important goods (e.g., educational achievement, civic engagement, and the ability to participate in communal life in modernized societies), it would be appropriate today to promote the worldwide development of this capability as a goal for public policy. This example is not intended to move from an "is" to an "ought" as per the naturalistic fallacy but only to demonstrate how the creation of new possibilities by human innovation can radically transform the surrounding culture, thereby creating new ways of flourishing and thus new demands to develop certain capabilities to allow for proper functioning.

Use of the Species-Norm and Extension to Nonhuman Animals

The final major contribution that CA can make to the more familiar human rights framework lies in its ability to make the connection to the prospect of animal rights more direct. Admittedly, the question of animal rights remains controversial, even nonsensical, to many people, and most jurisdictions do not take the well-being of nonhuman animals seriously beyond occasional "humane" laws that regulate the use of some animal species for food, research, companionship, or entertainment. Nevertheless, a public policy focus on the actual capabilities of human beings together with an understanding that we humans have dignity in part because of our capabilities logically leads to the question whether other beings with capabilities have their own form of dignity and, if so, what normative demands about our behavior towards them would follow as a result. This is to say that questions of animal rights complicate those of human rights, particularly since the successful implementation of the latter often has direct and serious repercussions for the well-being, if not actual lives, of the subjects of the former. To illustrate, we might design our public policies to fulfill the human right to housing by destroying (or preserving) the habitats of other creatures, just as we might elect to satisfy the human right to food by increasing the industrialization of the breeding and slaughter of animals for human consumption (or by shifting, where possible, to a more plant-based diet), and so forth. Thus, although conceptually not required, any justification of human rights that failed to consider both the likely impact of their implementation on the nonhuman realm and the question whether animals, too, have rights would appear short-sighted and incomplete.

To be clear, the prospect of contextualizing human rights claims alongside of the moral entitlements that other creatures might also be said to possess does not depend upon subjecting the concept of rights through the conceptual prism of capabilities. Nevertheless, doing so would be helpful because, as discussed in chapter 2, many philosophical justifications for human rights not only ground the moral worth of human beings with reference to specific capacities (e.g., the Kantian celebration of the human capacity for rational agency and autonomous legislation) but also ontologically distinguish human from nonhuman animals by appealing to a difference in capabilities of either degree or kind. Recall, however, Nicholas Wolterstroff's charge that capacities-grounded justifications for human rights cannot ultimately withstand the argument from marginal cases (AMC) because they can only guarantee the rights of some but not all human beings (namely, those who possess the relevant capacities in question) and thus cannot maintain any nonspeciesist or categorical distinction between humans and nonhuman animals.

It is here, then, where Martha Nussbaum's particular version of CA could prove instructive because she defends the universality of human rights and provides nonmorally arbitrary reasons for treating human and nonhuman animals differently without having to deny moral standing to animals. Against attempts to lump together mentally impaired humans with the higher animals due to their similar capacities for intelligence, Nussbaum points not only to the moral relevance of other human and animal capabilities beyond the rational or cognitive but also to the importance of the specific contexts in which creatures will primarily develop and exercise their species-specific capabilities. The capabilities to form associative affiliations or attachments with others, to understand and empathize with their suffering, to give and receive aid, to reproduce sexually, to rear offspring, and so forth are in many (but not all) cases either best realized or even only realizable with or among conspecifics. Thus, differential treatment between humans and other species would be warranted even in cases of comparable levels of intelligence (e.g., among "marginal" humans and the great apes or whales) because of the existence of other species-specific intrinsically valuable capabilities and because mentally impaired (or not fully rational) human beings can only actualize the full range of their capabilities among fellow humans.[23] From Nussbaum's perspective, then, the problem with the AMC is not only that it generally insists on isolating one morally relevant capability (as opposed to a plurality of them), but that it also assumes that the morally relevant distinction would be found at the level of capacities alone (as opposed to the contexts for their cultivation and functioning).

For reasons that will become clearer in the next section, Nussbaum's extension of her ten central capabilities to nonhuman animals is not without its problems. Still, she is among a growing list of philosophers, political theorists, and religious thinkers who correctly acknowledge that we can no longer ignore the question of animal entitlements when attempting to answer the same of human ones.

REVISITING THE QUESTION OF JUSTIFICATION

Recall that we asked at the conclusion of the previous chapter whether people who remain divided in their religious, philosophical, or cultural beliefs could come to an "overlapping consensus" on both universal standards of behavior and shared reasons for them. Nussbaum has offered her account of ten central human capabilities, which was based upon an intuitive idea of human dignity, as an affirmative response to that question. Legitimate concerns remain, however, over whether Nussbaum's version of CA successfully meets the maximalist challenge to human rights justification in light of its unclear or circular reasoning and arguably submerged metaphysical commitments.

On a straightforward reading of Nussbaum's articulation of CA, it is the capabilities of any complex living organism that give rise to certain social entitlements. Nussbaum previously even took pains to distinguish "basic capabilities" from more complex ones by defining the former as the "innate equipment of individuals that is the necessary basis for developing the more advanced capabilities, and a ground of moral concern" (2000a). In more recent work, however, she has disavowed the notion that dignity "rest[s] on some actual property of persons, such as the possession of reason or other specific abilities," and she now holds that the ten central capabilities are "ways of realizing a life with human dignity." She has accordingly conceded that these views represent a "shift from some earlier discussions of 'basic capabilities'" (2006b, 7, 161).

Now the problem with Nussbaum's shift in thinking is that she has left unclear why it is that human beings have the type of dignity that could justify their possession of ten basic social entitlements. In her more recent work, Nussbaum simultaneously depicts CA as beginning with an intuitive idea of human dignity and describes her conception of dignity as "not defined prior to and independently of the capabilities, but in a way intertwined with them and their definition" (2006b, 74, 161–62, 174). Without begging the question, however, one cannot ground a public policy pursuit of ten central capabilities for every person on an intuitive idea of human dignity and then maintain that the concept of human dignity and those ten central capabilities are intertwined. Admittedly, circular reasoning is part of what is entailed by a Rawlsian-inspired argument proceeding toward "reflective equilibrium," and because Nussbaum understands her procedural justification of CA accordingly, perhaps we ought not be surprised by it. Nevertheless, because Nussbaum intends for her capability approach to be universally valid in ways that Rawls does not for his political liberalism, she must do more than reason in a circular or tautological fashion if she is to be successful in countering the specter of relativism.

Nussbaum, however, would face a dilemma if she were to attempt to disentangle the concepts of human dignity and human capabilities. If she were to make a "naked" appeal to our dignity as human beings—without any accompanying argument about what it is about us that endows us with this dignity—her remarks would seem morally arbitrary and perhaps even speciesist. There are some indications that Nussbaum has already inclined toward this position. She writes: "the capabilities approach holds that the basis of a claim is a person's existence as a human being—not just the actual possession of a set of rudimentary 'basic capabilities,' pertinent though these are to the more precise delineation of social obligation, but the very birth of a person into the human community" (2006b, 285). The other option would be for Nussbaum to retain her earlier view that dignity rests on an actual property (or properties) of persons. But such an option would have metaphysical implications, which would be unsightly from the perspective of the political liberalism under which Nussbaum's account is to be cloaked.

Indeed, the second lingering concern about the type of justification Nussbaum offers is that it may not be as theoretically "free-standing" as described. As several critics have noted, to base one's conception of the central human capabilities on a Marxist-Aristotelian account of human flourishing is to participate in, or itself be an expression of, a historical comprehensive doctrine that might not adequately represent women's interests (Okin 2003, 296; Qizilbash 1997; Robeyns 2003, 67). To approach public deliberation through the lens of Rawlsian political liberalism or an "Aristotelian procedure in ethics" is simultaneously to fail to select other methods (e.g., an Augustinian one) (Skerker 2004). And to engage in the imaginative exercise of distinguishing humans from the Greek gods for the purposes of deciphering what is essential about us as human beings "may seem an implausible basis for a global ethic in a world with a highly divergent panoply of gods" (Alkire and Black 1997, 265). I would add that to base the extension of CA to animals using more or less Aristotle's classification of creatures is not to argue in a "freestanding" manner, even if she does not similarly appropriate the metaphysics connected to the original classification. Consider, for example, the Jain understanding that the whole world is alive via its attribution of souls (*jiva*) to objects not generally thought of (by non-Jains) as living; their prohibition of killing two- to five-sense creatures for food; and their teaching that even the "killing" of "one-sense creatures" (i.e., creatures with only the sense of touch—a class that includes turnips, trees, minerals, jewels, rivers, rains, lightning, and winds) should be minimized (Shah 1998; Embree 1988, 53–54).

That Nussbaum's theory trades on unacknowledged metaphysical or otherwise comprehensive ideas can be clearly seen in her attempts to adjudicate between human and animal interests. Nussbaum's theoretical position that differences in capabilities across species "affect entitlements not by creating a hierarchy of worth or value, but only by affecting what can be a good or a harm to a creature," together with her explicit rejection of any "natural ranking of forms of life, some being intrinsically more worthy of support and wonder than others," lead her to conclude that "there is no respectable way to deny the equal dignity of creatures across species" (2006b, 360, 383). But after acknowledging that requiring an "overlapping consensus" on such a position would make the prospect of recognizing animal entitlements even more difficult than it already is, she proposes instead that we "treat the question of equal dignity as a metaphysical question on which citizens may hold different positions" and thereafter settles for the "lower idea that all creatures are entitled to adequate opportunities for a flourishing life" (2006b, 383–84). Nussbaum's account certainly challenges many of our conventional practices that involve animal suffering and cruelty, but she generally privileges the interests of humans over animals in cases of real or potential conflict, such as when she fails to prescribe universal moral vegetarianism in part because she is unsure whether "such a diet could be made compatible with the health of all the world's children" (2006b, 402).

To be clear, my difficulties with Nussbaum do not primarily lie in her conclusions or manner of adjudication but in the process by which she reached either. If her premises were leading her to a view that she correctly ascertained would prove highly unpopular, she cannot simply declare it to be "metaphysical," and thus beyond the scope of political deliberation, without either succumbing to a failure of intellectual nerve, or implying that the premises themselves had heretofore submerged metaphysical entanglements.[24] In any event, by electing to resolve most conflicts between humans and animals in the favor of the former, she must at some level be committed to the superiority of humans over animals in either an ontological or purely practical sense, and yet her various theoretical arguments (e.g., her use of the species-norm, downplaying of the importance of rationality for a creature to have dignity, rejection of any hierarchy of species based on differences in capabilities) fail to substantiate the position she ultimately takes and universally recommends.

In sum, I do not primarily offer these criticisms to denigrate Nussbaum's working conception of the human being, her procedure for selecting which capabilities to promote as public policy goals everywhere, or her manner of adjudicating between human and animal entitlements (although, of course, legitimate questions can be raised about each of these points). Instead, my comments are principally designed to encourage her (and others) to cease trying to present her account of justification as purely "political" or "freestanding." Just as Rawls admitted that political liberalism would be unable to avoid implying a comprehensive doctrine's untruth if it refused to order the basic structure accordingly, so Nussbaum ought to concede that statements such as the following—"it matters a great deal what we ourselves think about our selfhood and our possibilities; what a being who stands apart from our experiences and ways of life think seems to matter little, if at all"—effectively dismisses the relevance of various theologically grounded accounts of human nature that many in society hold, and perhaps even implies their untruth (Rawls 1996, 138; Rawls 1999b, 183–84; and Nussbaum 1995a, 121).

The question now before us, then, is the following: if Nussbaum and others guided by political liberalism were to be more forthcoming about their reliance upon comprehensive ideas, would that mean that an adequate philosophical justification for human rights could not be supplied on minimalist grounds alone? That question is the subject of the final chapter.

Six

GROUNDING HUMAN RIGHTS IN A PLURALIST WORLD

As we have seen, it is no easy feat to provide a justification for human rights that would be robust enough to make sense of the powerful claims that the very idea makes as well as suitable under conditions of pluralism. In partial reaction to this difficulty, some have argued that the search for an underlying theoretical rationale is no longer even necessary, especially since human rights have already been institutionalized in various domestic, regional, and international laws. I would submit, however, that the desirability of identifying an adequate philosophical justification remains. Individuals and collectivities still legitimately press for principled reasons why they should comply with contemporary human rights standards, critics still object to their ever-expanding global reach in the absence of knowledge about their conceptual foundations, and proponents themselves could be aided by human rights theory when attempting to expand the catalog of provisions or adjudicate between conflicting claims. Much would therefore be lost if we were to ignore or collapse the distinction between the fact of human rights law and the open question of its extralegal moral force.

What then, would constitute a good justification for human rights in our pluralist world today? While we have not previously formalized a response to this question, a list of desirable attributes would be appropriate here. A good justification for human rights would arguably possess practical coherence, though not necessarily perfect correspondence, with the ways in which the term "human rights" is conventionally understood in both law and contemporary discourse for the sake of staying relevant to real world concerns. One way of procuring parity of this kind would be to adopt Michael Perry's rather sensible approach: analyze what is being claimed by the concept of human rights in core international human rights treaties and conventions (and, I would add, by human rights lawyers, theorists, activists, and even opponents), and then consider what higher principles or cognate ideas would have to be presumed to make those claims intelligible. If understood accordingly, a good justification for human rights would give appropriate expression to their universal applicability, moral urgency, and primary objective of specifying moral entitlements to certain kinds of minimal treatment or forbearance thereof by others.

A second desideratum in any theoretical defense of human rights would be its comparative persuasiveness, which is to say that our sought-after justification would improve upon or even overcome the shortcomings of its rivals. In light of the various approaches to justification that we have examined in this book, our ideal justification would assuage the minimalist's concern that any account too closely linked to a comprehensive conception of the good would not show proper respect for cultural and religious difference and thereby undermine the importance we render to conscience. It would likewise discharge the maximalist accusation that minimalist approaches are not "weighty" enough to handle the normative claims that human rights make—that every human being has moral worth and thereby ought to be treated in certain ways (and not treated in other ways). Our ideal justification would additionally outperform its alternatives in properly accounting for the provision of equal human rights, despite obvious variability among human beings in character, capabilities, choices, achievements, and social status or classification. Finally, the justification we are seeking would sufficiently address, though need not fully answer, the ways in which claims of animal rights do or do not affect the task of grounding human ones, particularly in light of concerns about implementation as well as the argument from marginal cases.

A third optimal feature in any adequate account of human rights is that it would show appropriate restraint. Without rejecting a priori any appeal to transcendent norms or nonrationally verifiable premises, the most desirable theoretical justification would contain as few controversial premises as possible to increase possibilities for a wide reception. This preference for parsimony would not invariably privilege minimalist over maximalist strategies of justification, for even the maximalists that we have considered only insist upon as many substantive convictions as are required by the logic of their approach. That is, Michael Perry may be Catholic, but his conclusion concerning the "ineliminably religious" character of the idea of human rights does not concomitantly require belief in specifically Christian, as opposed to Buddhist or still other, religious convictions. Likewise, both Max Stackhouse and Nicholas Wolterstorff may identify with different Protestant traditions, but their arguments concerning the indispensability of certain biblically grounded theological beliefs for human rights do not further oblige proponents to adopt a particular Protestant approach to biblical hermeneutics over a Catholic or Orthodox one or to take a stand on other theological matters (e.g., Christology, ecclesiology).

A final ingredient for a good justification of human rights is an ability to explain the type of universality at issue in the global project of advancing human rights today. Supporters need to be able to justify universality in scope, which means that all, not merely some, human beings should be treated as rightful bearers of a set of rights by virtue of their humanity alone. As discussed in the previous chapter, however, they need not also defend universality in time, whereby a good or liberty would have to have been applicable to all human beings across history to qualify as a genuine human right. Although there is notable overlap between the extension of "human rights" and "natural rights," any move to collapse the possible range of the former into the necessarily smaller and presocietal range of the latter would cause us to lose much desired specificity.[1] Thus, if we were to conceptualize human rights as the set of goods or liberties to which everyone should be entitled as a matter of basic justice in our modern and modernizing world today, we could make sense of a range of important human rights claims in international law that clearly postdate the formation of the earliest human communities, such as the rights of everyone to be "recognized everywhere as a person before the law" (Art. 6, UDHR), to nationality (Art. 15, UDHR; Art. 24.3, ICCPR; Art. 9, CEDAW; Art. 7, CRC), to free and compulsory elementary education (Art. 26, UDHR; Art. 13, ICESCR; Art. 10, CEDAW; Art. 28, CRC), and to various criminal justice proceedings when accused of committing a crime (Art. 14, ICCPR).[2] In turn, should the international community adopt a notably different set of social practices or institutions in the future, such as replace the post-Westphalian system of sovereign states with a world state or substitute the criminal justice model of conflict resolution for one of "restorative justice," the human right to nationality or to various criminal justice proceedings should be modified accordingly. In any event, our stipulation that universality in time is not required for universally validity is intended to prevent the invalidation of any human rights candidate simply because it refers to something contingent that originally arose in response to changing social–political conditions.

ASSESSING AND RETRIEVING MINIMALIST STRATEGIES OF JUSTIFICATION

We have reaffirmed the need for a theoretical defense of human rights and clarified ideal characteristics of the philosophical justification that is to be offered. Let us consider anew the intentions and limitations of the accounts of justification discussed in previous chapters before engaging in a selective retrieval of each.

The Enforcement-Centered Approach to Human Rights

Recall that the justification for human rights in enforcement-centered approaches ultimately resides in their function to serve as minimal standards of decency, delimit the bounds of acceptable pluralism between and among states, and accordingly contribute to international peace and security. These ideas are without neither merit nor precedence in the real world as elements of this goal-based orientation can be found in the post–World War II Human Rights Commission that was responsible for the creation of the Universal Declaration of Human Rights. Indeed, the preamble of the UDHR regards human rights to be crucial to the establishment of freedom, justice, and peace in the world; the avoidance of rebellion against tyranny and oppression; the development of friendly relations between nations; and the promotion of social progress.

We nevertheless found Rawls's particular enforcement-centered account of human rights in the *Law of Peoples* to be riddled with difficulties. His conception of internally homogeneous people-states is mythic, his equation of human rights with the morality of humanitarian intervention too severe and otherwise unnecessary to reduce legitimate occasions for third-party interference, and his account of justification ultimately vulnerable to charges of ethnocentrism or arbitrariness or both. Even if we were to follow Rawls in circumscribing the role of human rights so narrowly, we also concluded that his account of justification would still have to answer the questions why. Why do individual human beings have any rights at all, however large or small a set, by virtue of their humanity alone, and why would it be "indecent" to violate them? Why would it still be legitimate to interfere in the internal affairs of an otherwise sovereign polity in defense of human rights if the Society of Peoples were officially precluded from intervening to protect the moral worth or well-being of the victims themselves and if none of the anticipated outcomes that serve as the official rationale for human rights (i.e., the maintenance of international peace, security, and cooperation) were projected to come as a result? In short, we found that Rawls's defense of the human rights of individuals through the advantages that global compliance to human rights standards would bring for entire peoples presented enough problems to compromise the adequacy of his account as a response to the maximalist challenge to human rights justification.

But the shortcomings of the enforcement-centered approach to justification should not be taken to imply that nothing of value could be retrieved for our purposes. Quite the contrary, the approach's most productive idea is its insistence that human rights should not be viewed as the means to all good and worthwhile things. In our contemporary context where many strongly felt desires and items of importance quickly become transformed into calls for rights, it is helpful to be reminded that human rights are neither designed to provide individuals with totally satisfying, meaningful, wonderful, or exemplary lives; nor to establish "warmth, belonging, fitting, significance"; nor to remove the need for "love, friendship, family, charity, sympathy, devotion, sanctity, or for expiation, atonement, [or] forgiveness" (Henkin 1990, 186). Rather, we all should regard human rights much more modestly, even as Rawls does in part, as setting a decent social minimum benchmark beneath which no human being should ever fall.

If understood accordingly, human rights would be necessary to satisfy the demands of basic justice, but their fulfillment or realization would still not exhaust the topic of social or political justice much less all that could be said about morality.[3] If rights talk did not offer something distinctive in moral, sociopolitical, or legal discourse such that all matters of civility, fairness, reciprocity, respect, and so forth could be encapsulated into the moral vocabulary of rights, what would be the point of referring to a special class of claims as rights as opposed to as something else? Rawlsian conservatism, or the caution that we not dilute the strength or urgency of the concept of human rights through overextension, thereby compels us to discern which claims to human rights should instead be regarded as counterfeits.

Might some human rights claims or proposals be rejected for their exaggerated, excessive, or otherwise inappropriate character? Despite my strong feminist commitment to improving the status and well-being of women worldwide, I would regard Amartya Sen's proposal for the human right for women to be consulted in serious family decisions to fall in such a category. This is not primarily because enforcement of any legislation to that effect would be overly intrusive (assuming first that human rights are the kinds of things that ideally should be instantiated into law) but because the proposed requirement that every husband consult his wife in major familial decisions seems connected more to ideals of fairness, reciprocity, power sharing, and egalitarianism in marriage, not to basic justice per se. To use another example, I would also move to strike the latter portion of Article 12 of the UDHR—that "no one should be subjected to . . . attacks upon his honour and reputation. . . . [because] everyone has the right to the protection of the law against such . . . attacks"—from counting as a genuine human right and instead interpret it as a case of overzealous rights proliferation. Surely public figures who have disgraced themselves by their own conduct, or professionals who have seriously underperformed or been negligent in a critical task in their line of work, should not be able to claim a violation of their human right if their honor or reputation were publicly impugned for these reasons. We could, of course, apply similar scrutiny to the arguably hyperbolic elements in other human rights claims that are nonetheless either already recognized today in international human rights law or under consideration in other forums.

Finally, it is worth repeating that it can and should remain the prerogative of each political entity to secure additional rights for those within their jurisdiction in ways that transcend this social minimum. Once again, then, Rawls was right to observe that human rights could legitimately be a "subset" of the fuller schedule of guaranteed rights and liberties found elsewhere, such as in Western liberal constitutional democracies. As we have already noted, however, Rawls simply erred in making that subset much too small.

Consensus-Based Approaches to Human Rights

Recall that the question of whether we could preserve a broader range of human rights and conception of their role while still being able to justify them in ways that officially entailed minimum philosophical commitments is what led us to turn to consensus-based approaches to human rights. We saw in chapter 3 how these two-tiered accounts of justification do much to counter the charge that "human rights are Western," and they arguably describe the way the UDHR even came to be. They further allow us to see the unique contributions that each party to the "overlapping consensus" may have to offer, and they amply demonstrate how and why we need not procure total ideological alignment with others in order to pursue common ends. These benefits notwithstanding, our referrals back to the Rawlsian politically liberal concept of the "fundamental ideas" that predate the search for consensus itself, and to Maritain's hope for the identification of shared "key values" after the fact exposed the limitations of any approach that aims for mere convergence upon a list of practical human rights standards while leaving everything else undetermined. More specifically, what we found wanting was a shared set of deeper convictions about human rights that would either precede or follow the search for the cross-cultural consensus, guidelines about the correct procedure to follow when attempting to obtain one, and a suitably public or official justification for human rights that could transcend the myriad local varieties. In the absence of those features in any consensus-based account of human rights, we argued that the world community would be able to neither objectively distinguish permissible cultural instantiations of human rights from unacceptable deviations from universally valid norms nor evaluate the legitimacy of new candidates for human rights provisions. The world community would additionally be precluded from commending fidelity to human rights standards to those who have yet to join the consensus for reasons other than the popularity of the idea as measured by the fact of consensus itself, the threat of sanction for noncompliance, other appeals to self-interest, or their own particularistic justification that would likely prove unpersuasive unless the group in question shared similar comprehensive commitments.

Most importantly for our purposes, we judged that any consensus-based account of human rights would be woefully incomplete if it left unsettled how and why the results of convergence on minimum standards of conduct—however truly international, interreligious, and intercultural—should have normative force. To be sure, an empirical demonstration of widespread agreement on human rights might increase our confidence in the nonprovincial character of its results. But if we were to count success (or even its likelihood) in obtaining an overlapping consensus on human rights as sufficient for an official or public account of justification, we would be succumbing to the same logic as the relativists did in mistaking the empirical popularity of an idea for evidence of its moral validity. Put differently, because valuing something does not make it objectively valuable, we must locate the source of normativity elsewhere. In fact, I would argue that we should not even want the morality of a social practice such as discrimination based on religion or sex to be contingent upon widespread disapproval. Instead, it would be better for us to understand the growing convergence today on the impermissibility of religion- or sex-based discrimination as revealing that persons of diverse backgrounds have come to regard such forms of discrimination as problematic for principled reasons of their own, as opposed to establishing the wrongness of religion- or sex-based discrimination by its unpopularity.

While a consensus-based approach to human rights justification cannot be said to exhaust the issue of justification, we can still retrieve its key insight that it is possible, and in many cases desirable, for the content and public justification of human rights to be couched in more general terms than any underlying or supporting cultural, philosophical, or religious reasons. An additional virtue of this approach is its vivid demonstration that justification is and ideally should remain context sensitive: we commonly provide different rationales to different audiences for different ends. As philosopher A. John Simmons has noted,

> justifying an act, a strategy, a practice, an arrangement, or an institution typically involves showing it to be prudentially rational, morally acceptable, or both (depending on the kind of justification at issue). And showing this, in standard cases, centrally involves rebutting certain kinds of possible objections to it: either *comparative* objections—that other acts or institutions (etc.) are preferable to the one in question—or *noncomparative* objections—that the act in question is unacceptable or wrong or

that the institution practices or sanctions wrongdoing or vice.
Justification, we might say, is in large measure a "defensive"
concept, in that we ask for justification against a background
presumption of possible objections. (1999, 740)

That justification is always apologetic explains why most contemporary defenses of human rights, including the minimalist and
maximalist strategies examined in this study, take seriously the
well-trodden accusations that rights talk is culturally or morally parochial, illegitimately disruptive of a people's right to self-
determination, or otherwise antagonistic to social harmony and the
pursuit of communal ends. Moreover, that justification is normally
addressed to specific others and thus attuned to epistemological
context also explains why it is entirely appropriate for the theoretical defense we provide for human rights to vary according to dis-
cursive contexts as we tailor some of the reasons we offer to the
needs and modes of discourse of the particular communities we
hope to persuade.

The Capability Approach to Human Rights and the Limitations of Political Liberalism

Having identified as desiderata both the provision of deeper reasons
for international human rights standards at the public or official
level and an explanation of why cross-cultural consensus on them
should have justificatory force, we finally turned to the capability approach (CA) to see if it could supply what had been lacking in the
previous accounts. We examined Amartya Sen's and Martha Nussbaum's justification for human capabilities and human rights in particular. We observed that Sen largely adopts a counterfactual and
then a Maritain-like approach of inviting the world community to
jointly form affirm "key values" that could emerge from a highly interactive process of public deliberation and justification. Alternately,
we noted that Nussbaum pursues something closer to a Rawlsian political liberal strategy of beginning with "fundamental ideas" about
human dignity and flourishing before turning to her procedural

manner of justifying pursuit of her list of ten central human capabilities as public policy goals everywhere.

After noting points of contact as well as discontinuity between the concepts of human capabilities and human rights, we concluded that the human rights framework could be enhanced through selective appropriation of insights drawn from CA. It was not any particular listing of human capabilities that we found most useful about CA for our purposes but rather the following three points: (a) its clarification of what it actually means to secure a human right to someone; (b) its rightful acknowledgment of the unavoidability of presupposing a conception of the good for human beings when justifying human rights, and its helpful connotations of finitude and transcendence when assessing which provisions should even be counted among them; and (c) its removal of the sting from the "argument from marginal cases" while contextualizing human rights claims alongside of parallel concerns that are increasingly being raised about nonhuman animals.

With respect to the all-important matter of justification, our primary difficulty with Martha Nussbaum's version of CA was her underreporting of its reliance upon comprehensive, if not metaphysical, ideas and, thus, her exaggeration of its theoretically "freestanding" quality. These maximalist-leaning commitments were most prominently displayed in her reliance on Aristotelian thought (e.g., her use of an Aristotelian-inspired account of human flourishing, the "Aristotelian procedure in ethics," her Aristotelian-inspired taxonomy of creatures) as opposed to other viable alternatives, and in her ultimate privileging of human entitlements over animal ones, despite her theory's principled commitment to equal cross-species dignity. Nussbaum's desire to conform her account to the requirements of Rawlsian political liberalism is arguably motivating this underreporting of the role that these comprehensive commitments play in her Marxist-Aristotelian-inspired version of CA. As I have argued, however, her embrace of the Rawlsian manner of understanding the appropriate relationship between moral and political philosophy is precisely what is undercutting the full force of what she could contribute to the project of advancing human rights worldwide today.

To reiterate and expand upon some points made in the previous chapter, recall that a genuine "overlapping consensus" for Rawls would involve widespread agreement on not only the political conception of justice among persons firmly divided on questions about the good and the true but also on shared "fundamental ideas" that would be guiding the political conception itself. Following Rawls, Nussbaum provides ostensibly shared "fundamental ideas" for the furtherance of everyone's human capabilities and human rights, though she removes in her more recent writings the "ground" upon which that intuitive idea of human dignity was originally founded— every individual human being's possession of a set of intrinsically valuable basic capabilities. Without an appeal to the latter, however, the moral force of her intuitive idea would simply rest on the alleged fact that many people across cultures share that intuition. However, even if we were to assume for the sake of argument that diverse peoples do (in fact) share the conception of the human being and intuitive idea of human dignity upon which her account of basic social entitlements is based, Nussbaum would still not have provided a nonrelativistic defense of the propriety or validity of those ideas but would have only stated contingent empirical matters of questionable normative weight.

It is worth remembering that the author of the political liberalism upon which Nussbaum principally relies was more than willing to bite this relativist bullet. The "fundamental ideas" that Rawls insisted must drive the very search for an "overlapping consensus" are not themselves to be grounded metaphysically, objectively, or otherwise externally but as directly tied to the public, political culture of the very people seeking those regulatory principles of justice for themselves. That is, Rawls's shift from his classic defense of liberal egalitarianism in *A Theory of Justice* to a series of notable modifications in *Political Liberalism* was famously motivated by a realization that the arguments of the former contained, in his assessment, undesirable metaphysical implications. Rawls came to believe that "what justifies a conception of justice is not its being true to an order antecedent to and given to us, but its congruence with our deeper understanding of ourselves and our aspirations, and our realization that, given our history and the traditions embedded in our public life, it is the most reasonable doctrine for us" (1999a, 306–7). In place of truth, then, Rawls presented political liberalism as offering Western liberal democratic societies a way to affirm their identity. But Nussbaum's liberal cosmopolitan embrace of a more robust conception of universal human rights, her prescription of one ambitious list of central human capabilities for the governments of every nation to pursue as public policy goals, and her longstanding commitment to global feminism reveal that she would not be well-served by following Rawls's tactic of exchanging metaphysics for relativism. Nevertheless, I would submit that her unwillingness to jettison Rawlsian political liberalism is what is preventing her from making the very type of argument that could counter charges of relativism most successfully: an appeal to truth.

What we have seen, then, is the high cost of Nussbaum's turn to Rawlsian political liberalism. She had hoped to gain from a justificatory strategy of theoretical thinness the willingness of people who remain fiercely divided on questions of ultimate concern to commit nevertheless to pursuing the same list of ten central human capabilities as public policy goals everywhere. But for such prospects of widespread acceptability she has had to relinquish the claim that CA is superior to its rivals because it is ultimately built upon something genuinely real or true. Indeed, Nussbaum has fully acknowledged that any conception of human rights or human capabilities that is justified under political liberalism would be prohibited not only from appealing either to God as the locus of all value or to the existence of any self-evident truths but also even to statements such as the following: "men and women, black and white, we are deeply and truly equal. . . . Moral and religious conceptions that deny this equality, sexist and racist conceptions, are just *wrong*" (2001a, 899).

This inability to ground universal human rights on a vision of fundamentally real human moral equality should trouble many (if not most) egalitarians, feminists, postcolonial theorists, and deontologically oriented proponents of human rights. It would undoubtedly bewilder the maximalists, who would then retort that for all of Nussbaum's talk about human dignity and the intrinsic worth of certain human capabilities, her politically liberal grounding ultimately could not bear the normative weight of those ideas. Still worse in their eyes would be their observation that what Nussbaum and others in the tradition of political liberalism cannot explicitly commit to in theory is powerfully operative and arguably smuggled into the proposals that they nonetheless recommend in practice. That is, if Nussbaum and others persuaded by her were not beginning with the assumption that all human beings genuinely are the equals of others (i.e., men and women, whites and other races, young and old, the nonhandicapped and the physically or mentally impaired), why would they insist upon an ethical imperative that society develop everyone's capabilities equally? Similarly, if those commending "overlapping consensus" as a justificatory strategy were not already committed to a logically prior belief that individuals (in the singular or collective) have real—not merely conferred or constructed— moral standing, why would they put themselves through the trouble of designing the search for an overlapping consensus on human rights in a democratic fashion where individual conscience about religion and other matters of ultimate concern must be shown appropriate respect?

Simply put, to insist that morality (not simply prudence) requires one to respect or tolerate the "reasonable" comprehensive doctrines of others already assumes that the persons who hold them are worthy of being respected or tolerated.[4] This is to say, as noted previously, that the institutionalization of respect or toleration cannot simply be the product of public deliberation and consensus but must actually motivate them. Thus, unless one is either subscribing to a version of relativism as Rawls ultimately does or appealing to consequentialist considerations, a set of unacknowledged but powerful convictions about the truth of those liberal egalitarian commitments that political liberalism attempts to actualize is most likely standing behind any politically liberal theorist's concern for procedural fairness, respect for the conscience of persons (or peoples) through official silence about the truth-value of the political conception propounded, and purely political (as opposed to realist) conception of each human being as free and equal.

To be clear, nothing I have said so far should be taken to imply that theorists working in the tradition of Rawlsian political liberalism might still be correct in their observation that the actual citizens (or cultures) deliberating in public forums about matters of law, public policy, or justice need not necessarily appeal to their comprehensive religious or philosophical premises to pursue common ends. In fact, the very invocation of those commitments, particularly in diverse interreligious or multicultural settings, might in some cases work to impede, rather than facilitate, the ability to find common cause and thus make progress in practical matters (Sunstein 2000). Still, the fact that those who adhere to the dictates of political liberalism may not have to disclose their reliance upon comprehensive beliefs (if any) in the reasons they give to others once the system has been "set up," so to speak, does not let the theorists who recommend political liberalism as a strategy of justification similarly "off the hook" for the reasons described earlier.

We might be led to the conclusion that we cannot procure all that we normatively want in our philosophical justification of human rights by remaining theory-thin because such attempts have yet to demonstrate that they could give appropriate expression to what the idea of human rights entails: the moral worth and equality of human beings and the prohibition against sacrificing the rights of one or some for the sake of the many even if good outcomes were projected to follow. So if Nussbaum's approach, together with the other minimalist strategies of justification we have considered, cannot satisfactorily meet the maximalist challenge, does that mean that maximalists have been correct all along in their central contention that an appeal to religion is necessary to ground human rights? The answer, put simply, is no, although aspects of maximalism, like minimalism, might also be retrieved for our purposes of finding a suitable justification for human rights.

ASSESSING AND RETRIEVING MAXIMALIST
APPROACHES TO JUSTIFICATION

In contrast to minimalist strategies of justification, I noted in chapter 2 that maximalists unashamedly appeal to metaphysically realist premises when grounding human rights. On their reading, we all have rights by virtue of our humanity alone because we truly are entities of real value, inestimable worth, inherent dignity, and the like; the way to treat us in ways that properly reflect our worth is thus to respect the rights we all possess as human beings. If the underlying rationale for human rights truly pointed to a fact beyond any human creation as the maximalists contend that it must—to an alignment of the cosmos in ways hospitable to our deepest yearnings (Perry), to a Supreme Being or Absolute that stands apart from all that is conditioned (Küng), to the God whom the Bible reveals as either issuing universal and categorical moral requirements (Stackhouse), or as redemptively loving all who bear the *imago Dei* (Wolterstorff)—we would indeed have very compelling reasons to honor human rights. These maximalist justifications would be comparatively superior to minimalist ones because they would be based on a much more solid, powerful, and authoritative source than any constructivist account that was founded upon the vagaries of shifting sentiment, collective self-interest, or even widespread consent to their norms could ever provide.

In Western traditions of ethical reflection, we acknowledged that the most powerful accounts of human moral standing and cosmopolitanism (i.e., the idea that humanity ultimately forms one moral community) have historically been grounded religiously, as were the first inklings of consciousness about individual rights. The Stoics taught the idea of a divine force controlling human events and a divine power underlying morality, and the "biblically based" religions, of which several of the maximalists spoke, contributed to the formation of the idea of human rights through their gradually inclusive visions of who should be counted in the circle of moral concern and of how our social institutions should be arranged to safeguard human worth. Still, I already noted at the close of both chapters 1 and 2 that the historical fact that these nascent ideas of inherent human dignity and equality (or even the trajectory of natural law to natural rights to human rights) may have originally sprung from certain religious visions does not itself show that they must have taken, or still must now take, that route.

So we are left with the hunch that maximalists may be right about the crucial vulnerabilities in minimalist strategies of justification that deliberately avoid grounding human rights in the objectivity of value or real moral worth of all human beings. Several of these maximalists have nonetheless erred in concluding thereafter that we must (still) appeal to supernatural sources of meaning, authority, or value—or what is conventionally defined as "religious"—in order to do the opposite. Here we must emphatically insist that the conjunction of the religious with the ethically realist or metaphysical is still common but not conceptually necessary. There are philosophers who are committed to the objectivity of value and to the use of metaphysics in ethics in general and in human rights in particular who nevertheless avoid locating such commitments in any conventionally understood religious framework. To give a brief and small sampling of these approaches, Thomas Nagel defends realism about value in his classic *The View from Nowhere* (1986), in which truth is understood in terms of truths about practical reasons and where those reasons are further explicated through both objective and subjective points of view. Allen Wood defends the objectivity of values by arguing that such objectivity is a necessary presupposition of all rational deliberation (a required activity if we are to act at all). He further suggests that this metaethical position has normative implications for cosmopolitanism but grounds these patently metaphysical ideas within a naturalistic worldview, where "human beings are naturally evolved parts of the physical world, and no more than that" (2001, 868). William Fitzpatrick (2005, 2008) defends a robust form of this-worldly but nonnaturalistic ethical realism as the strongest (and perhaps only) way to account for the normative claim of the equal moral standing of all human beings, which he contends is implicit in any nonconsequentialist account of human rights. James Griffin (2008) also attempts to justify human rights nonreligiously by resurrecting the Enlightenment notion of the dignity of all persons as agents and then by arguing in a section titled the "metaphysics of human rights" that the interests we all have as human beings are real features of the world. We could add many other thinkers to this list of philosophical realists who do not rely upon explicitly religious premises in their arguments. While these or other like-minded secular realist accounts are not all feasible or mutually compatible, the point to underscore is that the type of appeal to a "context-transcending, metaphysical reality" that maximalists such as Stackhouse insist is required to justify the universal validity of human rights need not itself be religious (2005, 36).[5]

Two Exaggerated Claims

What, then, might have led some maximalists to bold overstatements about the conceptual necessity of religion for human rights? I offer two possible explanations, the first involving an overly broad definition of what religion has conventionally been understood to mean or to be and the second having to do with possible confusion and even conflation between the normative and the motivational.

In the first case, the answer might simply be that maximalists such as Michael Perry and Max Stackhouse provide an unconventionally expansive description of what religion is, so that anything that smacks of a realist or metaphysical bent could be readily assimilated into it. Recall that religion for Perry is principally about trust that the world is ultimately meaningful and ordered in a cosmologically significant manner such that morality must be recognized as ultimately not a product of our own creation. Recall further that, for Stackhouse, the idea of human rights necessarily implies that there is a "universal moral order under which all peoples and societies lie," and that religion is the very "human acknowledgment that we live under a power and morality that we did not construct and may not ignore, and particular religions are sets of ultimate convictions and hypotheses about the nature, character, demands, and implications of that reality" (1984, 2; 2005, 27). Under those working definitions, contemporary secular defenses of ethical realism (such as the ones noted earlier) would technically count as religious, as would the longstanding tradition of natural law, given its central ontological conviction that morality is somehow "built" into the world itself.[6] However, these perspectives are not conventionally understood as religious either because of their conceptual separation from historically extended religious traditions, or because of their epistemological nonreliance on transcendent sources of meaning and authority such as sacred texts or persons (Kohen 2007, 13–37; Amesbury and Newlands 2008, 136n24). While Perry and Stackhouse might still be right that ethical realism provides the strongest, and perhaps only, adequate justification for human rights, they would nevertheless be wrong to have presumed that religion must concomitantly be invoked to defend it.

The second possible reason why some maximalists might have overstated their case lies in a possible confusion between the normative and the motivational. Recall that all four of the maximalist theorists canvassed in chapter 2 stressed, to varying degrees, the inability for philosophy alone to propel people to pursue the good. Küng in particular lamented the ways in which philosophical models or "pure reason" often fails to spur people to act in accordance with the dictates of morality, especially if the morally correct course of action would necessitate personal sacrifices (1991, 43; see also Stackhouse and Healey 1996, 505). Recall further that such an inability, if true, would prove especially disastrous for any purely secular attempt to justify and protect nonderogable human rights. But the problem with this charge against philosophical or purely secular reasoning is that it is overdetermined. A philosophical model or secularly grounded normative claim that fails to entice people to act should not for that reason alone be regarded as inherently defective because it is inappropriate to expect one's justification for an ethical principle to provide nondefeasible reasons for people to follow it. Both experience and fiction provide ample examples of persons who do not meet the moral demands that they themselves acknowledge to be perfectly valid: they could be suffering from *akrasia*, exercising "bad faith" in prioritizing urgently felt nonmoral interests over moral obligations, or perhaps insufficiently trained to "do the right thing" in especially trying times. I would add that these existential difficulties of knowing what one must do but still not doing it (e.g., knowing that the existence of poverty in a world of wealth presents a serious moral problem but failing to act to alleviate it) is endemic to the human condition, whether one is operating out of an explicitly religious context or not. We need only be reminded of the Apostle Paul's consternation of being under the grip of sin, of being able to recognize what is right but not being able to do it, to concede this last point (Rom. 7:15–19).

The Limits of the Maximalist Approach to Human Rights Justification

What if maximalist theorists were to amend their objections to minimalist approaches in the ways suggested so that they no longer assimilated secular realist accounts of justification into religious ones, and no longer conflated normativity with practical efficacy? Would we then judge the overall maximalist approach to human rights justification superior to the overall minimalist strategy? It is important to acknowledge that while maximalists have consistently accused minimalists of argumentative incompleteness, of relying upon substantive commitments that they could not ultimately defend, maximalists themselves ultimately succumb to a parallel problem. All of the maximalists we have considered in this study attempt to show what they purport to be the necessary conceptual dependence of human rights upon one religious conviction or other. But they have not provided any affirmative reasons for believing in the truth or even the feasibility of those religious convictions in question and, thus, the truth or even feasibility of human rights claims themselves. Perry acknowledges that the question of the plausibility that every human being is sacred (a conviction he deems essential to the very idea of human rights) is "substantially a question about the plausibility of religious faith," yet he never defends in either of his two book-length studies on human rights the "(general) claim that the world has a normative order, much less the (particular) claim that every human being is sacred" (2000b, 39; and 2006, 161n3). Küng explicitly disclaims any attempt to "try to prove that religion is in fact focused on . . . a most real, primordial Ultimate Reality," and observes instead that religious convictions can only be held in "rational trust" (1987, 231–32; and 1991, 53). Stackhouse avoids demonstrating the truth or even the feasibility of the Christian theological convictions that he suspects might provide the only adequate grounds for human rights, and he concedes that our ultimate future may turn out to be Buddhist eschatological "emptiness" or "nothingness" instead of "God" because the "data" about the "ultimate end of things" obviously are not yet in (1984, 273; 2003, 9). Finally, Wolterstorff has waged a good part of his career defending Reformed epistemology against the evidentialist challenge to religious belief that is associated with classical foundationalism, and has consistently dismissed the need to marshal anything even resembling rational proofs for the existence of the God, even though God's redemptive love for humanity on his view might serve as the only adequate grounding for human rights (1983, 2008a).

Given the large role that faith plays in the formation of religious convictions, we might have expected nothing less from confessionally religious proponents of human rights. Still, we must acknowledge that transcendental arguments for human rights do not provide an affirmative justification for them or even reasons supporting their plausibility but only a diagnosis of what any preexisting belief in or commitment to human rights must logically entail.[7]

Although I have generally presented minimalism and maximalism in oppositional terms, we can now see how they ironically end in structurally similar positions. The minimalists canvassed in our study relied upon commitments that they ultimately could not defend because doing so would damage the integrity of the very type of justification they were hoping to offer. Rawls avoids appealing to the moral worth of individuals, consensus-based approaches evade having to provide a shared theoretical rationale for human rights, and Nussbaum's version of the capability approach sidesteps having to ground human dignity or equality metaphysically. Analogously, maximalists would not even attempt to provide a rational defense for human rights because doing so would undercut their central argument that the entire project of justifying them must ultimately rest upon some transcendent conviction of faith or other. Of course, a key difference between minimalist and maximalist approaches is that only the latter acknowledged the incompleteness of their arguments and embraced the central role of faith.

GROUNDING HUMAN RIGHTS IN A PLURALIST WORLD BY STRADDLING THE MINIMALIST–MAXIMALIST DIVIDE

While we have concluded that none of the aforementioned minimalist or maximalist approaches in their current forms can give us what we are looking for in grounding human rights, our examination of them has not been in vain. The way I would justify human rights could be described as neither purely minimalist nor maximalist, but both minimalist- and maximalist-leaning, thus in between the extremes of both poles. I would even argue that the language of the International Bill of Human Rights would support my negotiated and mediated approach.

The Justification

That the position I ultimately defend is neither strictly minimalist nor maximalist should be obvious for all the reasons provided in previous chapters. Against the general minimalist inclination to avoid controversy for the strategic purpose of increasing acceptability of human rights among diverse audiences, I have urged resistance to any short-circuiting of the critical edge of what human rights are supposed to mean and do. I have additionally called for an end to the minimalist tendency to downplay or even deny the deep philosophical commitments to which they implicitly subscribe when they justify such an ambitious claim as the universal validity of human rights. Against maximalists I have called for an end to their own exaggerated claims: that nonreligiously grounded justifications for human rights lack theoretical coherence (because the real issue is more about sufficient moral weight than about conceptual intelligibility), that the idea of human rights presupposes either that animals do not have rights of their own or that human rights will always trump theirs when and if animals do, and that religiously grounded ethical principles are invariably superior to secular reasoning in motivating people to act morally. Most importantly for our purposes, I have called for an end to the maximalist redescription of metaphysical commitments as religious ones, thus opening up space for a kind of justification that could fit in between the minimalist and maximalist poles—a justification that is neither theory-thin (as in the extremes of minimalism) nor invariably religious (as the maximalists insist it must be) but nevertheless premised on an underlying commitment to the real moral worth of all human beings.

My own account of justification consists of three primary parts. In the first I affirm many of Martha Nussbaum's arguments for essentialism, for we need not fear justifying human rights in ways dependent upon a normative conception of our nature as human beings. Of course, we ought to remain mindful that essentialist arguments have historically been put to exploitative or overly conservative ends (especially against women). But if we do not retain some basic account of who or what human beings fundamentally *are* and should be able to *be* or *do*, we will not be able to employ the powerful charge that some ways of treating human beings are simply "inhumane" and accordingly ought to be universally prohibited. Indeed, when core human rights treaties and conventions declare, to borrow Perry's terminology, that some things ought to be done for every human being and some things ought never to be done to any human being, they are making claims about a common humanity in light of our shared biological and sociopsychological constraints, vulnerabilities, wants, and needs. They are also instructing that certain features or characteristics that otherwise divide us—our differences in abilities or talents, gender, sex, race, nationality, culture, religion, socioeconomic status, and so forth—are not morally relevant insofar as they affect the allocation of the liberties and entitlements that are our human rights.

Our retention of essentialism about the good for human beings carries with it still further advantages. Although we ought still to distinguish the possession of human rights from their exercise and accordingly allow individuals in many circumstances to elect not to exercise what is in fact their right (e.g., to "take part in the government of his country," to "found a family," Art. 21, 16, UDHR), a commitment to essentialism would further allow us to make a range of important normative judgments that would otherwise be impossible. Consider hypothetically, for example, a person who would decide to continue to be enslaved by someone else even if given a real and meaningful choice of freedom, or who would refuse to press for just and fair judicial proceedings if falsely accused of a crime by the state, or who would still consent to receiving unequal remuneration for equal work even if her job were to remain secure in either scenario. Without an essentialist conception of the good for human beings and a normative conception of our common humanity, we would be obliged to respect and even affirm those choices just as much as we would their opposite; thus, we could not interpret the person in question as suffering from some sort of defective rational agency, "false consciousness," extreme privation, fear, low self-esteem, or learned helpfulness.

In the second part of my justification for human rights, I contend that we can make the most sense of the powerful claims that the idea of human rights make if we embed them within an ethically realistic framework. To be a realist is to be committed to the objectivity of value and to the idea that the good refers to real properties of things, not simply to linguistic artifacts of our social construction or to judgments that arise from only our conceptual schemes. Against various minimalists who follow in the tradition of political liberalism, I argue that we must posit the real and equal value of human beings to understand fully the moral imperative in international human rights law that implies that we show respect for all human beings by honoring the rights that everyone possesses simply by virtue of being human. To claim, as the ICCPR and ICESCR do in the preamble, that our dignity "inheres" in us is precisely to say that our value or worth is not something that we ultimately create or bestow upon ourselves or others. An ethically realistic commitment is accordingly maximalist-leaning in its concern that constructivist accounts of justification may not be robust enough to ground the profound demands that the idea of human rights makes. But this same commitment is simultaneously minimalist-leaning in its rejection of the maximalist contention that that belief in objectivity of value in general or the real worth of human beings in particular must invariably rest upon some religious foundation or other.

Third and finally for my official or public justification of human rights, I see no reason why we could not combine a minimalist-leaning strategy with a maximalist-inspired commitment to realism. We would only include as many controversial premises as necessary while simultaneously professing that statements about the moral worth and equality of all ages, races, and sexes, and so forth say something fundamentally true about ourselves and the world. In this merger of political liberalism with realism, we would begin with this "fundamental idea" of real human worth or dignity but then allow different cultures or traditions to affirm the deeper truth of that metaphysical commitment out of their differing religious or nonreligious frameworks. Some might believe that the value of humanity is somehow "built into" the structure of the world, and they may then proceed to account for it without appealing to supernatural sources of meaning, perhaps in one of the secular ways previously described. Others might believe that the ultimate source of a doctrine of equal human moral worth is to be found in a God who created us all in the divine likeness. Still others might ground these claims with reference to a metaphysical but impersonal force or power such as the tao.

Admittedly, this openness to a plurality of ways of grounding ethical realism would have practical consequences analogous to the ones described in our discussion of consensus-based approaches to human rights. That is, even if discrete parties were to support human rights because they believed that all humans really are of intrinsic worth, it is likely that the particular metaphysical reason undergirding that idea would affect their understanding of the resultant schedule of rights as well as their manner of implementation. Rather than conceal or suppress these points, however, I once again recommend that human rights proponents simply stop trying to pretend that neutrality can in all cases be maintained, for to conclude as I have that the idea of human rights is most adequately supported by a realist framework is already to offend a large number of theorists who have lost their taste for metaphysics in ethics altogether. To some degree, then, I share Max Stackhouse's prognosis of our contemporary situation, although not the specific conclusion he reaches, which is that we are witnessing a "failure of intellectual nerve" among scholars, philosophers, and theologians who are unwilling to engage in deep discussion and debate on questions pertaining to the possible superiority of one conception of the good over another (Stackhouse and Healey 1996, 512; Stackhouse 1998).

That a suitable justification for human rights under conditions of pluralism should have both minimalist- and maximalist-leaning tendencies would also fit well with our desideratum that our public justification show practical coherence with the manner in which the term "human rights" is conventionally understood in international law and popular discourse. In concert with the International Bill of Rights, I have proposed an account of justification that bends toward minimalism in eschewing any necessary recourse to either religion or a specific metaphysical or cosmological claim (to the exclusion of all others) while simultaneously inclining toward maximalism in its transcendence of legal positivism through its commitment to realism.

As noted previously, the minimalist strategy of restricting human rights theory for the sake of facilitating greater practice is reflected in the admittedly theory-thin aspect of the international human rights documents themselves. We recall how the drafters of the UDHR and other key international human rights documents knew all too well that they could not tie the justification of human rights too closely to any contentious philosophical, religious, or moral doctrines if human rights were to set minimum, universal standards of behavior especially for UN member-states. We also acknowledged in chapter 2 that any public or official justification of human rights that relied too heavily upon any one comprehensive conception of the good over others would not only be resented by those who do not share it but would also pose considerable tension with the conscience and belief-related rights that the documents are supposed to protect. For these and other reasons, the International Bill of Human Rights arguably makes clear by its silence on such matters that no particular philosophical or metaphysical tenet, sacred text, or teachings of "enlightened" persons (e.g., by any philosopher-kings or religious clerics) is required to understand what is entailed by either the concept or actual specifications of human rights. Johannes Morsink has called this the "universal epistemic condition" or "epistemic universality" of human rights, and David Little has similarly maintained that it must be possible to conceive of a "neutrally formulated normative regime" or else the "whole idea of human rights disappears" (Morsink 1999, 294; 2009, ch. 2; Little 1999, 166).

But minimalism is not the only trajectory represented in these international human rights documents: there is also a maximalist-leaning, antilegal positivist thrust that is at least suggestive of or compatible with ethical realism. While the legal authority of treaties and conventions such as the ICCPR depends upon their ability to have obtained enough signatories to enter into force, their moral authority has not been understood to rely solely upon any international or overlapping consent to their standards. Despite the pragmatic orientation of some of the reasons specified to promote human rights worldwide (e.g., in the words of the ICCPR, to achieve "civil and political freedom and freedom from fear and want"), human rights are nonetheless consistently described as having been "derive[d] from the inherent dignity of the human person" (preamble, ICCPR; see also Art. 1, UDHR).

It is notable, then, that all three documents in the International Bill of Human Rights employ the language of "recognition" and not "conferral," which suggests that the governments of the world and all people of good will are to acknowledge the preexisting moral authority of the normative claims that human rights make but are not themselves to be understood as endowing them with normativity through their approval. Mary Ann Glendon has observed that while legal positivism flourished in the United States and Europe and was dogma for the Soviet Union prior to World War II, the legally sanctioned atrocities committed by Nazi Germany "caused many people to reevaluate the proposition that there is no higher law by which the laws of nation-states can be judged" (2001, 176). To claim, then, that human rights are morally authoritative in ways that we did not ourselves create is to underscore conceptual continuity with the traditions of both natural rights and natural law that preceded them— traditions that have been overtly metaphysical in character. This is to say that the "ideal status of human rights" should be understood independently of "particular constitutional arrangements, legislative enactments, and judicial decisions" (Langan 1982, 72; see also Little 2006, 299n15). This is to suggest further that the UDHR's implicit "inherence view of human rights," or the idea that we have human rights simply because of our membership in the human family, means that they will not depend upon "any external force or agency" or "gifts of history or circumstance" (Morsink 1999, 290–96; 2009, ch.1). Once we understand this antilegal positivist thrust, that the source of normativity is something that we encounter but do not ourselves construct, human rights proponents could reasonably hope not only that the project of universal human rights might prove justifiable to diverse communities but also that the morality behind human rights would be justifiable and sound.[8]

This commitment to realism is precisely what distinguishes my appropriated version of political liberalism from the ones we have been considering in the Rawlsian tradition. More would be at stake than simply internal "coherence" among our considered judgments and beliefs as per the Rawlsian ideal of an argument proceeding toward "reflective equilibrium." Instead, at issue would be an attempt to ascertain real features or properties of the world, for example, truth. To see why truth as opposed to mere coherence would be necessary to break the specter of relativism, recall that beliefs about the institution of slavery in centuries past may very well have been in "reflective equilibrium" with other considered judgments (e.g., belief in the "naturalness" of slavery for some human beings, the legitimacy of enslaving captives of war, white superiority and the inferiority of other races). A commitment to truth and not simply to coherence would accordingly allow us to affirm that our modern understanding of the injustice of slavery and our legal prohibition of it everywhere represents not simply a change in perspective but also improvement.

To generalize from this example, I submit that the strongest defense of human rights is one that would conceptualize the gradual progression of the circle of individual rights-bearers as not simply modifications in law or a kind of Nietzschean ressentiment of the weak over strong but as indicative of actual social and moral progress. To ground those ideas of improvement, however, we would need to believe that prior practices (e.g., of denying rights to women, of enslaving some for the benefit others) were worse, that those who believed in the natural moral inferiority of certain classes of people were wrong, and that current abolitionist practices are better and closer to the truth. As noted earlier, however, these are all claims that theorists who stand in the tradition of Rawlsian political liberalism could not make objectively, given their methodological avoidance of the metaphysical enterprise altogether and positioning of all such claims about justice as tied relativistically only to the self-conception of Western liberal democracies.

Implications and Possible Objections

There are various implications and possible objections to the manner in which I have provided a justification for human rights, three of which deserve some attention here. According to the first possible objection, to assert as I have here that secular, metaphysically grounded justifications for human rights are not in principle inferior to religious ones is to claim that the former can successfully respond to the "argument from marginal cases" in ways that the maximalists have contended that they could not. In turn, if we were to combine the "inherence" view of human rights that is arguably present in the International Bill of Rights with a commitment to metaphysical realism, our secular account would be obliged to say something about the human properties or capacities upon which to premise the notion of human moral standing undergirding our conception of human rights.

Recall that Nicholas Wolterstorff was skeptical about the ability for any capacities approach to ground equal human rights in light of the notable variability among human capabilities as well as the superior capacities of some nonhuman animals over some human beings (e.g., infants, the mentally impaired) in important areas such as cognition. Although Wolterstorff was principally concerned about the exclusion of some classes of human beings from full and equal moral consideration for those reasons, it is curious that he does not refer to fetuses in his list of potentially vulnerable human beings who can be wronged, thereby leaving into doubt whether he regards fetuses, too, as bearers of inherent human rights.[9] While the morality of abortion is a complex question that cannot be resolved here, I would submit that the moral status of fetuses in relation to that of infants should depend, at least in part, upon the capabilities of either. This position would leave open the real possibility that late-term abortions would pose (more) morally difficult questions in ways that early abortions would not, in view of the significant differences in physical and cognitive development, brain activity, sentience, and the like of fetuses at different gestational ages.

My view, then, is a version of Nussbaum's insight that there is or should be a direct and morally significant relationship between a creature's possession of certain capabilities and the social entitlements due to it. Such a view would allow society to treat anencephalic infants differently than nonanencephalic ones, even by withholding care in the case of the former because of a crucial lack of certain capabilities, just as it might justify the same to patients in a persistent vegetative state (PVS) as opposed to non-PVS patients who are nonetheless terminally ill. To reiterate, for the purposes of public policy, we need not assume everyone's possession of equal capabilities to justify the provision of equal human rights, for a notion of a minimum or threshold amount could suffice. Finally, so long as we did not restrict the worth- or dignity-making feature of a creature to its possession or use of solely cognitive faculties, we need not worry about the prospect of low levels of rationality or intelligence pushing some human beings below the circle of moral concern.

The idea that a creature's particular capabilities can affect her schedule of rights without altering her moral status is entirely workable and defensible. If a human being is incapable of receiving a formal education because she is in a coma, the correct conclusion would not be the loss of moral standing but only that we should not require the state to continue pursuing futile attempts to provide her one. Of course, because that same individual would still have the capability of having her bodily integrity violated, her moral standing would require society to protect her from such harm. We could, of course, say something similar about nonhuman animals: the capacity for sentience and for other important capabilities such as movement and affiliation with conspecifics might be sufficient to ground their entitlements against many cruel and intensive forms of "factory farming" that are routinely deployed by large-scale agribusinesses today, just as the incapability of otherwise intelligent animals such as dolphins or primates to practice religion would obviously mean that society would not face any compulsion to secure any such belief-related rights to them.

As we have seen, then, our grounding of human rights on a conception of human capabilities will have ramifications for our treatment of nonhuman animals. To be clear, the account of justification for human rights that I have offered says nothing in principle against the idea of extending rights to nonhuman animals as well, but it also says nothing about how conflicts between human and animal entitlements should be resolved. My account even leaves open the interesting possibility presented by Christian ethicist Timothy P. Jackson. After disassociating the *imago Dei* from reason and volition and reconnecting it to a "particular human need and potential: to give and/or receive agapic love" as the capacity that endows all human beings with moral worth, Jackson references recent research on apes that suggests that they, too, display behaviors that resemble (human) altruism and empathy. He concludes: "If chimpanzees, say, genuinely love their neighbors, then they too are made in God's image. Better to expand the moral community to include some animals than to contract it to exclude some humans" (2003, 45, 72n53).

A second and entirely different objection to my manner of justifying human rights is that I may have overestimated what the language of "recognition" implies in the International Bill of Human Rights when I offered that it is suggestive of, or at least compatible with, realism. A Kantian constructivist might argue instead that the antilegal positivistic thrust of the idea of "recognition" need only evoke what is required to sustain practical reasoning. The argument would be that the sense of normative "oughtness" that precedes our legalization of human rights need not come from any grasp of some fundamental truth about the world but simply from a necessary truth about the ways in which we must experience it. Kantian constructivist Christine Korsgaard, among others, has argued that we can ground a sense of our necessarily valuing humanity as such without any metaphysical entanglements if we properly understand the psychology behind rational agency. Her point is not that we must understand ourselves as really metaphysically valuable but that we must come to construct the value of humanity and any normative claims that follow as a result from the fact that, as rational agents, we must act upon some reason or other if we are to function at all. This in turn implies that we must have a way of assessing what are good and bad reasons for acting, which in turn implies that we must regard some ends as valuable or worth pursuing. The loop is closed, then, through arguing that in order for us to regard some ends as worthy of being pursued, we must regard both ourselves and others as value-conferring beings, which is to say that we must regard ourselves as valuable (Korsgaard 1996, Korsgaard with Cohen et al. 1996; cf. Fitzpatrick 2005). As is typical of Kantian constructivist approaches, then, the rational and the moral would ultimately coincide. The worth or value of human beings would be intimately and necessarily connected with our ability to act as agents, and discussions of what is required for us to act as agents need not entail anything about what is metaphysically true or real in the world.

Whether Korsgaard and other Kantian constructivists are correct that we can still capture the idea of necessarily valuing humanity as such without appealing to metaphysics is something that lies beyond the scope of what can be resolved here. Still, it is worth observing that this way of grounding the moral worth of all rational agents would still fall short of grounding the equal moral worth of all human beings because rationality comes in degree and because some humans can be thought of as prerational or even postrational. What is more, as William Fitzpatrick has argued (convincingly in my view), this constructivist manner of grounding our moral standing would fail to capture something important about moral phenomenology. Put simply, the best reason not to violate someone or strip her of her human rights should have nothing to do with a complex series of arguments about what it would take for me to be a rational agent and accordingly act upon reasons by pain of logical contradiction. Instead, it should point to something completely external to myself—to the value that I would encounter in others (Fitzpatrick 2005). As Wolterstorff eloquently noted earlier, our actual experience of morality is that we encounter others as coming into our presence bearing legitimate claims upon us about how we are to treat them, just as we experience ourselves as coming into the presence of others bearing claims about how they should treat us (2008b, 671; 2005). To ultimately suggest, then, that all of this should instead be explained by logic and by the structure of practical reasoning itself would be to fail to give a satisfying account of our lived experience.

A final potential objection to my manner of justifying human rights is that it technically remains incomplete, in a manner parallel to my previous comments about the maximalist approach to human rights justification. As stated earlier, to claim that the universal validity of human rights is best or most properly grounded in an ethically realist framework is not itself to provide an affirmative justification for them but only a transcendental claim about the conditions for its possibility. Moreover, to state that the International Bill of Human Rights contains language that is suggestive of a realist or "inherence" view is to say nothing about whether the documents themselves are justified—only to point out what they imply and thus what defenders of those documents must establish.

It is precisely here, however, where our account of justification echoes again the maximalist strategy in needing to acknowledge its inability to provide a full or conclusive proof. Realism about value in general or the "metaphysics of human rights," to use Griffin's term, in particular is not something that one could provide arguments for that would be convincing to all. Instead, I would follow Thomas Nagel's earlier insight that we cannot really prove the possibility of realism, but we can work to refute the "impossibility arguments," thereby increasing our confidence in the realist framework the more often we rebut those incessant charges against it (1986, 143). As many philosophers have noted, it could well turn out that the bigger stumbling block about realism is not its ontological claim—that there are things or values that exist in the world independently of what we believe about them—but its epistemological ones. The concern, then, would be how we as humans would even come to know what those real or true things or values were. As J. L. Mackie famously argued in his "argument from queerness," the way in which we could come to account for our "knowledge of value entities or features and of their links with features on which they would be consequential" would seem to require that we possessed some unique ("queer") faculty or intuition or moral perception, which would purportedly be distinct from the ways in which we would come to know everything else (1977, 49).

An evaluation of these objections to realism is beyond the scope of this book, as is a full analysis of the viability of intuitionism to ground the idea of human rights, although it is worth acknowledging that intuitionism has contemporary contenders of its own. What I can and should say here, however, is the following. First, a commitment to realism and to the objectivity of value need not imply that we are attempting to do the impossible—receive unmediated access to reality so as to "see it as it really is" without use of our cognitive faculties or the interests and biases that we would inevitably bring to any such search. Second, it is not clear why we could not come to know about the existence of real values in the world the same way we come to know everything else—by reflection and experience. In fact, the notion of "recognition" in the International Bill of Human Rights that we considered previously would be helpful here, for it suggests a sensitivity or perception to something in the world, just as it connotes something experiential or empirical. Following Catholic theological ethicist Lisa Cahill, for example, if we were to understand human rights as both social practices and reflections on social practices, the fact that we would come to know about human rights contingently (i.e., through the circumstances of history) would not by itself erode their universal validity because we can only learn of anything that is universally valid (e.g., mathematics, the laws of physics) through the contingent practices of inquiry and reflection upon lived experience. Thus, it need not be that the idea of human rights emerged from some orienting "idea" that was brought about by either abstract intellectual argument or a set of propositions about the nature of the world that were disassociated from the practical context of social life and human interactions. Instead, it could be that our consciousness about what rights we have as human beings gradually emerged from communities, both religious or secular, that have committed themselves to the ideals of "respect, cooperation, and openness or inclusiveness to outsiders" and that have reacted to "negative 'contrast experiences' . . . of the gross violation of human dignity and well-being" (1999–2000, 44). Such a view that our reflections on experience could be genuine sources of moral knowledge would be reminiscent of David Hollenbach's interpretation of the experienced-based rationale for human rights as contained in the preamble to the UDHR and discussed previously in chapter 3: the "barbarous acts" and various atrocities committed during World War II so "outraged the conscience of mankind" that the international community moved to protect human rights everywhere (2003, 242). Indeed, as is well documented in the literature on modernity and the Enlightenment, many of our most cherished modern rights and freedoms, including the liberty of conscience, can be understood as arising from religious, moral, and political responses to crises in questions of religious and political authority (Freeman 2004, 387–89; and Stout 1988, 1994).

Postscript: What about the Absoluteness of Some Human Rights Claims?

The question remains whether we are really prepared to defend the idea that a religiously grounded metaphysics of human rights bears no principled advantage over secular alternatives. To answer this question, let us return to the concern about safeguarding the nonderogability of some human rights and couple it with Küng's earlier contention that only appeals to the "Unconditioned" or "Absolute" could justify the "absoluteness" or "unconditionality" of any ethical obligation (1991, 51). Although Küng sometimes implied that religion's ability to issue unconditional commands should always be counted as an asset over philosophy's purported inability to do the same, we should acknowledge that this "categoricity" could just as well work against, rather than with, the protection of nonderogable rights. On one of many possible readings of the pseudonymous Kierkegaard classic *Fear and Trembling,* for example, the God of Abraham might have been calling for a kind of "teleological suspension of the ethical" with respect to Abraham's binding of his son Isaac, wherein the normal injunction against human sacrifice and murder was to be waived to permit Abraham to "prove" his faith. Indeed, Küng has elsewhere conceded that religious traditions have often violated the ethical criterion of *humanum* for the sake of purportedly loftier goals, whether through the use of fire and torture by the Inquisition that lasted within Catholicism until well into the modern age, through monotheism's various wagings of the "holy war" to defend or propagate the faith, or through the (now illegal and all but defunct) practices of *sati* in parts of Hindu India (1987; 1991, 83–91). Any claim for the privileged space that religion has for commanding absolutely must thereby be considered alongside the historical record of these categorical "oughts" being used to inflict much violence and harm.

How then might nonderogable human rights be justified and sufficiently protected? Certainly not by turning to consequentialist considerations; we have already discussed in our evaluation of enforcement-centered approaches how utilitarian forms of consequentialism render everyone in principle susceptible to being sacrificed for the sake of projected good ends. Other constructivist approaches might also admit of comparable structural liabilities to "trade-offs" (of the rights of some for the sake of actualizing an ideal state of affairs for others) because if it is ultimately we who are bestowing value and thus rights upon individual human beings, it is we who would possess the power to remove that conferral if good outcomes were anticipated to result from doing so. These points notwithstanding, given the distinction we drew earlier between the normativity of a claim and what it might actually take for people to be motivated to follow it, the protection of nonderogable rights might actually depend more upon a community's grasp of contingent facts than upon any firmer or even absolutist commitment to their deontological grounding.

To see why this might be the case, let us recall Charles Taylor's reflections on Michel Foucault's famous discussion of the excruciating torture of Robert-François Damiens to show how the waning of beliefs about the direct relationship between cosmic order and morality might have actually worked in favor of the human right not to be tortured. Damiens was the unsuccessful French regicide who made an attempt on King Louis XV's life (1757) and was consequently burned, drawn, and quartered in order to make the "amende honorable." Taylor submits that it is not so much that we moderns ban torture today because we have an entirely new understanding of, or a heightened moral revulsion to, pain that was not shared by our forbearers. It is rather that our ancestors simply subordinated the negative significance of pain to other, purportedly weightier considerations:

> If it is important that punishment in a sense undo the evil of the crime, restore the balance—what is implicit in the whole notion of the criminal making *amende honorable*—then the very horror of parricide calls for a particularly gruesome punishment. . . . In this context, pain takes on a different significance: there has to be lots of it to do the trick. The principle of minimizing pain is trumped. . . . There are other, independent grounds in modern culture which have made us more reluctant to inflict pain . . . but surely we must recognize the decline of the older notion of cosmic-social order as one consideration which lends a rational grounding to modern humanitarianism. (1995, 49–50)

Thus, even if I am correct that metaphysical realism remains the strongest way to ground the idea of universal human rights as well as the unconditionality of some of those rights, it might still be the case that modern society's gradual loss and fading away of belief in a metaphysical or cosmic moral order was advantageous to the formation of many contemporary human rights standards.

If we were to generalize from this case, we might be led to see that the greater threat to the protection of nonderogable human rights today might not be the communal rejection or displacement of religious cosmologies, traditional metaphysics, or even secular deontological approaches in favor of pragmatic or consequentialist ones. Instead, the greater threat might be the various "special pleadings" to override the need to comply with human rights standards in times of crisis. If I am right about this, then it will take more than a firmer, principled commitment to the inherent moral worth and inviolability of all human beings to protect the nonderogability of certain human rights. Consider that while Küng remains committed to the absoluteness and unconditionality of universally valid ethical imperatives (which, for the purposes of our argument we will equate with nonderogable human rights), the other maximalists who nevertheless insist upon the importance of metaphysics for human rights do not. I have already noted in chapter 2 how Perry, in a discussion of the "ticking time bomb" scenario, argues against the idea of unconditional moral rights but seeks to preserve the absoluteness of some human rights as legal rights in international human rights law (2000b, 87–106). When asked about his position regarding the absoluteness of rights with respect to the rights not to be raped, tortured, or murdered, Stackhouse surprisingly speaks of "gradations in absoluteness" and acknowledged that sometimes "circumstances are so rotten and terrible" that one might be compelled to "moderate the behavior under rare circumstances to preserve the absolute principle itself" (2003, 10–11). Finally, as alluded to earlier, Wolterstorff adopts a different tactic altogether by interrogating the very notion of nonderogability and thus of any real as opposed to prima facie conflict against competing moral goods or demands, such as when he considers whether the right not to be tortured for any reason whatsoever really is a genuine human right (2008a, 316). In short, belief in the metaphysics of rights, or even in what maximalists have alleged to be their "ineliminably religious" roots, obviously would still not be sufficient to ground the absoluteness of some of those human rights provisions in question.

What kind of commitments might then protect the nonderogability of certain human rights? In addition to starting from a strong conviction about the real moral worth of all human beings, the next step might be to undermine or deflate projections about the likelihood that "good outcomes" would actually result from violating human rights standards, thus reducing the temptation to derogate to begin with. For instance, even if it would not matter from a deontological perspective whether interrogational torture practically "works" (i.e., if enough fear, pain, suffering, and humiliation could be inflicted on suspects to cause them to disclose actionable intelligence against their will), the fact that torture as a method of extracting useful information has consistently been shown to yield terribly unreliable information could matter a great deal practically in any community's weighing of whether to uphold or override the absolute ban on torture. Another way to reduce the temptation to torture in "emergency" situations would be to apply a "hermeneutics of suspicion" to the ticking time bomb scenario itself, thus scrutinizing both its plausibility and use in setting public policy. The thought experiment is designed for us to presume that the suspect in custody actually is the one who planted the bomb or knows who did or at least knows where it is; that the bomb was planted successfully and that it will indeed explode imminently unless it is found by counterterrorism officials and deactivated; and that the suspect would eventually reveal truthful and actionable intelligence in time for the authorities to intervene so long as the interrogator inflicts enough pain and terror to "break" him (Twiss 2007, 365–67). We might conclude, then, that protecting nonderogable human rights such as the absolute prescription against torture could easily involve much more than pure theory; it could also include educating counterterrorism officials, other public authorities, and members of the general public about the findings of empirical case studies and sociopsychological literature regarding what torture in fact can and cannot accomplish. By extension, a similar tactic of marshalling both principled and practical arguments might need to be deployed to safeguard other nonderogable human rights, such as the right to life. For example, one might seek either to demonstrate how use of the "supreme emergency" exception against the principle of discrimination in war has not been historically effective in achieving its own intended aims, or to scrutinize the plausibility of the "supreme emergency" exemption itself.

CONCLUSION

We can supply good reasons in support of our justification for the universal validity of human rights in a pluralist world, but we must ultimately concede that our account, like every other one we have discussed, will ultimately remain incomplete. We may not need to appeal to religion to ground the idea of human rights. We might not even need to appeal to metaphysics to persuade many parties to comply with human rights norms (which, admittedly, is one of the purposes of providing a theoretical rationale for human rights in the first place), even if metaphysically grounded accounts of human value remain the most adequate way to give appropriate expression to what the very idea of human rights entails. We might also find that the protection of nonderogable human rights will actually turn more on the inadequacies of the reasons given to violate what ought to be inviolable, as opposed to any grounding of human rights on a deeper deontological, metaphysical, or even religious foundation. While all this may be true, a fundamental role of faith, whether of a secular or religious nature, of belief and commitment in advance of evidence, must remain as an indispensable element in any attempt to ground human rights under conditions of pluralism today.[10]

The human rights project is undeniably teleological—it presupposes faith in moral progress, the ability to transform existing social realities, and the conviction that a more just and peaceful world is possible by our own efforts. Human rights, in the words of Jack Donnelly, express both a utopian ideal and a realistic practice for implementing that ideal, saying both "treat a person like a human being and you'll get a human being," and "here's *how* you treat someone as a human being" (1989, 19). This common faith will bend toward a cosmopolitan ideal in presuming that humanity in the end forms one moral community. In light of the obvious differences (in sex, race, religion, class, socioeconomic status, physical constitution, nationality, capabilities, life achievements, etc.) that divide and distinguish us from one another, it will take faith to believe that I am essentially like others in morally relevant ways, and they are like me. We have learned as a world community that it is no longer morally defensible to restrict our ethical consideration of others on account of either their involuntary characteristics (e.g., race, sex, or gender) or even certain features for which they may be partially responsible (e.g., their beliefs or religion). While in feudal societies the idea of different laws for different classes of people may have been considered just or appropriate (or at least minimally tolerated by those socialized under the discriminatory policies in question), contemporary human rights are overtly egalitarian in their aim to secure equal rights for everyone, regardless of social station or level of achievement. Still, in an analogous sense with the philosophical problem of other minds, we must ultimately conjecture, but cannot rationally defend, that others are ultimately like oneself, at least with respect to the important vulnerabilities and interests that give rise to the need for an egalitarian understanding of human rights. By linking human rights to faith in social progress and to a conception of our common humanity and equal moral worth, and then holding by faith that these claims are not simply projections of wish-fulfillment but are real or true, we are able to say that the progressive and hard-won expansion of the scope of ethical concern from the select few to the universal represents not simply changes throughout time but genuine improvement.

Notes

Introduction

1. While the UDHR is only hortatory in character, it has inspired more than sixty human rights instruments and legally binding treaties, has been enshrined in the national legislation and constitutions of many newly independent states, has arguably obtained the status of customary international law, and remains one of the most cited human rights documents in the world today.

2. Other components to the growing international human rights regime include the International Criminal Tribunals for Rwanda and the former Yugoslavia, regional human rights courts (in Africa, the Americas, and Europe), various nongovernmental organizations, and the world's first independent and permanent International Criminal Court (ICC). Although the ICC is a "court of last resort" that tries persons accused of the most serious crimes of international concern, its first president, Judge Philippe Kirsch, has publicly stated that the ICC is not a human rights court proper because Article 5 of the Rome Statute gives it jurisdiction only to prosecute war crimes, crimes against humanity, genocide, and aggression (Kirsch 2006).

3. The AAA initially expressed reservations about the proposed declaration on account of three reasons: (1) the need to tolerate cultural differences given the importance of culture for individual personality, (2) the absence of any "technique of qualitatively evaluating cultures," and (3) the impossibility of applying one moral code to "mankind as a whole" since "standards and values are relative to the culture from which they derive" (AAA 1947, 539–40).

4. Nongovernmental organizations such as Amnesty International (AI) and Human Rights Watch routinely criticize the United States for its use of capital punishment; systematic police brutality; large-scale manufacture of torture devices and anti-personnel mines; treatment of noncitizens, undocumented workers, and detainees suspected of terrorism; and apparent unwillingness to ratify several major international human rights treaties (namely, the ICESCR, the Convention on the Elimination of All

Forms of Discrimination Against Women [CEDAW], and the Convention on the Rights of the Child).

5. Much has been made of U.S. public policy responses to the terrorist attacks of September 11, 2001, especially but not exclusively under the two-term presidency of George W. Bush. While the "war on terrorism" has been waged in defense of freedom, human rights, and homeland security, any success on those fronts must be considered alongside the costly and deadly military campaigns in Afghanistan and Iraq; the detainment of prisoners at Guantánamo Bay, Cuba, and Bagram Air Base, Afghanistan; the denial of habeas corpus and infliction of torture or other "cruel, inhuman, or degrading treatment or punishment" on some high-value captives suspected of terrorism; the practice of "extraordinary rendition" (wherein the CIA delivers terrorism suspects into the hands of foreign intelligence services without extradition proceedings); and various infringements of civil liberties among U.S. citizens themselves.

6. Consider the following example: the United States finally ratified the ICCPR twenty-six years after the UN General Assembly unanimously adopted it and fifteen years after President Jimmy Carter had signed the covenant, but with an "unprecedented number" of reservations, understandings, and declarations: five reservations, five understandings, and one proviso (Ash 2005, 2–3). While article 6(2) instructs that capital punishment may be imposed "only for the most serious crimes" and article 6(5) prohibits the death penalty from being carried out on pregnant women or on anyone who committed those crimes while under eighteen, the United States officially reserved the right to execute any person other than a pregnant woman "duly convicted under existing or future laws permitting the imposition of capital punishment, including such punishment for crimes committed by persons below the age of eighteen years of age."

7. For example, during a January–February 2008 measles outbreak among unvaccinated children and infants too young to be vaccinated in San Diego, California, the Centers for Disease Control reported that more than seventy children had to be quarantined to maintain infection control (CDC 2008). Following an April 2009 swine flu outbreak in Mexico and surrounding areas that eventually led the World Health Organization to declare a global pandemic on June 11, 2009, many nations implemented policies to prevent or contain the 2009 H1N1 flu virus: travel advisories to selected countries; increased surveillance and monitoring of travelers;

temporarily closing of schools, businesses, and other public places; and mandatory quarantine for infected persons. Admittedly, the task of adjudication between conflicting claims may prove more difficult in other cases, for example, when a rape victim's right to physical integrity and privacy clashes with the defendant's right to a fair trial (O'Connell 2005).

Chapter 1: Prolegomena to Any Philosophical Defense of Human Rights

1. Although "culture" is most commonly the framework to which all moral values, ideals, and judgments are said to be relative, parallel arguments continue to be made with respect to traditions, civilizations, nations, religions, and conceptual schemes.

2. If theorists were to identify not radical but incommensurable differences across cultures, these protests of incommensurability could then be interrogated for their intelligibility. Philosopher Donald Davidson has persuasively argued that "different points of view make sense, but only if there is a common co-ordinate system on which to plot them; yet the existence of a common system belies the claim of dramatic incomparability" (1974, 184).

3. The much-touted "Asian values vs. (Western) human rights" debates of the 1990s centered on the claim that Asians had different and arguably better values than Westerners, which is why (Asian) collectivist concerns should take precedence over (Western-style) individual civil and political liberties. However, when the East Asian economy fell into a deep crisis in 1997–98, so did the bulk of these claims of superiority. See Sen 1997a, 1998, 1999a, 2003b, and Langlois 2001 for their interrogation of the notion that Asians on the whole are less supportive of individual freedom, more concerned with order and discipline, and consequently less interested in securing political and civil freedoms for themselves. See also Bell 2000 for a contrasting view that the "Asian values" debates were not principally about a cultural clash over human rights, but were about being in an unenviable position where some rights had to be restricted in order to secure more basic rights.

4. See especially Okin 1989 and Elshtain 1992 for Anglo-American feminist criticisms of liberal individualism. The label "communitarian" is usually one that is issued from the outside. Michael Sandel (1982) prefers the term "republican" and contends that what is at stake in the liberal-communitarian debate is not whether individual rights should be

sacrificed for the sake of the common good but whether principles of justice can truly be independent of any conception of the good. Alasdair MacIntyre (1991) denies that he has ever been a communitarian, and both Charles Taylor (1994) and Michael Walzer (1992) self-identify as liberals.

5. Thus, with respect to our earlier examples, we would be wise to acknowledge the presence of notable moral opposition to euthanasia even in jurisdictions where it is legally permitted. There is also sizable animal welfare and animal rights activism in societies where the human consumption of animals for food, clothing, entertainment, and experimentation remains largely uncontested by the public.

6. Many of these missionary enterprises manifested both evangelical and "civilizing" goals. In some contexts and for some missionaries, the acceptance of the civilizing function was unqualified. But for others, the missionaries' own partial (internal) resistance to secular authorities meant that the commitment to civilize was more problematic than was their dedication to preach the Gospel (Hutchison 1993). For an arguably more culturally sensitive approach to evangelism, consider the "policy of accommodation" of Jesuit missionaries such as St. Francis Xavier (1506–52) and Matteo Ricci (1552–1610) in the early modern period in India, Japan, and China.

7. More accurately, a relativist could still scrutinize the practices of a foreign culture by using the standards of her own (or even some third) culture, although the criticism would appear to have little or no normative force unless the foreign culture were "entitled to the thought that those standards are in some non-question-begging sense sound or correct" (Tasioulas 1998, 192–93). To be sure, the moral appraisal of a more powerful culture upon a less powerful one could still be politically effective even if interpreted relativistically, as when culture A fears the loss of foreign aid or other privileges from culture B and accordingly reforms its social practices to meet culture B's standards of conduct (Renteln 1988, 63–64).

8. Nothing, of course, precludes a theorist from affirming the modern Western origins of human rights without constraining their applicability to Western contexts alone. Neopragmatist philosopher Richard Rorty, for one, encourages the dissemination of human rights everywhere, even though he provocatively maintains that the sentimental idea upon which they depend—"membership in a biological species is supposed to suffice for membership in a moral community"—is neither transcultural nor

generally found "outside the circle of post-enlightenment European culture" (Rorty 1993, 115–17, 125). Human rights scholar Jack Donnelly affirms the universal validity of human rights even though he interprets them to have initially arisen in the West in response to "social and political changes produced by modern states and modern capitalist market economies" (1989, 50; 1999). British philosopher James Griffin has retrieved what he considers to be the Enlightenment notion of human dignity to defend the universal validity of human rights today (2001, 2008). The literature on others who argue similarly is extensive.

9. In the Sophoclean tragedy *Antigone,* the heroine was convinced that there were higher "unwritten and unchangeable laws" that required her to transgress the current legal decree against burying her slain brother. Natural law thinking can also be found in Cicero's work, particularly in Book I of *Laws* and Book III of the *Republic.* Aristotle is generally credited as the first philosopher to have developed a complex teleology that evaluates the appropriateness of human social conduct according to its "fittingness" with our nature as human beings.

10. The ICCPR and ICESCR also contain similar language that is reminiscent of earlier natural rights declarations (e.g., "inherent dignity," "equal and inalienable rights of all members of the human family").

11. These include the American Declaration of the Rights and Duties of Man, adopted by the Organization of American States at its founding meeting in 1948, and the 1944 "Statement of Essential Human Rights," which was produced by the American Law Institute (Glendon 2001, 57).

12. While the UN Charter affirms "faith in fundamental human rights" and Article 1 states that one of the UN's purposes is to "promot[e] and encourag[e] respect for human rights and for fundamental freedoms for all," the charter nowhere specifies which human rights are to be collectively advanced by its members. Nevertheless, delegates from Brazil, Canada, Chile, Cuba, the Dominican Republic, Egypt, France, Haiti, India, Mexico, New Zealand, Panama, and Uruguay supplied continued pressure for this type of specification (Glendon 2001; Waltz 2001). See also Nurser (2005) for an important discussion of the vital role that ecumenical and missions-minded Protestants and their organizations played in the formation of the Human Rights Commission and, thereafter, the UDHR.

13. Eleanor Roosevelt is remembered as having said, "I have always considered myself a feminist but I really would have no objection to the use

of the word [man] as the Committee sees it" (quoted in Glendon 2001, 68). Nevertheless, Hansa Mehta lobbied for the term "human" for fear that the phrase "all men" would be construed literally in some countries. Soviet-bloc delegates supported her efforts, as did representatives of the UN Commission on the Status of Women who were present as observers.

14. The Chinese character for *ren* is a composite of the characters for "man" and "two." The term is commonly translated as "humanity" or "humaneness," meaning sympathy or conscientiousness toward one's fellow human beings. Peng-chun Chang was widely regarded as one of the two most philosophically astute among the delegates. He was a noted Confucian humanist, philosopher, diplomat, and playwright who had held ambassadorial posts in Turkey and Chile, had emanated a zeal for promoting Chinese culture, and had been fond of drawing connections between Islam and Confucianism. According to both Glendon (2001) and Humphrey (1984), Lebanon's Charles Malik was a philosopher professor-turned-diplomat, former student of both Alfred North Whitehead and Martin Heidegger, and an outspoken advocate for the Arab League.

15. But see Wolterstorff (2008a, 52) for a rebuttal. To be sure, the origin or source of an idea could be relevant in other contexts when assessing its credibility. For instance, it would be reasonable to give more credence to the claims of experts than to those of others so long as experts restricted their comments to their fields of specialization. In a court of law, it would also be appropriate for judges and jurors to weigh the testimony of witnesses differently according to their source (e.g., eyewitness testimony, hearsay, conjecture) and not just their content.

16. In the "Asian values" debates, Amartya Sen (1997a) has cogently argued that the temptation to believe in the existence of "quintessential values" that distinguish Asians as a group from the rest of the world and that fit its heterogeneous population must be understood as itself part of an Eurocentric outlook. While Edward Said was principally concerned with orientalist depictions of Arab peoples and cultures, "the Orient" itself was understood to encompass most of Asia and the Middle East.

17. If human rights supporters were to argue accordingly, they would be using the same flawed logic to which adherents of cultural relativism had succumbed in moving simply from the fact that a group happens to approve of something to a claim about its truth-value. Of course, in a classical pragmatist conception of truth, experiential regularity and the

consensus that is formed by the relevant community of inquirers play a crucial role in what gets counted as truth (see James 1907). We will entertain the question whether an "overlapping consensus" on human rights can have justificatory force in chapters 4, 5, and 6.

Chapter Two: The Maximalist Challenge to Human Rights Justification

1. See UN Doc. A/CONF.157/PC/62/Add.18 (9 June 1993); and Mayer 1999, 22–23. While the Bangkok Declaration on Human Rights (1993), which was adopted by various representatives of Asian States and others and presented at the 1993 World Conference on Human Rights, might initially appear to be maximalist because it "contains the aspirations and commitments of the Asian region," it does not analogously describe the scope or source of human rights in terms of "Asian values." Instead, the Bangkok Declaration discourages any attempt to use human rights as a condition for development assistance, stresses the need to avoid applying a double standard, and affirms the "universality, objectivity and non-selectivity" of all human rights at the same time that it recognizes that they must be considered in the context of "national and regional particularities and various historical, cultural and religious backgrounds" (Art. 4, 7, 8, 10; UN Doc. A/CONF.157/ASRM/8 A/CONF.157/PC/59 [7 April 1993]).

2. The CDHRI also constrains the parameters of other rights and freedoms in implicitly Shariah-inspired ways. That no one can be restricted from marrying for reasons of "race, colour, or nationality" but not for reason of religion most likely stems from the traditional prohibition against Muslim women from marrying non-Muslim men while Muslim men are allowed to marry Jewish and Christian in addition to Muslim women (Art. 5a). These Qur'anic texts are often cited as evidence for this teaching: Qur'an 2:221, 5:5. Moreover, that women are to be regarded as equal to men in dignity though not necessarily in all rights and that husbands are to be held responsible for the support and welfare of the family also reflect common interpretations of Islamic law (Art. 6a-b).

3. See Küng and Kuschel 1993 for an account of the declaration, and see www.global-ethic-now.de/gen-eng/Oa_was-ist-weltethos/Oa-pdf/decl_english.pdf for its text in English. The declaration is followed by a list of signatories representing the Baha'i, Buddhist, Hindu, Sikh, Jain, Jewish, Christian, Muslim, pagan, Taoist, Zorastrian, and various indigenous religious traditions.

4. Perry's Christian example is the following: since God is love and every human being is a created and beloved child of God, all human beings ought to treat one another like fellow brothers and sisters. While others have argued differently, Perry does not interpret the Christian call to love the Other as grounded only in a divine command but as more deeply tied to a conception of authentic human flourishing. Put simply, loving the Other is the best way to fulfill and perfect our nature as human beings and is thus the best way for us to live (Perry 2006, 8–12; 2000b, 18–21).

5. Although one initially might have concluded otherwise in light of this statement, "the serious question is whether the morality of human rights can survive the death—or deconstruction—of God," Perry interprets Nietzsche's challenge not simply in terms of atheism but in terms of a loss of realism or "metaphysical order of any kind" (Perry 2006, 29, 173n86).

6. Although Swiss-born Hans Küng served from 1962 to 65 as an official theological consultant (*peritus*) to the Second Vatican Council, the Vatican officially stripped him of his canonical license to teach Catholic theology in 1979 because of his highly critical scrutiny of key Catholic tenets of faith (e.g., the doctrine of papal infallibility) in several publications. Küng nevertheless remained at the University of Tübingen from 1960 until his retirement in 1996 as professor of ecumenical theology and director of the Institute for Ecumenical Research, although he was not positioned under Catholic authorities from the time of his censorship onward. He is currently the president of the Global Ethic Foundation (*Stiftung Weltethos*).

7. Michael Perry was also concerned about the "effective sources" of moral strength and conviction for "virtuous pagans," or those who operate morally outside of a realist or metaphysical framework (2000b, 36–37; 2006, 15). Nevertheless, Perry spent more time exposing logical or conceptual difficulties with various secular attempts to ground the idea of human rights than he did lamenting their allegedly unstable character.

8. Lest we mistake this focus on obligations as implying that universal duties are more basic than universal rights, Küng has clarified that neither concept is logically prior than the other. He writes: "No one has claimed and will claim that certain human responsibilities must be fulfilled first, by individuals or a community, before one can claim human rights. These are given with the human person, but this person is *always at the same time one who has rights and responsibilities:* All human rights are by definition

directly bound up with the responsibility to observe them. Rights and responsibilities can certainly be distinguished neatly, but they cannot be separated from each other. Their relationship needs to be described in a differentiated way. They are not quantities which are to be added or subtracted externally, but *two related dimensions* of being human in the individual and the social sphere" (2005, sec. 3, emphasis in original).

9. Küng also correctly observes that the survival of humankind as an ethical ideal is completely compatible with violating the rights of individual human beings; thus, it is difficult to see how a concern for the species could adequately ground genuine concern for each and every human being.

10. "I cannot and will not try to prove that religion in fact is focused on a reality, indeed a most real, primordial Ultimate Reality. However, can atheistic opponents of religion provide proof that religion in the end focuses on nothing? Just as God is indemonstrable, so also this 'nothing' is indemonstrable. Our purely theoretical reason is bound to this world and simply does not reach far enough to answer this question; in that Kant was correct for all time. Positively put, we are concerned here with the famous '*Gretchen* question' of religion, which deals with nothing more and nothing less than the great question of *trust* in our lives. Despite all the apparent contradictions in this world, we nevertheless utter a yes in a tested, illusion-free, realistic trust in an ultimate ground, ultimate content, and ultimate meaning of the world and human life. Such is presumed in all the great religions. And this is a completely reasonable yes insofar as it has good reasons at its base, even though they may not, strictly speaking, be proofs" (Küng 1987, 233).

11. While Max Stackhouse's work on human rights predates Michael Perry's, Stackhouse has subsequently referenced Perry's understanding of what claims of universal human rights actually mean or imply: some things should be done to everyone while other things should never be done to anyone because each human being is morally inviolable (Stackhouse 2005, 37; 2004, 27). He has also followed Perry when arguing that the conceptual task of human rights justification requires a "universal, context-transcending metaphysical reality." That is, religion must be invoked because religion is the "human acknowledgment that we live under a power and morality that we did not construct and may not ignore," while particular religions are "sets of ultimate convictions and hypotheses about the nature, character, demands, and implications of that reality" (Stackhouse 2005, 27).

12. Stackhouse follows Küng in acknowledging the importance of religious traditions for providing "experience-gained wisdom" and networks of "events, traditions, relationships, commitments and specific blends of connectedness and alienation which shape the 'values' of daily experience and our senses of obligation" (Stackhouse 2005, 35).

13. In contrast, recall that Michael Perry provides a Christian interpretation of the normative grounds for human rights for ostensibly demonstrative purposes only and subsequently refrains from assessing the validity of that, or of any other, religious claim. In addition, while Hans Küng commonly refers to the Absolute or Ultimate Reality that grounds any universal ethic as "God," Küng emphasizes in the Declaration Towards a Global Ethic (as its principal architect) how the ancient wisdom of a plurality of religious traditions provides plural foundations for human rights (Küng 1987).

14. While Stackhouse acknowledges the Jewish and Hebraic origins of the idea of a universal moral law to which all are held accountable, he credits the early Christian church with radicalizing that idea in their insistence that this moral law is in some sense natural, so no one could claim ignorance of the demands of justice (1984, 38–40).

15. Although the particulars of Stackhouse's narrative of the emergence of the idea of human rights cannot be recounted in full here, highlights include the early church's radicalization of the prophetic elements of Judaism and their selective embrace of some aspects of Stoic thought, the formation of canon law, the establishment of various rights in ecclesiastical councils, the subsequent movements in conciliar Catholicism, modernity's liberal-Puritan synthesis, and the work of ecumenical Christianity in the twentieth century (1984).

16. By natural rights Wolterstorff does not mean to signify the rights that individuals would have even if they were not living in society (as in the fictional case of an asocial and purely natural human beings) but the rights that everyone would have even if not socially conferred or recognized by law (2008a, 33, 313).

17. Although others might use the term "natural law" to describe this phenomenon of universal accountability, Wolterstorff does not. In his own words: "the Hebrew prophets and the song writers . . . never suggest that we should think of this 'holding accountable' as taking the form of legislation, on analogy to Torah. Their picture is not that God somewhere, sometime, somehow issued legislation to all humanity, thereby holding

them accountable for acting justly, and then, on top of that, issued special legislation to Israel covering the same ground and more" (2008a, 86–87).

18. Wolterstorff does not assess the adequacy of other religiously grounded accounts of human rights, for he declares himself incompetent to ascertain whether the idea of natural human rights was also present in some form in "classical Indian and Chinese culture or in ancient Mesopotamian or Egyptian Culture" (2008a, 65). He does, however, affirm the importance of engaging the resources of both Judaism and Islam for human rights (2008a, 361; 2008b, 678).

19. Beyond their common appeal to God's universal love for humanity, other notable similarities between Wolterstorff and Perry include their reliance upon theological convictions that they do not themselves attempt to substantiate, their characterization of the problem facing human rights justification today in terms of Nietzsche's "death of God" challenge to morality, and their conclusion that it is unlikely that any adequate secular defense will emerge because all secular justifications have purportedly failed (Wolterstorff 2008a, 324–25, 325n3).

20. Wolterstorff's example of a "dignity-based but not capacities" approach is Ronald Dworkin's secular interpretation of the idea of human sacrality. While Perry charged Dworkin with a conceptual misuse of the idea of the sacred, Wolterstorff's primary problem with Dworkin's view (that each human being is simultaneously the highest product of natural creation and art-like self-creation) is that only the mature and properly functioning human beings (i.e., persons) stand behind Dworkin's account, thereby leaving it susceptible to the aforementioned criticism (Wolterstorff 2008a, 333–34). Wolterstorff's example of a "capacities but not dignity-based" approach is Alan Gewirth's principle of generic consistency, as described in Gewirth's much discussed *Human Rights: Essays on Justification and Application* (1982). Even if Gewirth's argument were sound, Wolterstorff charges that it would still only ground the rights of those with rational agency—not all human beings (2008a, 335–40). For a different critique of Gewirth's secular justification for human rights, see Kohen 2007, 38–63.

21. The "evidentialist challenge" that Woltertstorff ultimately rejects consists of two claims: (1) one ought not to accept some proposition about God if it is not rational to do so; and (2) it is not rational to accept propositions about God unless one does so on the basis of other beliefs that

provide adequate evidence for them "and with a firmness not exceeding that warranted by the strength of the evidence" (1983, 136).

22. "What are we to make of . . . talk about 'the inherent dignity' of all human beings . . . must we conclude that the idea of human rights is indeed ineliminably religious, that a fundamental constituent of the idea, namely, *the conviction that every human being is sacred—that every human being is 'inviolable,' has 'inherent dignity,' is 'an end in himself,' or the like—* is inescapably religious?" (Perry 2000b, 13, emphasis in original). Perry maintains that international human rights law is informed by a belief that every human being is sacred, and he elsewhere repeats the idea that nonreligious justifications for human rights must say something "functionally equivalent to 'the unashamedly anthropomorphic . . . claim that we are sacred because God loves us, his children'" (2000b, 16; 2006, 15).

23. There are other ways to counter Perry's claim that the idea of human rights is "ineliminably religious." One could reject Perry's understanding that a doctrine of universal human rights must rest upon *any* conception of inherent human dignity, whether religious or secular, and thereafter provide a justification for human rights without having to appeal to that concept. I consider some theorists who pursue this line of thought in the next two chapters.

24. The rights that are explicitly subject to certain restrictions include the freedom of movement for those lawfully within the territory of a State (Art. 12); a legal alien's right to contest his or her expulsion (Art. 13); the freedom of thought, conscience, and religion (Art. 18); the freedom to hold opinions without interference and to express them (Art. 19); the right of peaceful assembly (Art. 21); and the freedom of association (Art. 22). Beyond providing the familiar list of mitigating circumstances discussed earlier, Art. 19 adds that "respect of the rights or reputations of others" when provided by law and when necessary could also justifiably restrict one's human right to the freedom of expression.

25. Art. 4 of the ICCPR provides the following list of nonderogable human rights: the "inherent right to life" (Art. 6); the right to be free from "torture or cruel, inhuman or degrading treatment or punishment" (Art. 7); the right not to be enslaved or held in servitude (Art. 8 [1 and 2]); the right not to be imprisoned merely for failure to fulfill a contractual obligation (Art. 11); the right not to be held guilty for a crime when the act in question did not constitute a criminal offense at the time it was

committed (Art. 15); the right to "recognition everywhere as a person before the law" (Art. 16); and the right to freedom of thought, conscience, and religion (Art. 18). Note that paragraph 3 of Article 18 permits a certain class of limitations on the freedom of conscience, thought, and religion, but Article 4 prohibits any derogations from the same.

26. The "ticking time bomb scenario" imagines that the public authorities have detained a suspected or known but otherwise recalcitrant terrorist whom they believe to have actionable intelligence about a grave, imminent attack that is capable of killing hundreds, thousands, or even millions of civilians. After considering a version of this scenario, the Israeli High Court officially banned the use of torture among interrogators in 1999, thereby ending the use of "moderate physical and psychological pressure" against detainees, which had been legally permitted (and in many quarters, popularly supported) since 1987. Michael Perry considers a version of this "ticking time bomb" scenario and observes that many would find the absolute prohibition against torture "counterintuitive." He argues against the idea that some human rights as moral rights are unconditional but defends the importance of maintaining the absolute character of some human rights as legal rights in international human rights law (Perry 2000b, 87–106; cf. Wolterstorff 2008a, 316). Harvard law professor Alan Dershowitz has reached a nearly opposite conclusion. Although he concurs that the public would largely favor torturing a suspect to prevent an imminent case of mass terrorism, he himself opposes torture "as a *normative* matter," but would legally permit certain nonlethal forms of torture under carefully circumscribed and regulated contexts through the issuance of special "torture warrants" (2002, 2004).

27. Unlike our description of Hans Küng thus far, Stackhouse defends nonabsolutism in his concession to rare exceptions to otherwise unconditional moral prohibitions (e.g., not to kill fetuses or the terminally ill) to "modulate behavior under rare circumstances to preserve the absolute principle itself" (Stackhouse 2003, 11).

28. As we have seen, Wolterstorff's strategy of justification is typical of many in his attempt to isolate one or another morally relevant feature or property that could successfully distinguish all human beings from all other animals. A different and arguably better approach—and one that is discussed in chapter 5—is to identify not one but a plurality of capacities that could ground a creature's worth.

29. While not presented as exhaustive, Wolterstorff's list of natural human rights is notably shorter than the full catalog of provisions in the International Bill of Human Rights. He includes the free exercise of religion, free speech, freedom of assembly, habeas corpus, protections against bodily assault, and the right "not to be tortured for the pleasure of the torture," but he excludes the vast majority of positive rights (2008a, 314–16; 2008b, 678). On his reading, there are "relatively few positive rights that are truly human rights" because such benefits do not attach to the status of human beings as such but only to particular kinds of human being. For example, he does not regard the right to education as a genuine human right because it only applies to those human beings who are capable of being formally educated. Wolterstorff disqualifies the right to receive "periodic holidays with pay" for analogous reasons. Even "the benefit right of fair access to adequate means of sustenance" should not technically be counted as a human right because Wolterstorff could imagine cases where "turning off the life-support system of a terminally ill patient" does not wrong the patient in question (Wolterstorff 2008a, 314–16, 2; see also Art. 26, Art. 24, UDHR).

30. This is not simply a theoretical possibility. Michael Perry has interpreted the nonestablishment principle in the United States not as prohibiting official support for religion but as permitting government to positively affirm "certain few very basic religious beliefs" if it does so noncoercively; for example, "there is a God, who created us and who both loves and judges us; and because God created us and loves us, we are all sacred (inviolable, ends in ourselves, etc.)" (2000a, 310).

Chapter Three: An Enforcement-Centered Approach to Human Rights, with Special Reference to John Rawls

1. Rawls developed the idea of an "original position" as a device of representation among free and equal persons to specify a point of view from which a hypothetical fair agreement about the justice of domestic institutions could be reached. Under the "veil of ignorance," the contracting parties would be prevented from knowing their real native endowments, level of education, income or socioeconomic status, race, sex, and philosophical or religious views, thus preventing them from selecting principles that would merely augment their self-interest. Under such conditions, Rawls presumes that the parties would ultimately affirm two

principles of justice and their two priority rules, which he calls "justice as fairness." The first principle would protect equal basic liberties for everyone; the second, the fair equality of opportunity as well as a distributive principle that would permit social and economic inequalities only insofar as they improved the lot of the "worst off." Because Rawls has modified these principles of justice, his list and understanding of primary goods, and the parameters surrounding the "original position" in all of his major books, see §6, "The Idea of the Original Position," and §13, "Two Principles of Justice" (2001) for his most considered remarks on these topics.

2. Rawls runs two sessions of the international "original position": one for the representatives of well-ordered liberal peoples and the next for the same of all well-ordered decent peoples. While the representatives would know the type of people (i.e., liberal or decent) from which they came, they would be precluded from knowing their territorial size, natural resources, level of economic development, total population, and relative strength. In contrast to the domestic situation, the representatives would not be presented with rival principles of justice from which to choose but would "simply reflect on the advantages of these [eight] principles of equality among peoples and see no reason to depart from them or to propose alternatives" (1999b, 41). Philosopher John Tasioulas has charged Rawls's unwillingness to give rival accounts of international justice a hearing with an "overwhelming sense of argumentative deficit" (Tasioulas 2002, 377–78).

3. Alternatively, perhaps Rawls has become so sensitive to criticisms of liberalism in general and to human rights in particular that he has deliberately immunized his theory against falsification. Philosopher Thomas Pogge (1994) has observed that while liberal and decent peoples are supposed to be deliberating in isolation from each other in their respective original positions, liberal peoples are repeatedly enjoined to select principles of foreign policy to which other reasonable peoples would be amenable (Rawls 1999b, 14, 121–22). I will consider these and other criticisms later in the chapter.

4. Principles 1–5 arguably recapitulate the "law of nations" discussed (albeit briefly) in *A Theory of Justice*, when Rawls reconfigured the parties in the original position to be representatives of nations selecting "fundamental principles to adjudicate conflicting claims among states" (1999c, §58 at 331–35).

5. By "basic structure," Rawls means the way in which the "main political and social institutions of society fit together into one system of social cooperation, and the way they assign basic rights and duties and regulate the division of advantages that arise from social cooperation over time" (2001, §4 at 10–11; see also 1999c, §2 at 6; 1996, Lecture VII). Rawls clarifies that decent hierarchical societies could be either religious or secular and also "leaves in reserve" the possibility of other decent societies that are not organized in a consultative hierarchical fashion but might still be worthy of membership in the Society of Peoples (1999b, 4, 63–64).

6. In this hierarchical procedure of consultation, each person must belong to a group, each group must be consulted and represented by a higher body that shares their fundamental interests, and the highest body—the rulers of Kazanistan—must weigh the claims of each body in light of Kazanistan's "special priorities" and overall scheme of cooperation (1999b, 71–73, 77). Recall that Rawls elevates "decent societies" above "benevolent absolutisms" because only the former allows for any meaningful kind of civic political decision making (1999b, 4, 63, 92).

7. Following his critically acclaimed *Theory of Justice,* Rawls began clearly distinguishing between political philosophy and political conceptions of justice, on the one hand, and moral philosophy and metaphysical or "comprehensive doctrines," on the other. By a "comprehensive doctrine" Rawls means the moral, philosophical, or religious traditions of thought that encompasses "what is of value in human life, and ideals of personal character, . . . friendship, and of familial and associational relationships, and much else that is to inform our conduct" (1996, 13, 58–60).

8. While the relationship between rights and duties is a complex matter, legal scholar Fernando Tesón is correct to observe that a human right that is defined as "the behavior that the public authority merely *permits* because it is also the content of an obligation is at best a tautology (that which is prescribed is also permitted) and at worst an authoritarian distortion of the meaning of human rights as the legal expression of human freedom" (1995, 87).

9. Philosopher William Talbott has noted that decent societies could even legitimately exclude girls and women from education and all social roles outside of the family, provided that others paternalistically represented their interests in the hierarchical, decision-making process (2005, 12).

10. Although philosopher Joseph Raz similarly faults international law for falsely recognizing as a human right something whose systematic viola-

tion would not justify international action against the violating state, he takes issue with Rawls's assertion that the prohibition against genocide should be counted as a genuine human right. He argues that while genocide is clearly a grave moral wrong, it does not necessarily follow that everyone has the human right against the genocide of any people (Raz 2007, 13; cf. Rawls 1999b, 80n23).

11. In a footnote Rawls concurs with Henry Shue's and R. J. Vincent's understanding that subsistence rights are basic and that they are to be interpreted "as including minimal economic security" (1999b, 65n1). When referencing Amartya Sen's work on famines, Rawls might also have been implicitly agreeing to a human right to food (if available, though poorly distributed) and other necessary changes in the social and political structure, given Sen's well-known claim that no substantial famine has ever occurred in a country with a democratic form of government and a relatively free press (1999b, 109; Sen 1981a; Drèze and Sen 1989). Finally, Rawls's observation that there would also be "massive starvation in every Western democracy" were there "no schemes in place to help the unemployed" also highlights his support for "backup entitlements provided through public institutions"—or what others would normally regard as basic economic and social rights (Rawls 1999b, 109). His discussion of economic and social concerns in such a cursory manner (i.e., in the turn to nonideal theory, through a footnote, as derived from more primary civil and political rights) accordingly taps into a long history of privileging civil and political rights over economic and social ones—or even denying that the latter properly constitute rights at all (see, e.g., Cranston 1973; Williams 2005).

12. Admittedly, Rawls's noninternalization of "justice as fairness," a concept that figured so prominently in his earlier works, could be explained—and might even have been foreshadowed—by his concessions in the new introduction to the paperback edition of *Political Liberalism* (1996). He acknowledges there for the first time that there might be other reasonable liberal conceptions in addition to "justice as fairness," even though he remains committed to his vision as the most reasonable one (1996, xlviii–xlix). See Sen 1999b for a different set of reasons to resist any "grand universalism" through an extension of Rawls's "original position" to cover all persons of the world. For a defense of a global extension of Rawls's "difference principle" (so that it transcends the mere "duty of assistance" required of well-ordered societies to burdened

societies and regulates inter-societal economic and social inequalities through a global redistributive principle), see especially Beitz 1979, 2000; Buchanan 2000; Cabrera 2001; Pogge 1994, 2004; Moellendorf 1996.

13. Rawls's position on the universal validity of liberal norms arguably remains incoherent. To the aforementioned moral reasons for liberal toleration of decent nonliberal regimes, Rawls adds a prudential consideration: "All societies undergo gradual changes, and this is no less true of decent societies than of others. Liberal peoples should not suppose that decent societies are unable to reform themselves in their own way. By recognizing these societies as *bona fide* members of the Society of Peoples, liberal peoples encourage this change" (1999b, 61, 122). But herein lies the problem. If Rawls champions liberal toleration because the threat of censure or punishment (or even the offering of incentives) would most likely inhibit rather than encourage a decent people's internal struggle for reform, that argument would actually depend upon, rather than repudiate, the idea that liberal principles of justice are indeed the universally appropriate standard for all societies in the world. However, it is this latter conclusion that Rawls spends the majority of the *Law of Peoples* refuting.

14. Because the ability for citizens to play a meaningful role in political decision making is not mentioned in Rawls's list of human rights proper, a well-ordered people who sought to criticize any of those aforementioned elections as a "sham" could only do so by appealing to their own standards of fairness (i.e., of liberal justice or of decency), or even to Zimbabwe's own constitutional standards, but not to anything that objectively transcends them.

15. Rawls's account betrays statist tendencies in his initial assumption of intrastate unity (i.e., each people's sharing of "common sympathies," "feelings of nationality," and collective memories due to a combination of racial, linguistic, religious, or geographic considerations) and subsequent neglect to fine-tune this picture when turning to nonideal theory (1999b, 23n17). While acknowledging that the discussion is necessary, he does not take it up himself (1999b, 24–25).

16. Stephen Macedo (2004) urges us to value collective self-governance because it allows individuals to take joint responsibility for themselves and their common good. He thereby defends Rawls's toleration of decent societies such as Kazanistan because he regards them as making

their own choices about how best to organize their social, political, and communal life while meeting stringent criteria of inclusion, voice, and responsiveness.

17. Rawls does explicitly mention the challenges of immigration. But his assumption that immigration would no longer pose a "serious problem" if each society had an internally liberal or decent basic structure exists in some tension with his insistence that decent peoples must permit and even provide assistance for the right of emigration if for no other reason than for individuals to escape the "inequality of religious freedom" that would legally prevail in accordance with international law—the Law of Peoples and its schedule of human rights (1999b, 9, 74n15). Martha Nussbaum has criticized Rawls for failing to identify the many other reasons (beyond those he correctly lists) why individuals emigrate: malnutrition, ill health, and lack of education or opportunity in light of economic inequalities between and among political societies (2006b, 239).

18. The "significant practical relevance" that David Hollenbach finds in Rawls's distinction between the rights associated with Western liberalism and the more urgent or "basic rights" on which both liberal and decent peoples could agree is "related to the difference between moral norms that we judge should be enforced by law backed by police power and those where we think persuasion is the appropriate way to secure compliance" (2003, 250–51). While Hollenbach defends the ethical appropriateness of attempting to persuade Thai Buddhists of the value of constitutional protections for freedom of speech, he would not want liberal foreign policy to be devoted to it (ibid., 252–53). Instead, Hollenbach would have attempts at persuasion occur in the context of a "dialogue conducted in freedom," just as Rawls would have individual persons in civil society, not liberal peoples in the Society of Peoples, encourage decent societies to reform along more liberal lines.

19. King further notes that engaged Buddhists would ground the "duty of nonintervention" not on any idea of national sovereignty but upon the "duty to interact in ways that do not harm others" (2006, 648–49). After observing that Rawls has paid insufficient attention to interdependence, King rhetorically asks why Rawls has focused so much on protecting one's borders when they are already "so porous, unable to keep out the devastating pollution that drifts with the wind and water, unable to prevent the arrival of the poor seeking a better life, unable to prevent the

effects of the September 11, 2001 attacks from reverberating around the world?" (2006, 649).

20. This is not to suggest that oppressive states, in the absence of third-party humanitarian intervention, would experience no repercussions for their actions or policies, for they might still be subject to verbal censure by NGOs and human rights activists, litigation by relevant regional and international human rights courts, and removal from participating in cooperative ventures with other states, and so forth (Tasioulas 2002, 386–87).

21. According to Rawls, liberal and decent peoples would have no real way to influence outlaw "primitive societies" because they would lack contact with them, but they could find a "tactful approach" to remonstrate with outlaw "advanced civilizations" that sought trade or other cooperative arrangements. After describing a hypothetical outlaw state of this kind, an Aztec-like society that held its own lower class as slaves and subjected some of their younger members to human sacrifice, Rawls instructs that they should be made to realize that their practices do not represent a "system of cooperation" and thus could not be part of the very "international system of cooperation" that they seek (1999b, 93–94n6). Nowhere in Rawls's defense of humanitarian intervention does he appeal to the value, worth, or even the interests of the individual human beings who would be enslaved or sacrificed. Rawls's suggested retort to the Aztec-like society is also likely to prove unpersuasive for its historical inaccuracy because many nations of the world participated in international schemes of cooperation even while they were perpetuating patently unjust institutions on the domestic front (i.e., the United States from the colonial period onward maintained trade and other cooperative agreements with foreign peoples such as France and Spain even while its institution of slavery remained firmly intact).

Chapter Four: Consensus-Based Approaches to Human Rights

1. Rawls defines "reasonable" persons as those who respect liberal democracy and do not use the apparatus of the state to repress the different, but still "reasonable," comprehensive doctrines of their fellow citizens (1996, 60–61). He hopes to brand as unreasonable without having to declare them false certain views that are incompatible with democratic society, such as certain "fundamentalist religions" and secular ideas of "autocracy and dictatorship" (1999d, 178–79). He nonetheless admits

that a society might not be able to avoid "entirely implying [a] lack of truth" if it decides not to act upon an unreasonable view, such as when a modern liberal democracy refuses to use the state's political power to enforce the medieval Church's doctrine *extra ecclesia nulla salus* (there is no salvation outside the church) to organize the basic structure of society accordingly (2001, 183–84; 1996, 138).

2. Rawls not only extends these concepts to cover global justice and human rights in the *Law of Peoples* but he is often read as having suggested that the rigorous account of political liberalism discussed in *Political Liberalism* would only be justifiable to liberal constitutional democracies that share the legacy of the Protestant Reformation and the European Wars of Religion (see, e.g., 1996, xxiii–xxviii).

3. The nine core international human rights treaties include the ICCPR and ICESCR, the International Convention on the Elimination of all Forms of Racial Discrimination (ICERD), the Convention on the Elimination of All Forms of Discrimination against Women (CEDAW), the Convention against Torture and Other Cruel, Inhuman, or Degrading Treatment or Punishment (CAT), the Convention on the Rights of the Child (CRC), the International Convention on the Protection of the Rights of All Migrant Workers and Their Families (ICRMW), the International Convention for the Protection of All Persons from Enforced Disappearance, the Convention on the Rights of Persons with Disabilities (CRPD), and their various optional protocols. There are many other international instruments on human rights that do not have legally binding force but that provide moral and practical guidance to signatories and other nonstate actors.

4. Until the 1960s, UN bodies were wary of criticizing the human rights violations of member-states. South Africa was the first exception and others followed thereafter. Since 1991 "humanitarian intervention" has been asserted by various nations seeking to justify third-party military action in Haiti, Somalia, Iraq in Gulf War I and II, Bosnia, Kosovo, East Timor, Sierra Leone, the Ivory Coast, and elsewhere. Nevertheless, the juridical status of humanitarian intervention remains unclear and hotly contested, especially in cases where the UN Security Council did not explicitly authorize military action.

5. Political philosopher Charles Beitz has argued that such interference might be seen as paternalistic because it would be based on the assumption that the recipients of intervention would be "better off" as a result.

It might also appear unjustifiable because the intervening agents would be acting in accordance with standards that the recipients had no reason to accept. Beitz speculates that this interference-justifying role has most likely led many to aspire to a "nonparochial or culturally neutral doctrine" of human rights (2001, 272–73).

6. Rawls turns to the "public culture itself as a shared fund of implicitly recognized basic ideas and principles," but he does not equate this "public culture" with the "background culture" wherein all comprehensive doctrines are to be found. Although he is often misread as having done so, Rawls was well aware that "everyday ideas about consensus politics and how to achieve consensus have misleading connotations," which is why he explicitly sought to distinguish his notion from more common idiomatic uses (2001, 188). In his "Reply to Habermas," which is included in the expanded paperback edition of *Political Liberalism,* Rawls discusses two other types of justification after the first (*pro tanto*) level: an individual would justify the political conception by embedding it in her own comprehensive doctrines as either true or reasonable, and then political society as a whole would justify the "shared political conception by embedding it in their several reasonable comprehensive views," which is to say that individuals in the final stage would take the views of others into account (1996, 386–87).

7. The framers of the UDHR were admittedly concerned about the possibility of not being able to reach an agreement on human rights at all, which is why they were willing to make concessions to avert that disastrous outcome. Perhaps this is why they specified several human rights provisions at a high level of generality. For example, Article 3 states that "everyone has the right to life, liberty and security of person" but makes no mention of either the permissibility or prohibition of euthanasia, capital punishment, or abortion—much to the chagrin of those who wanted to protect fetuses or ban capital punishment or both.

8. That these rights are no longer credibly in dispute by defenders of human rights is neither to deny that their execution remains far from perfect, nor to ignore the variability of their parameters when implemented in specific contexts.

9. Beitz considers a hypothetical scenario of a racist society that practices forced sterilization on a despised minority race as a means of population control. He argues that if we were to require universal consent and agreement for something to count as a genuine human right, we would

be forced to strike from the list the injunction against genocide because the prohibition would neither be a part of, nor consistent with, that racist society's beliefs and practices (2001, 274).

10. For Gandhi's views on religious pluralism, see Gandhi 1980. For a larger discussion of compatibility and tensions between Hinduism and human rights, see Elder 1996, Traer 1991, Carmen 1988, Mitra 1982. There is also the natural law argument for religious liberty that purports to be grounded on (universal) reason alone (see, e.g., George 2005, 143).

11. William F. Schulz, executive director of Amnesty International USA and an ordained Unitarian Universalist minister, not only separates his theoretical commitment to human rights from the best way for "the average American" to be induced to humanitarian action but also provides a nonmoral and nonreligious answer to the latter question. Although he acknowledges that we should all care about human rights abuses because they are morally wrong and illegal, he contends that the best way to promote human rights is to appeal to neither our conscience nor our sense of moral indignation but to our prudential interests in living in a rights-friendly world (2001; see also Rorty 1993).

12. Joseph Chan's point is that the vocabulary of rights is most useful not when there is mutual love and care as in an ideal marriage or a strong parent–child relationship but when relationships dissolve or are otherwise severely deficient (e.g., in a divorce, when parents do not fulfill their obligations to their children, or when grown children neglect to provide adequate care for their parents in their old age). Rights would then be necessary to protect the vulnerable party from neglect, harm, or even exploitation (1999, 220–22).

13. Consider the case of Kuwait, which reserves the right to allow only males to "stand and vote in elections" in contrast to the nondiscrimination requirement of the ICCPR's Article 25(b). Kuwait also registered that its "personal-status law, which is based on Islamic law," will in all cases determine the interpretation of the various marriage and family issues that are addressed in Article 23.

14. Amnesty International and Human Rights Watch have reported on various incidents in Nigeria, Somalia, Afghanistan, Iraq, and Iran where women who have been found guilty of adultery by Shariah courts have subsequently been stoned to death after being placed in a hole up to their chest or neck. All of those states are signatories to the ICCPR, even though Article 7 provides that "No one shall be subjected to torture or

to cruel, inhuman or degrading treatment or punishment." While Article 6.1 permits the sentence of death in countries that have not abolished the death penalty only for "the most serious crimes," the UN Human Rights Committee that monitors states parties' compliance with the convention has repeatedly ruled that the punishment of death by stoning for those who have committed adultery is grossly disproportionate to the nature of the crime and thus stands in violation of international law.

15. The ICRC is the appointed legal guardian of the Geneva Conventions and is entrusted with overseeing the treatment of prisoners of war. ICRC representatives conducted interviews in the fall of 2006 with detainees at the U.S. military prison in Guantánamo Bay, Cuba, and issued a forty-three-page secret report in February 2007. That report, which concluded that the prisoners' ill treatment constituted torture, was then provided to the CIA and ultimately to upper-level U.S. officials (including President George W. Bush). Its findings converge with a February 2004 ICRC report about the improper treatment of prisoners by U.S. coalition forces in Iraq.

16. The quoted passage comes from the controversial August 1, 2002, memo sent from Assistant Attorney General Jay S. Bybee to Attorney General Alberto R. Gonzales that is popularly referred to as the "Bybee memo" or the "torture memo." The memo offered an interpretation of the language of a 1994 federal statute that ratified the UN Convention against Torture and made torture a crime. The memo argued that ratification of the statute could itself be unconstitutional if it interfered with the president's constitutional powers as commander in chief. The memo was leaked to the press and published by the *Washington Post* in June 2004, and then quietly rescinded by the Justice Department on December 30, 2004. See also the U.S. Code Title 18 §2340 for another definition of torture.

17. The post–*Theory of Justice* Rawls does not argue that his two principles of justice would be reasonable or rational for every human society. Instead, his task has been to examine the reasons that can be given in support of a liberal democratic regime on the assumption that it is something that we already wish to support: "what justifies a conception of justice is not its being true to an order antecedent to and given to us, but its congruence with our deeper understanding of ourselves and our aspirations, and our realization that, given our history and the traditions

embedded in our public life, it is the most reasonable doctrine for us" (1999a, 306–7). As noted previously, this is also why Rawls does not push decent hierarchical societies to become internally liberal, for he does not believe that Kazanistan's "public political culture" supports liberal ideas such as nondiscrimination on the basis of sex or religion, democratic notions of popular sovereignty, or equal treatment before the law in all cases.

18. The "fundamental ideas" that Rawls considers include those of society as a fair system of cooperation over time, of citizens as free and equal persons, and of a well-ordered society as one regulated by a political conception of justice (1996, 14; 2001, 5).

Chapter Five: The Capability Approach to Human Rights

1. Martha Nussbaum and Amartya Sen originally developed their ideas independently although they began collaborating in 1986 at the Helsinki-based World Institute for Development Economics Research after they noticed that certain aspects of Nussbaum's Aristotelian scholarship resembled Sen's approach in development economics (see, e.g., Crocker 1995).

2. Martha Nussbaum presents CA as a necessary condition of justice, though not as providing a full theory of justice because the latter would cover other important issues left unsettled by her account: the appropriate role of the public sphere vis-à-vis incentives to private actors, what to do after citizens have reached the minimum threshold of capability, matters relating to private and public property, justice between generations, civil disobedience, and redistributive justice between nations (2000b, 75n75). Amartya Sen has also acknowledged that CA does not offer a full theory of justice (1992; 1995, 268).

3. Whether a society that subscribed to a liberal egalitarian conception of justice would also be required to correct for inequalities that arise from situations for which individuals are partly responsible is a matter of internal debate. Ronald Dworkin (2000) would have individuals take responsibility for bad outcomes that result in part from their choices (e.g., if they are economically devastated in the aftermath of a natural disaster but did not previously buy insurance against it).

4. Rawls has defined "primary goods" as the "various social conditions and all-purpose means" that all free and equal citizens would need to exercise their moral powers and pursue their conceptions of the good. These

include "basic rights and liberties," "freedom of movement and free choice of occupation against a background of diverse opportunities," "powers and prerogatives of offices and positions of authority and responsibility," "income and wealth," and the "social bases of self-respect" (2001, §17 at 57–61; 1999c, §11 at 54–55). When attempting to show the superiority of CA over Rawls's resourcist model, Sen has been criticized for primarily invoking Rawls's concern for "income and wealth" instead of his full complement of primary goods, thereby giving an impression of a greater difference between the two models than there actually might be (Beckley 2002, 111; Pogge 2002, 190–94).

5. But consider Pogge's critical question about how the compensation to the naturally disfavored (e.g., the handicapped) is to be financed: If "justice [according to the capabilities framework] requires special compensatory benefits for the naturally disfavored in proportion to how disfavored they are, why should justice not also require special compensatory burdens on the naturally favored in proportion to how favored they are?" (Pogge 2002, 209; see also Berges 2007 for a rebuttal).

6. Proponents of CA make comparable remarks about the undesirability of using gross national product (GNP) per capita instead of basic capabilities to compare the quality of life across nations. They contend that the GNP per capita approach neither answers the question of actual distribution nor takes into account other important elements in life that are not always well correlated with wealth and income, such as "life expectancy, infant mortality, educational opportunities, employment opportunities, political liberties, [and] the equality of race and gender relations" (Nussbaum 2000b, 61).

7. The "expensive tastes" problem is one in which some individuals have preferences that would require a disproportionately greater share of society's resources to satisfy in order for them to attain a comparable level of happiness as the more moderate or self-controlled. For some theorists, the appropriateness of requiring society to compensate individuals for their "expensive tastes" would depend, at least in part, on whether such tastes were deliberately cultivated (e.g., a taste for pre-phylloxera claret and plover's eggs), or were involuntary or otherwise beyond one's own control (see, e.g., Dworkin 1981, 228–40; Cohen 1989, 912–17; Arneson 2000). Under the phenomenon of adaptive preferences, a person learns to adjust to "doing without." In a study designed to determine how widowers and widows measure their health and well-being, Amartya

Sen found that women significantly underreported their ill conditions even though they were empirically worse off than men. He accounts for this by noting that women, especially poor women, have long been habituated to the absence of good health and thus neither complain about it nor expect that their health will improve (Sen 1995; Nussbaum 2000b, 136–42).

8. While Nussbaum's open and revisable list does not succumb to these problems, Sen still does not endorse it. He has, however, acknowledged the Aristotelian roots of the ideas of capabilities and functionings and interpreted her attempt to protect "minimal rights against deprivation" as extremely useful and practical (Sen 1992, 39n3; 1999c, 24; 2005, 159; Robeyns 2003, 68–70). Sabina Alkire has compared Nussbaum's Aristotelian-inspired articulation of CA with the natural law ethic of John Finnis, Germain Grisez, and their collaborators to provide an alternative list of types of practical reasons that are specified at the level of general objectives (e.g., security, life, health) and are to be used as a way to focus public deliberation (Alkire 2002; Alkire and Black 1997).

9. See G. A. Cohen (1989, 1993) and Richard Arneson (1989, 2006) for the contrary view that society ought instead to concern itself with the actual quality of life that people attain, not simply their opportunities, freedoms, or capabilities. Robeyns has also forcefully argued that disparities in achieved functionings in assessments of group inequalities imply real inequality in capabilities "except if one can give a plausible reason why one group would systematically chose different functionings from the same capability set" (2003, 84).

10. Although Nussbaum attempts to match all ten rubrics of human capabilities with possible analogs in the UDHR, she has conceded that this last capability is not addressed directly therein but is reflected in various international environmental instruments and in several draft texts on human rights and the environment (2004a; 1999, 28, 44–47).

11. Nussbaum does not, however, simply seek to affirm the status quo, for she remains highly critical of Israel's treatment of non-Orthodox forms of Judaism and judges the virtual impossibility in India of free egress from one religion to another to be morally unacceptable (2000b, 189).

12. Admittedly, talk of "trade-offs" of either rights or capabilities would be more difficult to square with Nussbaum's version of CA given her understanding that justice requires the securing of all ten central human

capabilities, at least up to their minimum thresholds. Still, even Nussbaum concedes that "in practical terms priorities may have to be set temporarily" under certain circumstances (2003, 40; 2006b, 175; cf. Wasserman 2006; Wolf 1995).

13. According to Nussbaum, we human beings cooperate with others out of a wide range of motives beyond self-interest, including a "love of justice itself" and a "moralized compassion" to attend to those who have "less than they need to lead decent and dignified lives" (2006b, 92, 132, 156–59).

14. Nussbaum's Aristotelian-inspired view is that sensitivity to context need not lead to cultural or moral relativism, for objectivity and particularism are not invariably opposed. In her own words, "the fact that a good and virtuous decision is context-sensitive does not imply that it is right only *relative to*, or *inside*, a limited context, any more than the fact that a good navigational judgment is sensitive to particular weather conditions shows that it is correct only in a local or relational sense. It is right absolutely, objectively, anywhere in the human world, to attend to the particular features of one's context. . . . If another situation should ever arise with all the same ethically relevant features, including contextual features, the same decision would again be absolutely right" (1993, 257).

15. Nussbaum does not intend by these comments to draw a categorical break between humans and animals, for she believes that our rationality and animality are "thoroughly unified," and that the former is not the sole basis for our dignity because it is only one aspect of who we essentially are (2006b, 92, 132, 159).

16. Harnessing Aristotle in support of this internalist position, Nussbaum does not even interpret his famous "human function" passage of the *Nichomachean Ethics* I.7 as an endorsement of metaphysical biology or an externalist account of human nature. Instead she reads it as an invitation to engage in dialogue about which functions are so important and central that "their absence will mean the absence of a human being or human life" (1995a, 94). It is, of course, a separate and contestable matter whether this reading of Aristotle is correct. But the heart of Nussbaum's internalism is her conviction that we cannot but judge for ourselves what are the most important "doings and beings" of the truly human form of life (1993, 260–61; 1995a; cf. Putnam 1990).

17. When discussing a hypothetical scenario involving a successful vote in India to replace its pluralistic constitution for one declaring India a

Hindu state, Nussbaum concludes that equal freedom of conscience is simply not negotiable for a decent pluralistic democracy. Thus, while informed desire and consent should play a role in political justification, the "independent moral argument must take priority" (Nussbaum 2004b, 200–201). This is to say that Nussbaum's willingness for her list of ten central capabilities to be ever-revisable and remade is not unlimited, especially since the possibility of never-ending change exists in some tension with her other claims of the capabilities' moral objectivity and intrinsic worth.

18. Martha Nussbaum has argued that there are two rhetorical advantages to deploying the language of capabilities instead of rights. First, the discourse on capabilities is not as strongly linked to a particular cultural or historical tradition as rights talk is and thus does not even give the appearance of privileging a Western idea. Second, the language of capabilities might better advance gender justice by "foreground[ing] and address[ing] inequalities that women suffer inside the family," since rights talk is more commonly associated with law and state action in the public sphere and a more "hands-off" approach in the private sphere (2003, 39). I would submit, however, that any gains in rhetoric would be more apparent than real. For critics who object to the modern Western "taint" of rights talk would most likely also find fault with the Western influences behind Nussbaum's focus on human capabilities (viz., Marx and Aristotle) as well as some of the items advanced by CA's proponents (e.g., the capabilities identified by Nussbaum having to do with our emotional development, interactions with other species, opportunities for sexual satisfaction, and play). As for the second claim, since Nussbaum has designed her list of ten central capabilities to function in a parallel political and legal way as rights do—they are to be regarded as constitutionally protected, basic social entitlements that each state must minimally deliver to its citizens—it is not entirely clear how and why talk of capabilities could advance gender justice in a way that a focus on rights could not. In fact, the promotion of rights need not always occur through law—public appraisal and advocacy could prove just as effective as actual legislation (see Sen 2004b, 319–20). Despite Nussbaum's position that it is rhetorically advantageous to talk about capabilities instead of about rights in some contexts, she has also acknowledged two ways in which the latter is comparatively superior to the former. First, the discourse on rights is itself more normative—it more succinctly captures the ethical

judgment that we have valid and urgent claims to certain forms of treatment that we ought to be able to hold against our own governments (2000b, 100; 2006b, 290). Second, rights talk remains connected to notions of individual choice and autonomy while the language of capabilities is still often tied to illiberal forms of Aristotelianism that endorse perfectionism and requisite functioning (2000b, 101). This latter point is tied to Nussbaum's instruction for the "Aristotelian [to] diverge from Aristotle" in light of his total lack of a conception of political liberty to be free from state interference in certain areas of choice, unacceptable comments on slaves and women, and the undesirable consequences entailed by his comments on leisure (1990a, 239).

19. But a critic of CA, Thomas Pogge, has argued that the forms of redress that CA requires would be extremely cumbersome, for if individual capabilities were used as a "metric of advantage that governs the compensatory fine-tuning of the distribution of resources so as to take account of persons' vertically diverse capacities to convert resources into valuable functionings," society would be required to "grad[e] all citizens for their natural aptitudes toward each of the capabilities on the list, determin[e] their specific deficits, and ensur[e] that these deficits are duly neutralized through suitable compensatory benefits" (2002, 210–11). He adds that even if there were a "large body of rules" and a "large administrative bureaucracy," the "task could not be accomplished in a way that [was] even approximately equitable" (ibid.). While Pogge correctly recognizes that CA would require more monitoring and social assessment than would a resourcist model or perhaps even the human rights framework as traditionally conceived, he has overlooked the fact that many of the items on Nussbaum's list need only to be satisfied to an adequate (not necessarily equal) level, thus making the task of assessment less cumbersome. It is also worth underscoring that many public and private institutions in several liberal democratic societies have already acknowledged that granting the formal equal right to compete for all (e.g., for entrance to competitive educational institutions, for jobs) may not prove sufficient to redress past wrongs or guarantee genuinely real opportunities for all, which is why some have enacted various affirmative action programs.

20. While a full explanation of this idea cannot be provided here, the general worry is a potential to compromise the genuinely free exchange of ideas in a nation with notable class stratification if limits were not set upon the total amount of political contributions that any given individ-

ual, corporation, or special-interest group could make to a political candidate or party in any given year or election cycle.

21. Mobility is truly a universal human need. Even those who are either paralyzed from the neck down or who are in a coma have needs for their bodies and limbs to be moved around (by others), given the danger of bed sores and amputation in worst-case scenarios, if not moved.

22. Maurice Cranston discusses the ways in which we convert strongly felt desires into a kind of a moral imperative, such as when our natural survival instinct and aversion to die a violent death lead to claims about everyone's "right to life" (1973, 25).

23. Nussbaum's view is that society should work tirelessly to bring those who live with disabilities up to the same threshold capability that it sets for other (nonimpaired) citizens. Doing so might involve devoting more resources to remedial and special education, providing appropriate forms of guardianship, and perhaps even engineering away certain medical conditions (e.g., Down syndrome), although she is careful to note that CA would not require this last action (2006b, 186–210).

24. In contrast to the case of equal species dignity, Nussbaum contends that the idea of equal human dignity "is not a metaphysical idea, but a central element in political conceptions that have long been prevalent in modern constitutional democracies" (2006b, 383). This statement not only fails to take seriously the maximalist challenge to human rights justification (i.e., that a particular kind of metaphysics is required to justify a doctrine of human rights) but also suggests that she is conflating unpopular ideas with metaphysical ones.

Chapter Six: Grounding Human Rights in a Pluralist World

1. It is worth noting that the framers of the UDHR did not understand their task to have been completed once they placed constraints on the legitimate reach of governmental power. However, most classical natural rights theorists in their late seventeenth and eighteenth century did in their critique of feudal rule, absolute monarchy, and the divine right of kings.

2. I do not mean to imply that human rights did not exist in premodern times, only that many vital human rights that are legally recognized today in various domestic, regional, and international statutes would be neither intelligible nor even necessary were it not for the radical changes to religious, social, economic, and political life that were brought about by modernity and industrialization.

3. That is, Rawls and others have repeatedly noted that other issues such as civil disobedience, matters pertaining to public and private property, population pressure, environmental concerns, the ethics of war, and re-distributive justice between nations would have to be addressed as well.

4. To reiterate a point made earlier in our final assessment of the enforcement-centered approach to human rights, an attempt to ground respect for cultures nonrelativistically but still consequentially (e.g., for the sake of maintaining peace, security, and social cooperation among peoples) would encounter additional problems of its own. The account would in principle always be willing to "sacrifice" the human rights of some for the "greater" benefit of others and would accordingly provide insufficient protection for non-derogable human rights. And the account would still remain incomplete because a critic of consequentialism would still be able to ask what is so harmful or wrong about war, what is good or so advantageous about social cooperation, and so on, and any satisfactory answer to those questions would ultimately have to hinge upon some value claim about the good for human beings.

5. Obviously, naturalist and nonnaturalist positions would be mutually in-compatible. James Griffin's personhood account of human rights would also likely prove troubling to those intending to extend human rights to everyone because his "human" in "human rights" is not simply a mem-ber of *Homo sapiens* but a "functioning . . . human normative agent" such that "infants, the severely mentally retarded, [and] people in an irre-versible coma" would be excluded from the class of bearers of human rights (2008, 34, 50). To soften the blow, Griffin repeatedly stresses that human beings can still possess moral standing without having human rights, which is to say that the retraction or failure to extend human rights to any given member of *Homo sapiens* does not on its own imply that one can then justifiably do (or not do) anything to him or her.

6. Admittedly, what complicates our understanding of what exactly Perry means by "religious" is his brief consideration of John Finnis's account of natural law as one possible way to provide "non-religious support for the morality of human rights," which he couples with doubt that "a natural-law morality of human rights" could stand alone without theo-logical support (Perry 2006, 18–19). Stackhouse, in comparison and contrast, interprets the natural law presupposition that there is "norma-tive, objective, moral order in the universe and that it can be known by

unaided (not revealed) human reason" as still "profoundly religious" in character (1984, 8). Despite Stackhouse's attempt to assimilate natural law into the realm of religion, the conventional distinction between philosophical arguments and religious ones is that the former eschews reliance upon special revelation while the latter ordinarily does not.

7. Cf. "But still, this question intrudes: If, as their (bedrock?) conviction holds, the other, *even the Other,* truly does have inherent dignity and truly is inviolable, what *else* must be true; what *must be true for it to be true that the Other has inherent dignity and is inviolable?*" (Perry 2006, 29).

8. That is, to say that certain individuals or communities are justified in believing in human rights is not to say that human rights principles themselves are justified. As philosopher Chris Eberle has noted, rational justification is radically perspectival in that it is a function of an individual's "evidential set" (i.e., "the fund of beliefs and experience she assumes to be true or reliable" while evaluating a particular claim) and the "manner in which she employs evidence available to her" (2002, 62). Thus, justification must be distinguished from soundness, or the objective adequacy of an argument for a given conclusion.

9. I posed this very question to Nicholas Wolterstorff at a panel on his *Justice: Rights and Wrongs,* at the 2009 annual meeting of the Society of Christian Ethics, and his response left much to be desired according to the logic of his book's own argument. His understanding of whether fetuses have rights seemed to turn on whether they had the relevant capacities in question. For comparison, note that Max Stackhouse has been explicit in his remarks that no one, including demented Alzheimer's patients, the terminally ill, and fetuses, should be treated as expendable.

10. While Michael Ignatieff observes that the secular humanist must, for the sake of internal consistency, reject the idea that "there is something inviolate about the dignity of each human being," for its unwarranted worshipful attitude, he nevertheless declares that our commitment to human rights "needs sustaining by some faith in our species" (2001, 83–87). Even Richard Rorty, who wants us to cease our search for a "philosophical or religious preface" to liberal democratic politics, who wants us instead to conceptualize the "human rights culture" as a way of life entirely contingent upon the particular experiences of the modern West, nevertheless encourages us to widen our circle of concern gradually to encompass the Other, and to act as if pain and cruelty were the

worst things we can inflict upon others even though we can supply no "rational," nonneutral, or otherwise foundationalist defense for these claims. The point is that what Rorty disavows theoretically he is nevertheless entirely committed to practically, for he has for all pragmatic purposes assumed common human vulnerabilities and some trust in the idea that an unfamiliar "featherless biped" should be treated more like kin than like enemy (Rorty 1983, 1990).

References

Abdel-Nour, Farid. 2004. "Farewell to Justification: Habermas, Human Rights, and Universalist Morality." *Philosophy & Social Criticism* 30, no. 1: 73–96.

Ackerley, Brooke A. 2000. *Political Theory and Feminist Social Criticism.* Cambridge: Cambridge University Press.

Alkire, Sabina. 2002. *Valuing Freedoms: Sen's Capability Approach and Poverty Reduction.* Oxford: Oxford University Press.

Alkire, Sabina, and Rufus Black. 1997. "A Practical Reasoning Theory of Development Ethics: Furthering the Capabilities Approach." *Journal of International Development* 9, no. 2: 263–79.

Alves, Jose Lindgren. 2002. "Declaration of Human Rights in Postmoderity." *Human Rights Quarterly* 22, no. 2: 478–500.

American Anthropological Association (AAA). 1947. "Statement on Human Rights Submitted to the Commission on Human Rights, United Nations." *American Anthropologist* 49, no. 4: 539–43.

Ames, Roger. 1988. "Rites as Rights: The Confucian Alternative." In *Human Rights and the World's Religions,* edited by Leroy Rouner, 199–216. Notre Dame, IN: University of Notre Dame Press.

Amesbury, Richard and George Newlands. 2008. *Faith and Human Rights: Christianity and the Global Struggle for Human Dignity.* Minneapolis: Fortress Press.

Anderson, Elizabeth. 1999. "What Is the Point of Equality?" *Ethics* 109, no. 2: 287–337.

An-Na'im, Abdullahi Ahmed. 1990a. "Human Rights in the Muslim World: Socio-Political Conditions and Scriptural Imperative." *Harvard Human Rights Journal* 3:13–52.

———. 1990b. "Problems of Universal Cultural Legitimacy for Human Rights." In *Human Rights in Africa: Cross-cultural Perspectives,* edited by Abdullahi An-Na'im and Francis M. Deng, 331–67. Washington, DC: The Brookings Institution.

———. 1992. "Toward a Cross-Cultural Approach to Defining International Standards of Human Rights: The Meaning of Cruel, Inhuman, or Degrading Treatment or Punishment." In *Human Rights in Cross-cultural Perspectives: A quest for Consensus,* edited by Abdullahi Ahmed An-Na'im, 29–43. Philadelphia: University of Pennsylvania Press.

———. 1996. "Islamic Foundations of Religious Human Rights." In *Religious Human Rights in Global Perspective: Religious Perspectives,* edited by John Witte Jr. and Johan D. van der Vyver, 337–60. The Hague: Martinus Nijhoff Publishers.

———. 2002. "The Cultural Transformation." In *Cultural Transformation and Human Rights in Africa,* edited by Abdullahi Ahmed An-Na'im. London: Zed Books.

Arneson, Richard. 1989. "Equality and Equality of Opportunity for Welfare." *Philosophical Studies* 56:77–93.

———. 2000. "Perfectionism and Politics." *Ethics* 111, no. 1: 37–63.

———. 2006. "Distributive Justice and Basic Capability Equality: 'Good Enough' Is Not Good Enough." In *Capabilities Equality: Basic Issues and Problems,* edited by Alexander Kaufman, 17–43. New York: Routledge.

Artz, Donna E. 1996. "The Treatment of Religious Dissidents under Classical and Contemporary Law." In *Religious Human Rights in Global Perspective: Religious Perspectives,* edited by John Witte and Johan D. van der Vyver, 485–516. The Hague: Martinus Nijhoff Publishers.

Ash, Kristen. 2005. "U.S. Reservations to the International Covenant on Civil and Political Rights: Credibility Maximization and Global Influence." *Northwestern University International Journal of Human Rights* 3 (Spring), www.law.northwestern.edu/journals/jihr/v3/7/Ash.pdf.

Ayer, A. J. 1952. *Language, Truth, and Logic.* New York: Dover Publications.

Balfour, Ian, and Eduardo Cadava. 2004. "The Claims of Human Rights: an Introduction." *South Atlantic Quarterly* 103, nos. 2–3: 277–96.

Bary, Wm. Theodore de. 1983. *The Liberal Tradition in China.* Hong Kong and New York: Columbia University Press.

———. 1994. "Neo-Confucianism and Human Rights. " In *Human Rights and the World's Religions,* edited by Leroy Rouner, 183–198. Notre Dame, IN: University of Notre Dame Press.

Beckley, Harlan. 2002. "Capability as Opportunity: How Amartya Sen Revises Equal Opportunity." *Journal of Religious Ethics* 30, no. 1: 107–35.

Beitz, Charles. 1979. *Political Theory and International Relations.* Princeton, NJ: Princeton University Press.

———. 2000. "Rawls's Law of Peoples." *Ethics* 110, no. 4: 669–97.

———. 2001. "Human Rights as a Common Concern." *American Political Science Review* 95, no. 2: 269–82.

Bell, Daniel A. 2000. *East Meets West: Human Rights and Democracy in East Asia*. Princeton, NJ: Princeton University Press.

Benhabib, Seylah. 2004. "The Law of Peoples, Distributive Justice, and Migrations." *Fordham Law Review* 72:1761–87.

Berges, Sandrine. 2007. "Why the Capability Approach Is Justified." *Journal of Applied Philosophy* 24, no. 1: 16–25.

Blackburn, Simon. 1993. *Essays in Quasi-Realism*. New York: Oxford University Press.

Bloom, Irene. 1996. "Confucian Perspectives on the Individual and the Collectivity." In *Religious Diversity and Human Rights*, edited by J. Paul Martin, Irene Bloom, and Wayne L. Proudfoot, 114–51. New York: Columbia University Press.

———. 1998. "Fundamental Intuitions and Consensus Statements: Mencian Confucianism and Human Rights." In *Confucianism and Human Rights*, edited by Wm. Theodore De Bary and Tu Weiming, 94–116. New York: Columbia University Press.

Brandt. 1959. *Hopi Ethics: A Theoretical Analysis*. Chicago: University of Chicago Press.

Brauman, Rony, and Philippe Petit. 2004. "From Philanthropy to Humanitarianism: Remarks and an Interview." *South Atlantic Quarterly* 103, no. 2–3: 397–17.

Buchanan, Allen. 2000. "Rawls's 'Law of Peoples': Rules for a Vanished Westphalian World." *Ethics* 110, no. 4: 697–721.

Burke, Roland. 2006. "'The Compelling Dialogue of Freedom': Human Rights at the Bandung Conference." *Human Rights Quarterly* 28, no. 4: 947–65.

Cabrera, Luis. 2001. "Toleration and Tyranny in Rawls's 'Law of Peoples.'" *Polity* 34, no. 2: 163–79.

Cahill, Lisa Sowle. 1999–2000. "Rights as Religious or Secular: Why Not Both?" *Journal of Law and Religion* 14, no. 1: 41–52.

Carmen, John B. 1988. "Duties and Rights in Hindu Society." In *Human Rights and the World's Religions*, edited by Leroy S. Rouner, 113–28. Notre Dame, IN: University of Notre Dame Press.

Centers for Disease Control (CDC). 2008. "Oubreak of Measles—San Diego, California, January–February 2008." *Morbidity and Mortality Weekly Report* 57 (February 22):1–4.

Chan, Joseph. 1999. "A Confucian Perspective on Human Rights for Contemporary China." In *The East Asian Challenge for Human rights,* edited by Joanne Bauer and Daniel Bell, 212–37. Cambridge: Cambridge University Press.

———. 2000. "Human Rights and Confucian Virtues." *Harvard Asia Quarterly* 4, no. 3: 51–54.

Ching, Julia. 1998. "Human Rights: A Valid Chinese Concept?" In *Confucianism and Human Rights,* eds. Wm. Theodore de Bary and Tu Wei-Ming, 67–82. New York: Columbia University Press.

Cohen, G. A. 1989. "On the Currency of Egalitarian Justice." *Ethics* 99, no. 4: 906–44.

———. 1993. "Equality of What? On Welfare, Resources, and Capabilities." In *The Quality of Life,* edited by Martha Nussbaum and Amartya Sen, 9–29. Oxford: Clarendon Press.

Cohen, Joshua. 2004. "Minimalism about Human Rights: The Most We Can Hope For?" *Journal of Political Philosophy* 12, no. 2: 190–213.

Cranston, Maurice. 1973. *What Are Human Rights?* New York: Taplinger Publishing.

Crocker, David A. 1995. "Functioning and Capability: The Foundations of Sen's and Nussbaum's Development Ethics, Part 2." In *Women, Culture, and Development: A Study of Human Capabilities,* edited by Martha Nussbaum and Jonathan Glover, 153–98. Oxford: Oxford University Press.

Dallmayr, Fred. 2002. "'Asian Values' and Global Human Rights." *Philosophy East & West* 52, no. 2: 173–89.

Davidson, Donald. 1974. "On the Very Idea of a Conceptual Scheme." In *Inquiries into Truth and Interpretation,* 183–98. Oxford: Oxford University Press.

Dershowitz, Alan. 2002. *Why Terrorism Works: Understanding the Threat, Responding to the Challenge.* New Haven, CT: Yale University Press.

———. 2004. "Tortured Reasoning." In *Torture: A Collection,* edited by Sanford Levinson, 257–80. Oxford: Oxford University Press.

Donnelly, Jack. 1989. *Universal Human Rights in Theory and Practice.* Ithaca, NY: Cornell University Press.

———. 1999. "Human Rights and Asian Values: A Defense of 'Western' Universalism." In *The East Asian Challenge for Human Rights,* edited by Joanne Bauer and Daniel Bell, 60–87. Cambridge: Cambridge University Press.

————. 2003. "The Universal Declaration Model: A Liberal Defense." In *International Human Rights in the 21st Century: Protecting the Rights of Groups*, edited by Gene Marin Lyons and James Mayall. Lanham, MD: Rowman and Littlefield.

Drèze, Jean, and Amartya Sen. 1989. *Hunger and Public Action*. Oxford: Clarendon Press.

Dworkin, Ronald. 1981. "What Is Equality? I: Equality of Welfare." *Philosophy & Public Affairs* 10:185–246.

————. 2000. *Sovereign Virtue*. Cambridge, MA: Harvard University Press.

Eberle. Christopher J. 2002. *Religious Convictions in Liberal Politics*. Cambridge: Cambridge University Press.

Elder, Joseph W. 1996. "Hindu Perspectives on the Individual and the Collectivity." In *Religious Diversity and Human Rights*, edited by J. Paul Martin, Irene Bloom, and Wayne L. Proudfoot, 54–86. New York: Columbia University Press.

Elshtain, Jean Bethke. 1992. *Meditations on Modern Political Thought: Masculine/Feminine Themes from Luther to Arendt*. University Park: Pennsylvania State University Press.

Embree, Ainslie Thomas, ed. 1988. *Sources of Indian Tradition: From the Beginnings to 1800*, vol. 1. New York: Columbia University Press.

Engle, Karen. 2001. "From Skepticism to Embrace: Human Rights and the American Anthropological Association from 1947–1999." *Human Rights Quarterly* 23, no. 3: 536–59.

Esack, Farid. 2001. "Islam and Gender Justice: Beyond Simplistic Apologia." *What Men Owe Women: Men's Voices from World Religions*, edited by J. Raines and D. Maguire, 187–210. New York: State University of New York Press.

Falk, Richard. 1992. "Cultural Foundations for the International Protection of Human Rights." In *Human Rights in Cross-cultural Perspectives: A Quest for Consensus*, edited by Abdullahi An-Na'im, 44–64. Philadelphia: University of Pennsylvania Press.

Fitzpatrick, William J. 2005. "The Practical Turn in Ethical Theory: Korsgaard's Constructivism, Realism, and the Nature of Normativity." *Ethics* 115, no. 5 (July): 651–91.

————. 2008. "Robust Ethical Realism, Non-Naturalism and Normativity." In *Oxford Studies in Metaethics*, vol. 3, edited by Russ Shafer-Landau. Oxford: Oxford University Press.

Fox, Robin. 2002. "The Ground and Nature of Human Rights: Another Round." *The National Interest* 68 (Summer): 113–23.

Freeman, Michael. 2000. "Universal Rights and Particular Cultures." In *Human Rights and Asian Values: Contesting National Identities and Cultural Representations in Asia*, edited by Michael Jacobsen and Ole Bruun, 43–58. Surrey, U.K.: Curzon Press.

———. 2004. "The Problem of Secularism in Human Rights Theory." *Human Rights Quarterly* 26:375–400.

Gandhi, Mohandas K. 1980. *All Men Are Brothers: Autobiographical Reflections*, edited by Krishna Kripilani. New York: Continuum.

Geertz, Clifford. 1989. "Anti Anti-relativism." In *Relativism: Interpretation and Confrontation*, edited by Michael Krausz, 12–34. Notre Dame, IN: University of Notre Dame Press.

George, Robert P. 2005. "Natural Law and Human Rights: A Conversation." In *Does Human Rights Need God?* edited by Elizabeth M. Bucar and Barbra Barnett, 135–44. Grand Rapids, MI: Eerdmans.

Gewirth, Alan. 1982. *Human Rights: Essays on Justification and Application.* Chicago: University of Chicago Press.

Glendon, Mary Ann. 1993. *Rights Talk: The Impoverishment of Political Discourse.* New York: Free Press.

———. 2001. *A World Made Anew: Eleanor Roosevelt and the Universal Declaration of Human Rights.* New York: Random House.

Griffin, James. 2001. "First Steps in Any Account of Human Rights." *European Journal of Philosophy* 9, no. 3: 306–27.

———. 2008. *On Human Rights.* Oxford: Oxford University Press.

Gutmann, Amy. 2001. "Introduction." In *Human Rights as Politics and Idolatry*, edited by Michael Ignatieff. Princeton, NJ: Princeton University Press.

Gyatso, Tenzin (His Holiness the XIV Dalai Lama of Tibet). 1998. "Human Rights and Universal Responsibilities." In *Buddhism and Human Rights*, edited by Wayne R. Husted, Damien V. Keown, Charles S. Prebish. Surrey, Great Britain: Curzon Press.

Hassan, Riffat. 1996. "Rights of Women within Islamic Communities." In *Religious Human Rights in Global Perspective: Religious Perspectives*, edited by John Witte Jr. and Johan D. van der Vyver. The Hague: Martinus Nijhoff Publishers.

Hatch, Elvin. 1983. *Culture and Morality: The Relativity of Values in Anthropology.* New York: Columbia University Press.

Hayfa, Tarek. 2004. "The Idea of Public Justification in Rawls's *Law of Peoples*." *Res Publica* 10:233–246.

Henkin, Louis. 1990. *The Age of Rights*. New York: Columbia University Press.

Herskovits, Melville. 1948. *Man and His Works*. New York: Alfred A. Knopf.

Hollenbach, David. 2003. *The Global Face of Public Faith: Politics, Human Rights, and Christian Ethics*. Washington, DC: Georgetown University Press.

Humphrey, John P. 1984. *Human Rights and the United Nations: A Great Adventure*. New York: Transnational Publishers.

Huntington, Samuel. 1993. "The Clash of Civilizations?" *Foreign Affairs* 72, no. 3: 22–49.

———. 1998. *The Clash of Civilizations and the Remaking of the World Order*. New York: Simon & Schuster.

Hutchison, William R. 1993. *Errand to the World: American Protestant Thought and Foreign Missions*, rprt. ed. Chicago: University of Chicago Press.

Ignatieff, Michael. 2001. *Human Rights as Politics and Idolatry*. Princeton, NJ: Princeton University Press.

Ivanhoe, Philip J., ed. 2009. *Mencius*. Trans. Irene Bloom. New York: Columbia University Press.

Jackson, Timothy P. 2003. "A House Divided, Again: Sanctity vs. Dignity in the Induced Death Debates." In *In Defense of Human Dignity: Essays for Our Time*, edited by Robert P. Kraynak and Glenn Tinder, 139–64. Notre Dame, IN: University of Notre Dame Press.

———. 2005. "The Image of God and the Soul of Humanity: Reflections on Dignity, Sanctity, and Democracy." In *Religion in the Liberal Polity*, edited by Terence Cuneo, 43–72. Notre Dame, IN: University of Notre Dame Press.

James, William. 1907. *Pragmatism: A New Name for Some Old Ways of Thinking*. New York: Longmans, Green, and Co.

Johnson, Luke Timothy. 1996. "Religious Rights and Christian Texts." In *Religious Human Rights in Global Perspective: Religious Perspectives*, edited by John Witte Jr. and Johan D. van der Vyver, 65–96. The Hague: Martinus Nijhoff Publishers.

Joyce, Richard. 2001. *The Myth of Morality*. Cambridge: Cambridge University Press.

Kant, Immanuel. 1795. "Perpetual Peace". In *Perpetual Peace and Other Essays*. Trans. Ted Humphrey. Indianapolis: Hackett, 1983.

Kelsay, John, and Sumner B. Twiss, eds. 1994. *Religion and Human Rights*. New York: The Project on Religion and Human Rights.

King, Sally. 2001. "A Global Ethic in the Light of Comparative Religious Ethics." In *Explorations in Global Ethics: Comparative Religious Ethics and Interreligious Dialogue,* edited by Sumner B. Twiss and Bruce Grelle, 118–40. Boulder, CO: Westview Press.

———. 2006. "An Engaged Buddhist Response to John Rawls's *The Law of Peoples.*" *Journal of Religious Ethics* 34, no. 4: 637–61.

Kirsch, Philippe. 2006. "The Role of the International Criminal Court in Enforcing International Criminal Law." Washington College of Law, American University, June 1. Available at C-Span Video Library, www.c-spanvideo.org/program/192823-1.

Kohen, Ari. 2007. *In Defense of Human Rights: A Non-Religious Grounding in a Pluralistic World.* Routledge: London and New York.

Korsgaard, Christine. 1996. *Creating the Kingdom of Ends.* New York: Cambridge University Press.

Korsgaard, Christine, with G. A. Cohen, Raymond Geuss, Thomas Nagel, and Bernard Williams. 1996. *The Sources of Normativity,* edited by Onora O'Neill. Cambridge: Cambridge University Press.

Küng, Hans. 1987. "What Is True Religion?" Toward an Ecumenical Criteriology." In *Toward a Universal Theology of Religion,* edited by Leonard Swidler, 231–50. Maryknoll, NY: Orbis Books.

———. 1991. *Global Responsibility: In Search of a New World Ethic,* trans. John Bowden. New York: Crossroad.

———. 1998. *A Global Ethic for Global Politics and Economics.* Oxford: Oxford University Press.

———. 2005. "Global Ethic and Human Responsibilities." High-Level Expert Group Meeting on Human Rights and Human Responsibilities in the Age of Terrorism, April 1–2, Santa Clara University. www.scu.edu/ethics/practicing/focusareas/global_ethics/laughlin-lectures/globalethic-human-responsibility.html.

Küng, Hans, and Karl-Josef Kuschel, eds. 1993. *A Global Ethic: The Declaration of the Parliament of the World's Religions.* London: SCM Press.

Langan, John, SJ. 1982. "Defining Human Rights: A Revision of the Liberal Tradition." In *Human Rights in the Americas: The Struggle for Consensus,* edited by Alfred Hennelly, SJ, and John Langan, SJ, 69–101. Washington DC: Georgetown University Press.

Langlois, Anthony J. 2001. *The Politics of Justice and Human Rights: Southeast Asia and Universalist Theory.* Cambridge: Cambridge University Press.

Lindholm, Tore. 1992. "Prospects for Research on the Cultural Legitimacy of Human Rights: The Cases of Liberalism and Marxism." In *Human Rights in Cross-cultural Perspectives: A Quest for Consensus,* edited by Abdullahi An-Na'im, 387–426. Philadelphia: University of Pennsylvania Press.

Little, David. 1990. "A Christian Perspective on Human Rights." In *Human Rights in Africa: Cross-cultural Perspectives,* edited by Abdullahi An-Na'im and Francis M. Deng, 59–103. Washington, DC: Brookings Institution.

———. "Rethinking Human Rights." *Journal of Religious Ethics* 27, no. 1: 151–71.

———. 2006. "On Behalf of Rights: A Critique of Democracy and Tradition." *Journal of Religious Ethics* 34, no. 2: 287–310.

Lizhi, Fang. 1990. "First Word." *Omni* 12, no. 6: 8.

Macedo, Stephen. 2004. "What Self-Governing Peoples Owe to One Another: Universalism, Diversity, and the Law of Peoples." *Fordham Law Review* 72:1721–38.

MacIntyre, Alasdair. 1984. *After Virtue: A Study in Moral Theory,* 2nd ed. Notre Dame, IN: University of Notre Dame Press.

———. 1991. "I'm Not a Communitarian, But . . ." *The Responsive Community: Rights and Responsibility* 1, no. 3: 91–92.

Mackie, J. L. 1977. *Ethics: Inventing Right and Wrong.* New York: Penguin.

Maritain, Jacques. 1949. "Introduction." In *Human Rights: Comments and Interpretation; A Symposium Edited by UNESCO,* 9–17. July 25, 1948, Paris. London: UNESCO and Allan Wingate. http://unesdoc.unesco.org/images/0015/001550/155042eb.pdf. Reprint, Westport, CT: Greenwood Press. 1973.

———. 1951. *Man and the State.* Chicago: University of Chicago Press. 1999.

Mayer, Ann Elizabeth. 1999. *Islam and Human Rights: Tradition and Politics,* 3rd ed. Boulder, CO: Westview Press.

Mernissi, Fatima. 1987. *The Veil and the Male Elite: A Feminist Interpretation of Women's Rights in Islam.* Reading, MA: Addison-Wesley/Perseus Books.

———. 1992. *Islam and Democracy: Fear of the Modern World,* rev. ed. Reading, MA: Addison-Wesley/Perseus Books.

Mitra, Kana. 1982. "Human Rights in Hinduism." In *Human Rights in Religious Traditions,* edited by Arlene Swidler. New York: The Pilgrim Press.

Moellendorf, Darrel. 1996. "Constructing the Law of Peoples." *Pacific Philosophical Quarterly* 77, no. 2: 132–45.

_216_
References

Moody-Adams, Michelle. 2002. _Fieldwork in Familiar Places: Morality, Culture and Philosophy._ Cambridge, MA: Harvard University Press.

Morsink, Johannes. 1999. _The Universal Declaration of Human Rights: Origins, Drafting, and Intent._ Philadelphia: University of Pennsylvania Press.

——. 2009. _Inherent Human Rights: Philosophical Roots of the Universal Declaration._ Philadelphia: University of Pennsylvania Press.

Muzaffar, Chandra. 1999. "From Human Rights to Human Dignity." In _Debating Human Rights: Critical Essays from the United States and Asia,_ edited by Peter Van Ness. London and New York: Routledge.

Nagel, Thomas. 1986. _The View from Nowhere._ Oxford: Oxford University Press.

Nozick, Robert. 1974. _Anarchy, State, and Utopia._ New York: Basic Books.

Nurser, John. 2005. _For All Peoples and All Nations: The Ecumenical Church and Human Rights._ Washington, DC: Georgetown University Press.

Nussbaum, Martha. 1990a. "Aristotelian Social Democracy." In _Liberalism and the Good,_ edited by R. Bruce Douglass, Gerald M. Mara, and Henry S. Richardson, 203–52. New York: Routledge.

——. 1990b. _Love's Knowledge: Essays on Philosophy and Literature._ New York: Oxford University Press.

——. 1992. "Human Functioning and Social Justice: In Defense of Aristotelian Essentialism." _Political Theory_ 20, no. 2: 202–46.

——. 1993. "Non-Relative Virtues: An Aristotelian Approach." In _The Quality of Life,_ edited by Martha C. Nussbaum and Amartya Sen, 242–69. Oxford: Clarendon Press.

——. 1995a. "Aristotle on Human Nature and the Foundations of Ethics." In _World, Mind, and Ethics: Essays on the Ethical Philosophy of Bernard Williams,_ edited by J. E. J. Althan and Ross Harrison, 86–113. Cambridge: Cambridge University Press.

——. 1995b. "Human Capabilities, Female Human Beings." In _Women, Culture and Development: A Study of Human Capabilities,_ edited by Martha Nussbaum and Jonathan Glover, 61–104. Oxford: Oxford University Press.

——. 1997a. "Capabilities and Human Rights." _Fordham Law Review_ 66: 273–300.

——. 1997b. _Cultivating Humanity: A Classical Defense of Reform in Liberal Education._ Cambridge, MA: Harvard University Press.

———. 1999. "Capabilities, Human Rights, and the Universal Declaration." In *The Future of International Human Rights*, edited by Burns H. Weston and Stephen P. Marks, 25–64. Ardsley, NY: Transnational Publishers.

———. 2000a. "Aristotle, Politics, and Human Capabilities: A Response to Antony, Arneson, Charlesworth, and Mulgan." *Ethics* 111, no. 1: 102–40.

———. 2000b. *Women and Human Development: The Capabilities Approach.* Cambridge, New York: Cambridge University Press.

———. 2001a. "Political Objectivity." *New Literary History* 32:883–906.

———. 2001b. *Upheavals of Thoughts.* Cambridge: Cambridge University Press.

———. 2002. "Women and the Law of Peoples." *Politics, Philosophy, and Economics* 1, no. 3: 283–306.

———. 2003. "Capabilities as Fundamental Entitlements: Sen and Social Justice." *Feminist Economics* 9, no. 2–3: 33–59.

———. 2004a. "Beyond 'Compassion and Humanity': Justice for Nonhuman Animals." In *Animal Rights: Current Debates and New Directions*, edited by Cass R. Sunstein and Martha C. Nussbaum, 299–320. Oxford: Oxford University Press.

———. 2004b. "On Hearing Women's Voices: A Reply to Susan Okin." *Philosophy & Public Affairs* 32, no. 2: 193–205.

———. 2006a. "Capabilities as Fundamental Entitlements: Sen and Social Justice." In *Capabilities Equality: Basic Issues and Problems*, edited by Alexander Kaufman, 44–70. New York: Routledge.

———. 2006b. *Frontiers of Justice: Disability, Nationality, Species Membership.* Cambridge, MA: Belknap Press.

Nussbaum, Martha, and Amartya Sen. 1989. "Internal Criticism and Indian Rationalist Traditions." In *Relativism: Interpretation and Confrontation*, edited by Michael Krausz, 299–326. Notre Dame, IN: University of Notre Dame Press.

O'Connell, Rory. 2005. "Do We Need Unicorns When We Have Law?" *Ratio Juris* 18, no. 4: 484–503.

Okin, Susan Moller. 1989. *Justice, Gender and the Family.* New York: Basic Books.

———. 2003. "Poverty, Well-Being, and Gender: What Counts, Who's Heard?" *Philosophy & Public Affairs* 31, no. 3: 280–316.

O'Neill, Onora. 1996. *Towards Justice and Virtue: A Constructive Account of Practical Reason.* Cambridge: Cambridge University Press.

Othman, Norani. 1999. "Grounding Human Rights Arguments in Non-Western Culture: Shari'a and the Citizenship Rights of Women in a Modern Islamic State." In *The East Asian Challenge for Human Rights,* edited by Joanne R. Bauer and Daniel A. Bell. Cambridge: Cambridge University Press.

Pannikar, Raimon. 1982. "Is the Notion of Human Rights a Western Concept?" *Diogenes* 120:75–102.

Parliament of the World's Religions. 1993. "Declaration toward a Global Ethic." *Global Ethic Foundation,* September 4, www.weltethos.org/pdf_decl/Decl_english.pdf.

Perry, Michael J. 2000a. "Freedom of Religion in the United States: Fin de Siècle Sketches." *Indiana Law Journal* 75, no. 71: 295–332.

———. 2000b. *The Idea of Human Rights: Four Inquiries.* Oxford: Oxford University Press.

———. 2006. *Toward a Theory of Human Rights: Religion, Law, Courts.* Cambridge: Cambridge University Press.

Pogge, Thomas. 1994. "An Egalitarian Law of Peoples." *Philosophy & Public Affairs* 23, no. 3: 195–224.

———. 2002. "Can the Capabilities Approach Be Justified?" *Philosophical Topics* 30, no. 2: 167–228.

———. 2004. "The Incoherence between Rawls's Theories of Justice." *Fordham Law Review* 72:1739–1759.

Putnam, Hilary. 1990. *Realism with a Human Face.* Cambridge, MA: Harvard University Press.

Qizilbash, Mozaffar. 1997. "A Weakness of the Capability Approach with Respect to Gender Justice." *Journal of International Development* 9, no. 2: 251–62.

Rawls, John. 1993. "The Law of Peoples." In *On Human Rights: The Oxford Amnesty Lectures 1993,* edited by Stephen Shute and Susan Hurley, 41–82. New York: Basic Books.

———. 1996. *Political Liberalism,* paperback ed. New York: Columbia University Press.

———. 1999a. "Kantian Constructivism in Moral Theory." In *John Rawls: Collected Papers,* edited by Samuel Freeman, 303–58. Cambridge, MA: Harvard University Press.

———. 1999b. *The Law of Peoples.* Cambridge, MA: Harvard University Press.

———. 1999c. *A Theory of Justice,* rev. ed. Cambridge, MA: Harvard University Press. First published 1971.

———. 1999d. "The Idea of Public Reason Revisited." In *The Law of Peoples with The Idea of Public Reason Revisited*. Cambridge, MA: Harvard University Press.

———. 2001. *Justice as Fairness: A Restatement*. Cambridge, MA: Belknap Press of Harvard University Press.

Raz, Joseph. 2007. "Human Rights without Foundations." March. Oxford Legal Studies Research Paper No. 14, available at Social Science Research Network, http://ssrn.com/abstract=999874.

Renteln, Alison Dundes. 1988. "Relativism and the Search for Human Rights." *American Anthropologist* 90, no. 1: 56–72.

Robeyns, Ingrid. 2003. "Sen's Capability Approach and Gender Inequality: Selecting Relevant Capabilities." *Feminist Economics* 9, no. 2–3: 61–92.

Rorty, Amelie Oksenberg. 1989. "Relativism, Persons, and Practices." In *Relativism: Interpretation and Confrontation*, edited by Michael Krausz, 418–40. Notre Dame, IN: University of Notre Dame Press.

Rorty, Richard. 1983. "Postmodernist Bourgeois Liberalism." *The Journal of Philosophy* 80, no. 10: 583–89.

———. 1993. "Human Rights, Rationality and Sentimentality." In *On Human Rights: The Oxford Amnesty Lectures 1993*, edited by Stephen Shute and Susan Hurley, 111–34. New York: Basic Books.

Rosemont, Henry, Jr. 1988. "Why Take Rights Seriously? A Confucian Critique." In *Human Rights and the World's Religions*, edited by Leroy Rouner, 167–182. Notre Dame, IN: University of Notre Dame Press.

———. 1998. "Human Rights: A Bill of Worries." In *Confucianism and Human Rights*, edited by Wm. Theodore De Bary and Tu Weiming, 54–66. New York: Columbia University Press.

Said, Edward. 1979. *Orientalism*. New York: Random House.

Sandel, Michael. 1982. *Liberalism and the Limits of Justice*. Cambridge: Cambridge University Press.

———. 1998. *Democracy's Discontent: America in Search of a Public Philosophy*. Cambridge, MA: Harvard University Press.

Schulz, William F. 2001. *In our Own Best Interest: How Defending Human Rights Benefits Us All*. Boston: Beacon Press.

Sen, Amartya. 1981a. *Poverty and Famines*. Oxford: Clarendon Press.

———. 1981b. "Public Action and the Quality of Life in Developing Countries." *Oxford Bulletin of Economics and Statistics* 43, no. 4: 287–319.

———. 1990. "Justice: Means versus Freedoms." *Philosophy & Public Affairs* 19, no. 2: 111–21.

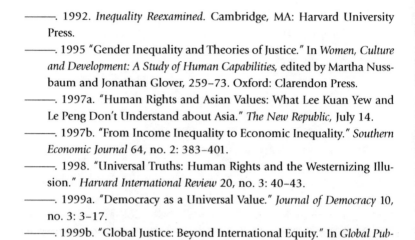

———. 1992. *Inequality Reexamined*. Cambridge, MA: Harvard University Press.

———. 1995 "Gender Inequality and Theories of Justice." In *Women, Culture and Development: A Study of Human Capabilities,* edited by Martha Nussbaum and Jonathan Glover, 259–73. Oxford: Clarendon Press.

———. 1997a. "Human Rights and Asian Values: What Lee Kuan Yew and Le Peng Don't Understand about Asia." *The New Republic,* July 14.

———. 1997b. "From Income Inequality to Economic Inequality." *Southern Economic Journal* 64, no. 2: 383–401.

———. 1998. "Universal Truths: Human Rights and the Westernizing Illusion." *Harvard International Review* 20, no. 3: 40–43.

———. 1999a. "Democracy as a Universal Value." *Journal of Democracy* 10, no. 3: 3–17.

———. 1999b. "Global Justice: Beyond International Equity." In *Global Public Goods: International Cooperation in the 21st Century,* edited by Inga Kaul, I. Grunberg, and M. A. Stern, 116–25. New York: Oxford University Press.

———. 1999c. *Development as Freedom.* New York: Anchor Books.

———. 2003a. "Continuing the Conversation: Amartya Sen Talks with Bina Agarwal, Jane Humphries, and Ingrid Robeyns." *Feminist Economics* 9, no. 2–3: 319–32.

———. 2003b. "Democracy and Its Global Roots." *The New Republic,* October 6, 28–35.

———. 2004a. "Capabilities, Lists, and Public Reason: Continuing the Conversation." *Feminist Economics* 10, no. 3: 77–80.

———. 2004b. "Elements of a Theory of Human Rights." *Philosophy & Public Affairs* 32, no. 4: 315–56.

———. 2005. "Human Rights and Capabilities." *Journal of Human Development* 6, no. 2: 152–66.

Shah, Natabhuai. 1998. *Jainism: The World of Conquerors,* vol. 2. Portland, OR: Sussex Academic Press.

Shestack, Jerome. 1998. "The Philosophic Foundations of Human Rights." *Human Rights Quarterly* 20, no. 2: 201–32.

Shue, Henry. 1996. *Basic Rights: Subsistence, Affluence, and U.S. Foreign Policy,* 2nd ed. Princeton, NJ: Princeton University Press.

Simmons, A. John. 1999. "Justification and Legitimacy." *Ethics* 109, no. 4: 739–71.

Skerker, Michael. 2004. "Nussbaum's Capabilities Approach and Religion." *Journal of Religion* 84:379–409.

Stackhouse, Max. 1984. *Creeds, Society and Human Rights: A Study in Three Cultures.* Grand Rapids, MI: Eerdmans.

———. 1998. "The Intellectual Crisis of a Good Idea." *Journal of Religious Ethics* 26, no. 2: 263–68.

———. 2003. "Lecture: Sources of Basic Human Rights Ideas: A Christian Perspective." *The Pew Forum on Religion & Public Life.* January 27.

———. 2004. "A Christian Perspective on Human Rights." *Society* 41, no. 2: 23–28.

———. 2005. "Why Human Rights Needs God: A Christian Perspective." In *Does Human Rights Need God?* edited by Elizabeth M. Bucar and Barbra Barnett, 25–40. Grand Rapids, MI: Eerdmans.

Stackhouse, Max, and Stephen E. Healey. 1996. "Religion and Human Rights: A Theological Apologetic." In *Religious Human Rights in Global Perspective: Religious Perspectives,* edited by John Witte Jr. and Johan D. van der Vyver, 485–516. The Hague: Martinus Nijhoff Publishers.

Stout, Jeffrey. 1988. *Ethics after Babel: The Languages of Morals and Their Discontents.* Boston: Beacon Press.

———. 1994. *Flight from Authority: Religion, Morality and the Quest for Autonomy.* Notre Dame. IN: University of Notre Dame Press.

Steckley, John. 2008. *White Lies about the Inuit.* Ontario, Canada: Broadview Press.

Sunstein, Cass R. 2000. "Practical Reason and Incompletely Theorized Agreements." In *Reasoning Practically,* edited by Edna Ullmann-Margalit, 98–122. New York: Oxford University Press.

Swidler, Leonard. 1999. "Toward a Universal Declaration of a Global Ethic." In *For All Life: Toward a Universal Global Ethic,* edited by Leonard Swidler, 1–36. Ashland, OR: White Cloud Press.

Talbott, William. 2005. *Which Rights Should Be Universal?* New York: Oxford University Press.

Tasioulas, John. 1998. "Consequences of Ethical Relativism." *European Journal of Philosophy* 6, no. 2: 172–202.

———. 2002. "From Utopia to Kazanistan: John Rawls and the Law of Peoples." *Oxford Journal of Legal Studies* 22, no. 2: 367–96.

Tatsuo, Inoue. 1999. "Liberal Democracy and Asian Orientalism." In *The East Asian Challenge for Human Rights,* edited by Joanne R. Bauer and Daniel A. Bell, 27–59. Cambridge, MA: Cambridge University Press.

Taylor, Charles, ed. 1993. "Explanation and Practical Reason." In *Philosophical Arguments*. Cambridge, MA: Harvard University Press.

———. 1994. "The Politics of Recognition." In *Multiculturalism: Examining the Politics of Recognition*, edited by Amy Gutmann, 25–74. Princeton, NJ: Princeton University Press.

———. 1999. "Conditions for an Unforced Consensus on Human Rights." In *The East Asian Challenge for Human Rights*, edited by Joanne Bauer and Daniel Bell, 124–44. Cambridge: Cambridge University Press.

Tesón, Fernando R. 1995. "The Rawlsian Theory of International Law." *Ethics and International Affairs* 9:79–99.

Tierney, Brian. 1997. *The Idea of Natural Rights: Studies on Natural Rights, Natural Law, and Church Law, 1150–1625*. Atlanta: Scholar Press.

Tilley, John. 2000. "Cultural Relativism." *Human Rights Quarterly* 22, no. 2: 501–47.

Toner, Christopher. 2005. "Just War and the Supreme Emergency Exemption." *Philosophical Quarterly* 55, no. 221: 545–61.

Traer, Robert. 1991. *Faith in Human Rights: Support in Religious Traditions for a Global Struggle*. Washington, DC: Georgetown University Press.

Tuck, Richard. 1979. *Natural Rights Theories: Their Origin and Development*. New York: Cambridge University Press.

Twiss, Sumner B. 1996. "Comparative Ethics and Intercultural Human Rights Dialogues: A Programmatic Inquiry In *Christian Ethics: Problems and Prospects*, edited by Lisa Sowle Cahill and James F. Childress, 357–78. Cleveland, OH: Pilgrim Press.

———. 1998a. "A Constructive Framework for Discussing Confucianism and Human Rights." In *Confucianism and Human Rights*, edited by Wm. Theodore De Bary and Tu Weiming, 27–53. New York: Columbia University Press.

———. 1998b. "Moral Grounds and Plural Cultures." *Journal of Religious Ethics* 26, no. 2: 271–82.

———. 2004. "History, Human Rights, and Globalization." *Journal of Religious Ethics* 32, no. 1: 39–70.

———. 2007. "Torture, Justification, and Human Rights: Toward an Absolute Proscription." *Human Rights Quarterly* 29:347–67.

UNESCO. 1949. *Human Rights: Comments and Interpretations*. Reprint, Westport, CT: Greenwood Press, 1973.

Villa-Vicencio, Charles. 1999–2000. "Christianity and Human Rights." *Journal of Law and Religion* 14, no. 2: 579–600.

Waldron, Jeremy, ed. 1988. *Nonsense upon Stilts: Bentham, Burke and Marx on the Rights of Man.* New York: Routledge.

Waltz, Susan. 2001. "Universalizing Human Rights: The Role of Small States in the Construction of the Universal Declaration of Human Rights." *Human Rights Quarterly* 23, no. 1: 44–72.

Walzer, Michael. 1977. *Just and Unjust Wars: A Moral Argument with Historical Illustrations.* New York: Basic Books.

———. 1992. "The Politics of Recognition." In *Multiculturalism: Examining the Politics of Recognition,* edited by Amy Gutmann, 25–74. Princeton, NJ: Princeton University Press.

———. 1994. *Thick and Thin: Moral Argument at Home and Abroad.* Notre Dame and London: University of Notre Dame Press.

———. 2004. "The Politics of Rescue." In *Arguing about War,* 67–81. New Haven, CT: Yale University Press.

Wasserman, David. 2006. "Disability, Capability, and Thresholds for Distributive Justice." In *Capabilities Equality: Basic Issues and Problems,* edited by Alexander Kaufman, 214–34. New York: Routledge.

Williams, Bernard. 2005. "Human Rights and Relativism." In *The Beginning Was the Deed: Realism and Moralism in Political Argument,* edited by Geoffrey Hawthorn, 62–74. Princeton, NJ: Princeton University Press.

Witte, John. 2007. *The Reformation of Rights: Law, Religion and Human Rights in Early Modern Calvinism.* Cambridge: Cambridge University Press.

Wolf, Susan. 1995. "Martha C. Nussbaum: Human Capabilities, Female Human Beings: Commentary by Susan Wolf." In *Women, Culture and Development: A Study of Human Capabilities,* edited by Martha Nussbaum and Jonathan Glover, 101–15. Oxford: Oxford University Press.

Wolterstorff, Nicholas. 1983. "Can Belief in God Be Rational If It Has No Foundations?" In *Faith and Rationality: Reason and Belief in God,* edited by Alvin Plantinga and Nicholas Wolterstorff, 135–86. Notre Dame, IN: University of Notre Dame Press.

———. 2005. "God, Justice, and Duty." In *Religion in the Liberal Polity,* edited by Terence Cuneo, 15–42. Notre Dame, IN: University of Notre Dame Press.

———. 2008a. *Justice: Rights and Wrongs.* Princeton, NJ: Princeton University Press.

————. 2008b. "How Social Justice Got to Me and Why It Never Left." *Journal of the American Academy of Religion* 76, no. 3: 664–79.

Wood, Allen. 2001. "The Objectivity of Value." *New Literary History* 32, no. 4 (Autumn): 859–81.

Zakaria, Fareed. 1994. "Culture Is Destiny: A Conversation with Lee Kuan Yew." *Foreign Affairs* 73, no. 2: 109–126.

Zizek, Slavoj. 2004. "From Politics to Biopolitics . . . and Back." *South Atlantic Quarterly* 103, nos. 2–3: 501–21.

INDEX

with, 22–26; and
enforcement-centered
approach, 63, 71–72, 135; and
natural law, 19–22;
prescriptive problems with,
26–28
euthanasia, 13, 176n5
evangelical goals of missions,
176n6
evidentialist challenge to theism,
49, 183n21
"expensive tastes" problem,
198n7
extraordinary rendition, 174n5

fair opportunity protections, 109
fair process protections, 109
faith's role in formation of religion,
151
Fear and Trembling (Kierkegaard),
166
feminists, 13–14
feudalism, 172
Finnis, John, 37, 199n8, 204n6
Fitzpatrick, William, 148, 163
flexibility in implementation,
110–12
flu pandemic, 174n7
Foucault, Michel, 167
Fox, Robin, 22
France: Corsican independence
movement in, 69; natural law
in, 20; and UDHR drafting
process, 88
Franciscans, 19
Francis Xavier (saint), 176n6
freedom of association, 63
freedom of movement, 121,
174n7, 184n24, 203n21

freedom of religion and
conscience: in capability
approach, 114; and consensus-
based approach, 92; in
consensus-based approach,
86; de jure vs. de facto
protections of, 119; in Eastern
philosophy and religion, 89;
and maximalist approaches,
55; as nonderogable right,
185n25
fundamental ideas, 138, 140,
142

Gandhi, Mohandas, 88, 89,
195n10
Gaudium et spes (Second Vatican
Council), 83
Geertz, Clifford, 12
gender inequality assessment,
106
gender issues: and capability
approach, 107, 201n18; and
UDHR drafting process, 24.
See also women
generic consistency principle,
183n20
Geneva Conventions, 92, 196n15
genocide: and consensus-based
approach, 81; and
enforcement-based approach,
189n10; group right to be free
from, 63; in Rwanda, 2; in
Sudan, 3
Genocide Convention (1948), 1
Gewirth, Alan, 183n20
Glendon, Mary Ann, 158
Glorious Revolution (England,
1690), 20

republican government, 75–76
resource-distribution models, 103
restorative justice model, 134
restraint, 132–33
Ricci, Matteo, 176n6
rights dimension of moral order,
    49, 180n9
Robeyns, Ingrid, 106, 199n9
Romulo, Carlos, 23
Roosevelt, Eleanor, 23, 24,
    177–78n13
Rorty, Amelie, 15
Rorty, Richard, 37, 176n8,
    205–6n10
Rosemont, Henry, Jr., 25
Rwanda: genocide in, 2–3;
    International Criminal
    Tribunal for, 173n2

sacredness, 37, 54, 151, 184n22
Said, Edward, 178n16
Sandel, Michael, 13, 175n4
sati practices, 167
Saudi Arabia, UDHR drafting
    objections, 86
Schulz, William F., 195n11
Scotus, Duns, 19
Second Vatican Council, 83, 180n6
secular approaches: and ethical
    realism, 149; and maximalist
    justifications, 35–36, 54–55;
    and natural law, 20;
    Wolterstorff's critique of, 47, 49
Sen, Amartya: on adaptive
    preferences, 198–99n7; and
    "Asian values" debates,
    178n16; and capability
    approach, 101, 103, 107,
    109–10, 140–46, 197n1;

proposed right for women to
    be consulted in serious family
    decisions, 136–37; and
    subsistence rights, 189n11;
    universal norms defended by,
    112–13
senilicide, 12
senses as central human capability,
    105
Shari'ah: and CDHRI, 32, 179n1;
    in consensus-based approach,
    83, 86, 93–94; *zina* offenses
    under, 94, 195–96n14
Shestack, Jerome J., 3
Shue, Henry, 189n11
Simmons, A. John, 139–40
situationism, 17
Sivaraksa, Sulak, 90
slavery: and consensus-based
    approach, 81, 92; and cultural
    relativism, 16; right to be free
    from, 63, 184n25
Smith, Adam, 110
social climate, 103
Socrates, 115
Sophocles, 19
South Africa: UDHR drafting
    objections, 86; UN criticism of
    human rights violations,
    193n4
sovereignty, 57, 73
Soviet Union: legal positivism in,
    158; and UDHR drafting
    process, 23, 88
Spain, Basque separatist movement
    in, 69
species norm, 116, 119, 123–25
Sri Lanka, ethnoreligious conflict
    in, 69